[LOVE] RACHEL

to Amanda and Anthony —

A Daughter's Memoir
of Love, Betrayal and Grace

With best regards,

Rebecca M. P___

REBECCA

Fulton Books, Inc.
Meadville, PA

Originally published by Fulton Books 2019

ISBN 978-1-63338-822-2 (Paperback)
ISBN 978-1-63338-823-9 (Digital)

Library of Congress Control Number: 2018968509

Printed in the United States of America

In Memoriam

Rachel Gweneth Williams Madden, 1908-1996

Gwenda Alice Williams Craig, 1910-1997

John Rogers Painter, 1944-1983

ACKNOWLEDGEMENTS

Heartfelt thanks to my former writing group, led by Patti Dann, whose insights were vital to many revisions: Phyllis Dolgin, Lenore Migdal, Beth Rosen, Rochelle Rosenbaum, Leni Goodman, Phyllis Birne, and the late Ursula Karolsen and Dorothy Johnson. Without the friendship and candor of my sister in spirit, Mary Josephine Kaiser, I could not have pulled together several key threads of this memoir. I've been sustained throughout by the interest, patience, and copy-editing skills of my husband, Martin Goldberger, and by the conceptual challenges and support of my dear friend Oscar Aquino. Blessings on those who read previous drafts of the manuscript, for their feedback and encouragement: Nancy di Benedetto and Lee J. Strauss for their skilled editing suggestions; Rhonda Rosenstock, Doris Schechter and Miriam Katin for their candid responses as readers.

Special thanks to Miriam for the artistry of her sketches for the book's front and back covers.

In this memoir, some names have been changed to protect the privacy of those concerned, and a few have been substituted for names the writer has forgotten.

CONTENTS

CHAPTER ONE

The Lost Love

Mummy slipped the last dish into the rack and unplugged the rinse water. Taking a deep breath, she reached into the cupboard and pulled a bag from the box of Red Rose tea. I watched her from the kitchen table, dangling my six-year-old legs. Many washings had faded the flowery blouse tucked into her canvas shorts, keeping white the ankle socks inside her scuffed leather shoes. A nearly invisible hairnet covered her wispy brown curls. Glancing at me, she dropped the teabag into a mug drying on the rack, poured boiling water from the teakettle into it, and sighed.

I had my play clothes on with no one to play with. There were no little girls in the neighborhood and my brother Johnny, a year and a half older, had snuck off with his pals before I could run after them. It was 1953 on Painter's Berry Farm in northwest Washington State, a few miles from Lake Stevens and the town of Marysville.

Papa had died unexpectedly. Our mother, a New Zealander he'd married shortly before our country entered the War, was left to run the farm and look after Johnny and me. She'd married the first farm manager she'd hired, but he'd disappeared on a drinking binge. Other than me, Mummy had no family or close friends she could talk to on this side of the Pacific.

Fishing out her teabag, she glanced at me and dropped it into the smallest cup from the rack, half-filled it from the tea-kettle, and opened the fridge for a bottle of fresh cow's milk with a layer of cream on top. She poured a fair amount into her mug, and a drop into the small cup, which she placed before me.

Try it, dear, she said, taking the chair across from me. I stared at the drink I'd never been offered before, and did as she did—breathing in its rising steam, blowing on the hot surface, and taking a tiny sip.

Would you like to hear a story from my life in New Zealand, before I came to this country?

How could I not? It would be like hearing about part of my own life that I'd missed because I hadn't been born yet.

As she warmed her chapped hands around the thick mug, her voice seemed to float in from far away. *Your mother once had a true love, Beck, long before I met your father. But we were separated by the war.*

Gazing out the window, she tried a real swallow. So I did, too.

We used to work together at a large important plant nursery in New Zealand. His name was Douglas Elliott, and he came from an upper-class family.

Her eyes settled on the row of fragrant rosebushes she'd traded for a truck-bed of raspberry seedlings. To enjoy them better, she'd planted them alongside the row of raspberries closest to the farmhouse.

Your mother's side of the family is descended from Welsh landed gentry. It sounded as though her family was as good if not better than my father's, though it wouldn't be recognized as such in this country.

When I was in my twenties I worked side by side with Douglas for four years. He was very shy, but I knew he loved me, and I loved him.

Douglas, she explained, had a bedridden mother, whose illness was unknown because she was a Christian Scientist and refused to see a doctor. His older brother had left home to work with their father in what sounded like the legal profession, while Douglas stayed and looked after his mother. Evidently, Mrs. Elliott was not at all pleased with her younger son's friendship with his co-worker Rachel. Mummy said it took him four years to get up his nerve to invite her to his home for tea.

She recalled walking up a long path lined with trees toward the Elliott residence, where he escorted her into an elegant sitting room. A servant brought in a silver tea service, and when they were alone he began by saying that he loved her.

I knew he was about to ask me to marry him, Mummy said, looking out the window and taking another deep breath. The rest came out in choppy bits. From what I gathered, at the very moment Douglas began to propose, Mrs. Elliott—whose bedroom was too far away to hear anything—screamed something shocking at her son. My mother didn't say what. The gist, though, was that Douglas obeyed his mother and his teatime with his guest came to a terrible end. My mother quit working with Douglas and moved to another town, where she became the nurse companion to a wealthy society lady whose family appreciated her nursing skills and her company.

Years passed, and so did Mrs. Elliott. Britain declared war on Germany, and the Nazis were about to bomb London, where Douglas had gone to study horticulture at the world famous Kew Gardens. By then he knew that Mummy had been engaged to another man and was probably already married. Regardless, he wrote to her as Miss Rachel Williams, at her parents' address in New Zealand. In case anything happened to him, he wanted her to know that he'd never stopped loving her and would always love her. She cabled him the sad truth that her engagement had been broken. Douglas shot back a cable asking her to marry him.

I accepted, but he was far away and our whole engagement was by correspondence.

"But Mom, why did you marry Papa if you really loved Douglas?"

Instead of answering, she offered more history. *Well dear, the family I worked for wanted to reward me with a vacation in Canada. They booked me first class on a luxury liner sailing from New Zealand to Victoria, British Columbia, just north of us in Canada.* In those days, she explained, well-bred people used formal letters of introduction, and she'd been given one to meet my father. Papa was highly regarded among her patient's society friends. One of them was a strange rich woman who'd consulted with him in Canada and insisted that her friend's nurse should meet him.

Papa was much older than Mummy, and died from an accident when I was three. My earliest memories were of people filling up our living room to hear him speak. He and Mr. Barley were co-owners of the berry farm, and lived in separate houses on the property. They were both Theosophists, as were most people who traveled to our place, but it was my father they'd come to see.

When I arrived at the berry farm, Mom recalled in a different tone, *your father opened the door and shouted, "Those are the eyes!" He said he'd had visions of a pair of eyes in his dreams—mine— which meant that I was the woman destined to fulfill his life.*

For several weeks my mother stayed with Mrs. Barley, who'd been recently widowed, while Papa, who lived alone in a smaller house on the property, tried to convince her to marry him. During that time, she said, the ship she was booked on to sail back to New Zealand was the first passenger vessel sunk by the Japanese in the war. No more passenger ships were allowed in the Pacific, she explained, so she had to stay either in Canada or the States for the rest of the war. That meant Douglas would have to wait for her until the war was over, and she had to find out if he was willing to do so. My father—her escort, not yet her husband—drove her to the nearest telegraph office so she could cable her fiancé. She told me it went like this:

MUST STAY FOR DURATION WHAT ARE YOUR
PLANS LOVE RACHEL

Everyone understood, Mom added, that duration meant the length of the war.

I waited and waited for word from Douglas, but he didn't respond. It broke my heart. I was under so much pressure and there was no way I could return to New Zealand. So I stayed in the States and married your father.

Many years later, when Mom returned from her first trip back to New Zealand, she described how shocked she'd been when Auntie Gwenda showed her the actual cable Douglas had received from her, that ended their engagement in 1940. It did not end **LOVE RACHEL**, as she'd dictated to the Western Union clerk. In fact, the name underneath the cable's message was **RACHEL PAINTER**. But she'd still been Rachel Williams, having not yet married my father! Gwenda, who'd always looked up to her sister, confessed that she'd never understood the cruel way Rachel had chosen to inform "poor Douglas" that she was marrying someone else! How did this happen?

Mummy wracked her brains, dimly recalling that after she'd paid for the cable, Roger had opened the door for her to leave the telegraph office, and she was already outside when the clerk called out, "Sir, what's your last name?"

Roger told him, and though it seemed rather odd, he shrugged it off and I forgot about it. To defend herself from Gwenda's accusation of cruelty toward Douglas—when it was he who'd broken *her* heart!—my mother reconstructed what might have happened. The man behind the counter must have assumed they were married and, as they were leaving, might have realized that he'd forgotten the wartime requirement that all cables had to be signed with a first and last name. So he asked the man who'd opened the door for what looked like his wife what was his surname. And without checking with his actual customer, the clerk removed **LOVE** and inserted **PAINTER** after **RACHEL**, so the cable's word count and cost would remain the same. Mummy said she'd probably lost Douglas because of this simple error, for after he received the cable she never heard from him again.

That story haunted my life until after my mother's death. It clouded every aspect of what I believed possible for my own chances to find love. If my far more deserving mother, whom I loved more than anything, could lose the love of her life because of one word switched in a telegram, I could not imagine fate treating me any better.

CHAPTER TWO

My Mother's Call

In a moment like no other in my life, a crisp fall Friday afternoon in Manhattan, 1996, I was close to 50, home from a week of teaching college in the Bronx. Shoes off and feet up, I drifted into a satisfying reverie of my students' earnest young faces as they began to own what they were learning.

An unexpected ring pierced the silence. As I lifted the heavy old receiver, background static told me the call was long distance.

Becky, I need you to come out here. I'm terminal.

I'd been teaching freshman writing and literature to mostly Latino immigrants at a community college, having left a more lucrative career that threatened to corrode my sense of integrity. Though it felt like a calling, the rewards were hard to reconcile with an adjunct professor's low pay and job insecurity.

Students had started giving me modest, touching thank-you gifts—a pink crystal heart dangling in front of a small mirror on a mirrored base; a pair of Asian metal balls that hummed when rolled in the hand to relieve tension; an inscribed plaque from an entire class. The gifts I valued most arrived incrementally: complete sentences, intelligible grammar, and coherent ideas in English that could help pave their way out of poverty.

Mom's call came mid-semester, when my classes were just hitting their stride.

You did tell me that you wanted to take care of me when I was near the end.

A rather goofy but serious thought arose. I was finally inhabiting an old cliché: ready and able. For years I'd prayed—verbally and in wordless longing—for the chance to stay with and take care for my mother before she died. I wanted time to finally convince her of my love for her, and to shield her from the not unusual hell of dying old and neglected.

During the phone call, a thrill passed over me like a wave of grace, as I realized that my prayers had been heard. This knowledge that I was ready and able was deeper and stronger than the confidence I'd gradually gained in the classroom.

Out popped my childhood name for her, true to my tenderness and vulnerability where she was concerned, heedless of the years I'd spent in so-called adulthood. "Of course, Mummy. I've always wanted to. I just need to make a few arrangements. When would you like me to come?"

She'd been authorized to enter the Hospice program, which would provide an array of domestic, medical, social, and spiritual services that would make her final days as free of pain and anxiety as possible. The program required a live-in caregiver.

My mother's voice darkened. *You'll have to come soon.* In few words, she informed me that her longtime boyfriend had broken off with her. Knowing that she was dying, he'd demanded something that she could not agree to, under threat of leaving her. Why had he chosen this moment to reveal he was capable of cruelty?

"How about if I come Tuesday?"

All right, dear. I can manage till then.

It was uncanny how everything fell into place for my trip. Instead of panic at the sight of an empty suitcase, I knew just what to pack and trusted that anything I forgot could be obtained while I was out there. A neighbor agreed to collect my mail and water my plants. The English Department found other professors to cover my courses. I'd saved a discount coupon for car service to the airport, and the plane was on time.

During the five-hour flight to Seattle I contemplated the finality of this time with my mother. There was elation at my good fortune to be able to stay with her, tempered by a somber sense of cosmic punctuality, of final reckoning. My mother's life held mysteries I needed to resolve, or at least uncover, for the sake of my remaining life.

A gifted nurse, Mom had blessed me with extraordinary care when I was a child suffering for years from a chronic, humiliating affliction. But as I grew older, her tender, patient kindness was overtaken by a force entirely alien to healing and nurture.

Yet to me, and those who knew her, both in her native New Zealand and in her adopted homeland, she was a Great Soul, a ministering angel who ennobled others, a sage capable of dispensing life-changing wisdom. On one hand, she was an unsung heroine whose memory did not deserve to fade into obscurity. On the other, I was the anomaly in her life of benevolence. My mother and I seemed to reenact an unresolved version of King Lear in female form and his forsaken daughter Cordelia.

From childhood, the truest thing I knew about myself was that I loved my mother and had expressed it without reserve. This remarkable woman, whose grace and wisdom I would be first to acknowledge, she had also given me the most intimate taste of what might be called personal evil. I so wanted to find out before the end why someone so loving and inspiring to others would not accept that she was loved by the person most devoted to her.

With one possible exception. I'd heard about Douglas, my mother's lost love, since I was a little girl. Only after her death did I discover letters from him that she'd saved and possibly forgotten. They flooded my heart with the spirit of his hope, wit and devotion to her. After the experiences we shared in the final weeks of her life, the discovery of these letters would reframe my understanding of perhaps the greatest source of pain in my life.

A taxi pulled up just as I'd stepped out of the airport van from SeaTac to Bremerton. The driver had no trouble finding the address, but was unfamiliar with the hairpin turns winding down to my mother's house—ones I would soon be navigating with ease. As promised, I was with her on Tuesday.

CHAPTER THREE

The Beloved Name

On the plane to SeaTac, I could not focus on the paperback best-seller in front of me. Thoughts drifted by of my brother, with whom I could have shared my mother's last days, had he survived. Nothing led me to think of my deceased father and three subsequent stepfathers. Instead, I reached out to the memory of some-one I'd never met. Douglas Elliott's name had not come up that often when I was a child, but Mom uttered it with a fond, wistful tone you would not hear when she spoke of my father.

Rachel Williams met Douglas in Palmerston North, New Zealand, in the early 1930s, when they were in of a group of nurses and their friends. Soon after, when a tubercular spot appeared in her chest X-ray, she reached an impasse in her nursing career. No drugs yet existed for TB, there was no treatment other than fresh air and rest. The small British colony had yet to weave its safety net of socialized medicine, and a long sojourn in a sanatorium was beyond Rachel's means. She had to forego hospital work and find healthier employment.

Douglas was the younger son of a respected family, who pursued his interest in horticulture at Duncan & Davies, New Zealand's foremost plant nursery and supplier of seeds to the multitude of gardeners Down Under. Rachel enjoyed gardening, and asked Douglas about a girl's chances at a career in horticulture. D&D was expanding, and Douglas may have put in a good word for her, for she left the hospital to spend what may have been the happiest four years of her life working with him—until that episode with his mother.

Douglas Elliott was the love of my life, she declared in a letter when I was in my twenties. I'd grown up haunted by her account of how she'd been cut off from him by a telegraph clerk's fluke error in wartime. It did not occur to me that her story about him might have served to justify the marriage that produced my brother and me.

Since childhood I'd been my mother's confidante, privy to topics too complex and distressing for a child to sort out. She seemed to assume that I possessed an adult's maturity in a child's body. All I knew was how difficult it was to converse with children my age, and how comfortable I felt listening to grownups talk. I was eager to learn more about Douglas, but Mom kept him at an elusive distance. I hoarded the scraps she'd dropped about him until after her death, when I came across more pieces to that puzzle.

At Duncan & Davies my mother acquired an encyclopedic sounding knowledge of things botanical. Scented flowers, especially roses, became her passion. Her knowledge of both the Latin and English names of plants was formidable. I marveled at the way she gently padded her fingers into the earth around their roots, like a mother checking a baby's bottom. She seemed to commune directly with nature, measuring the health of a plant as well as the soil from which it grew.

Throughout my childhood, our shabby-modest homes were upgraded by the glorious flowerbeds she planted around them and the exquisite flower arrangements displayed inside. Their scents could defog the mind and transport one into spells of aromatic bliss. My strongest floral memories were of her long bank of roses on the berry farm, and a blue and white iris by the back door that smelled like beatified Cool-Aid. She loved dogwood trees for the precision of their creamy pink flowers, and copper beeches for the two-tone velvety shimmer of their leaves.

She could be judge and executioner of plants as well. When a long-tended specimen was not flourishing sufficiently she simply chucked it. *No point getting sentimental, dear,* she said, *when something is beyond redemption.*

After the death of her fourth husband, Mom was able to purchase the waterfront home she'd long admired from her rented apartment nearby, and sent me a photograph of herself smiling proudly at the base of a forklift. She'd hired this gap-jawed machine and paid for the truck full of boulders the forklift was to install, at her direction, to construct an artful but imposing rock barrier between her residence and the apartment building that would have otherwise loomed directly over her property. Douglas would have been impressed at this bold landscaping project. I was sure she'd thought of him in the midst of it.

On occasions when my mother shared some of her botanical lore, I heard in her voice the closest thing to contentment, perhaps joy. She'd acquired this knowledge in Douglas's company, and it remained his life's work. He became one of New Zealand's best-known gardening authorities, with a weekly radio program and a book about the country's native flowers that became a collector's item.

My mother had described Douglas as a bashful mother's boy, though capable of disconcerting honesty. As some kind of moral lesson, she once confided that, while employed at Duncan & Davies, she'd been invited to speak to a group of weekend gardeners, and was expected to provide them with tips for beginners. Unnoticed by her, Douglas—who was far more knowledgeable and possibly responsible for her invitation to speak rather than himself—sat in the back throughout. She thought her talk went well, she'd offered several clever anecdotes and got some laughs. The audience gave her a hearty round of applause.

In the greenhouse the next day, Douglas broke a long silence by saying, *Rachel, you gave them nothing they could use.* With a sidelong glance, Mom confessed that she'd felt rather superior to these dabblers, and had not bothered to prepare anything substantive for them. Basking in the glow of hopeful faces, she'd ignored the part of herself that loved Chaucer's description of the humble teacher: "Gladly would he learn, and gladly teach."

Oh, Douglas, she'd said, *how could you not tell me you were coming? I would have gone over everything with you beforehand!* My mother's shame at his disappointment in her might have been assuaged only by using the memory to warn me against this form of arrogance.

CHAPTER FOUR

Mangaotawhito and Beyond

Eldest of three sisters, Rachel Williams was wise beyond her years. Her father respected her views so much that he included his young daughter in his discussions of world affairs with his gentleman peers. When far afield mending fences on their sheep ranch, he would have a farmhand go and fetch her so he could have someone interesting to talk to. Rachel's sister Gwenda, two years younger, relied on her for guidance and insight not forthcoming from their reclusive mother. (Githa, the youngest sister, was reportedly slow-witted and seldom mentioned by my mother.)

In 1922, Rachel was one of the first girls in New Zealand to receive a government scholarship to attend boarding school, at a time when there were no state-sponsored high schools. Gisborne was the only large town on what was called the Gisborne East Cape, a three-day trip south by stagecoach from the Williams' sheep station. At the Gisborne High School for Girls she excelled in science, history and literature, and wrote a prize-winning essay on Shakespeare. Apparently, in the 1920s, there were no scholarships for women to attend university, if they were even allowed to attend. Though she'd graduated with honors, Rachel had to return home, where her mother, who'd once been the head nurse at Wellington General Hospital, had become obese and reclusive, reading in bed most of the day. It fell upon Rachel to manage the household, look after her younger sisters, and serve as hostess to the family's few visitors.

Sheep stations on the North Island were, as many in New Zealand and Australia, huge and labor-intensive. The ranchers toiled from dawn to nightfall, grazing, culling, breeding, shearing, birthing and doctoring sheep. There were hired hands to manage, sheepdogs and horses to train and tend, and supplies to fetch from faraway markets. Though neighboring stations tried to stay attuned to each other's wellbeing and help out when possible, long stretches of working life passed in isolation. Though their survival required intelligence and ingenuity, there were few opportunities to socialize. Rachel decided that her family, especially her witty father and shy sister Gwenda, needed to end their social isolation. At boarding school, she'd become popular with upper-class girls, adopted their accent, and learned how to play tennis. She would make good use of all this.

Morgan Williams was a born storyteller and poet. The letters he'd sent Rachel at boarding school, brimming with local news and hilarious insights, were all penned in metered rhyme. To her lifelong regret, she had not saved them, assuming that all her classmates' fathers wrote similar letters. When she finished school she found him drinking too much and longing for more stimulating company.

Rachel decided that Mangaotawhito (mahn-gah-tah-FEET-oh, a Maori word for the stream that flowed through the property) could be a social hub for tennis parties, drawing guests from the countryside as far north as Ruatoria. Her father perked up when she pointed to an area near the house that could be leveled and seeded for a lawn tennis court. He and Gwenda pitched in to do this, assisted by several curious Maoris.

If they were to properly receive company, Rachel realized, the interior of the farmhouse needed improvement. No one knew how to hang wallpaper, so she taught herself. This proved hazardous, as the farm had only a pole ladder that tended to wobble and slide. She proudly solved this problem by planting the ladders' legs in her father's rubber boots.

One day a mysterious package appeared in the Mangaotawhito mail drop, far from the farmhouse at the station's entrance on the East Cape's narrow coastal road, near the Maori village of Tikitiki. Inside what looked like a wooden doghouse on sticks, with a latched door and a corrugated iron roof, a canvas mailbag lay protected from the elements. Soon a Maori boy, more curious than fluent in English, peeked in and spotted the package. As my mother told it, the boy ran up the long winding drive to the farmhouse to notify her father.

"Package, Boss! Big package in mailbox!"

"Is that so?" Mr. Williams responded. "How big is it?"

"Big, Boss. Big."

"How wide is it?"

"Wide, Boss. Wide."

Running out of patience, my grandfather asked, "Well, how long is it, do you suppose?"

A radiant smile appeared on the boy's face. Savoring the word's strangeness, he answered, "Ob-long."

It must have been the tennis net Rachel had ordered from Auckland.

Mangaotawhito's mail drop, about a century
after my grandfather built it.

Very few knew how to play tennis in those parts, so primers on technique had to be secured, as well as racquets and balls for their guests. Rachel made the court available for practice sessions, teaching Gwenda and several others to play.

The key to being a gracious hostess was simple, my mother explained. Always put people at ease. When folks arrived for a tennis party, she told me, she would offer everyone tea, then step right away into the bathroom and pull the handle of their old-fashioned toilet, causing a deafening crash from the water tank near the ceiling. *Of course I didn't need to go just then. But if I acted as if it was perfectly natural to make such a racket, I figured nobody would feel embarrassed. It worked like a charm!*

Photos of Wimbledon winners appeared in the papers, and local players were keen to look the part. Girls wore calf-length white pleated skirts and short- or long-sleeved white blouses like the great Suzanne Lenglen. Men wore loose white trousers of wool or linen, and rolled up the cuffs of long-sleeved cotton or linen shirts—tennis whites of the day. Relatives in New Zealand recalled that my mother and Gwenda had competed in tournaments at Ruatoria. Though Mom never mentioned it, that was probably where she'd won the uninscribed silver dish she kept at the back of our china cabinet.

While his daughters played tennis, Mr. Williams attracted a throng of older folk, the non-athletic, and players resting between matches. Rachel hoped their company would compensate for his less than companionable marriage. My mother said she was determined never to become as fat as her mother, and never forgave her for treating her father so coldly. During one of their parental rows, she heard her mother hissing at him: *You killed my love!* In Rachel's eyes, it was her mother who'd made herself unlovable.

Morgan Williams, older than in the tennis days, but still dapper.

Mangaotawhito became a lively venue for tennis parties. Everyone was invited—sheep station owners and workers, their children and relatives, Maori neighbors, and what passed for high society in those parts: wealthy wool merchants and their families. The latter occasionally hosted balls, and Rachel took seriously a courtesy invitation sent in appreciation of her tennis parties. It was at a mansion overlooking Ruatoria, hours away on horseback.

To prepare for this event, Rachel sewed a lavender gown from silk fabric she'd ordered at some expense from Auckland. She'd saved up and bought silk stockings and shoes suitable for dancing, and arranged to change out of her riding clothes and into the gown at a friend's place in Ruatoria. She combed her hair into a simple twist that could withstand the journey and pass for elegant on the dance floor, and borrowed a pair of her mother's earrings.

As the ball drew near, so did potential disaster. There were signs of chicken pox. Rachel avoided the eagle eye of the resident former nurse matron of Wellington Hospital, who might have discovered that her daughter was running a fever, with blisters emerging on her torso. Late on the afternoon of the big event, thick clouds darkened the sky and a thunderstorm threatened to destroy all her plans. Regardless Rachel carefully rolled up her ballgown and dance shoes inside bed linens protected by oilcloth, packed the ensemble into saddlebags, cinched up her favorite horse, pulled a hooded slicker over her riding gear and rode off into the elements.

That dance, my mother reminisced, was the peak experience of her social life in New Zealand. Though unable to carry a tune, she had a sense of rhythm, and was light on her feet. Her dance card filled quickly, and I imagined all the men vying for a whirl with the Adele Astaire of the Gisborne East Cape.

The best thing about it—Mom noted with a slight grin of triumph—*the chicken pox stayed discreetly inside my gown!* After the ball, when she undressed at her friend's house, she was delighted to see that the lining of her gown was soaked through and all her pox blisters had burst from so much dancing, but *nothing showed on the outside.* Not only that, she recalled, but *running a fever had given my sallow complexion a rosy glow.*

I didn't think to ask whether she'd given a moment's thought to being contagious. More contagious was the thrill of dancing at a ball.

In time Mangaotawhito's tennis scene began to fade. Guests found it awkward when Mr. Williams repeated stories that were no longer amusing. Rachel wondered why people began to make excuses not to attend the parties, and why her father had fewer people surrounding him. She decided to linger nearby, unnoticed, and find out.

Daddy, are you aware that yesterday you told Harriet Winstead and her children the same joke three times?

Is that true, Rachel? To her father, being a bore was a far worse transgression than being a drunkard.

I'm afraid so, Daddy. That's why people are starting to avoid you.

From that day forward, she claimed, her father drank only tea. She considered it one of his greatest accomplishments. Without her saying, it also demonstrated his exceptional regard for her.

My mother was in her late twenties when her father became less able to manage the sheep station, and spoke of selling it. Not wanting to stay at Mangaotawhito, she sought training for a profession, since she could not attend university. Even though Rachel was estranged from the peevish woman she felt her mother had become, training as a nurse was one of the few career options available to women of that era. In perhaps a rare moment of maternal encouragement, Mrs. Williams gave Rachel the gold chain and pocket watch she'd used as a nurse, along with her insignia pin, and probably her blessing, though my mother never spoke of it. I found the pin, watch and chain in Mom's jewelry box after her death. To my knowledge, she'd never worn them.

I also came across a copy of my grandparents' marriage certificate. It stated that Alice Mary Evans married David Morgan Williams at age 37. Though she'd left a responsible position at Wellington Hospital to marry him, her profession as a nurse was not recorded. The document described her as a "spinster," while Mr. Williams, 39, was identified as a "bachelor farmer." Perhaps Grandmother Williams had cause to become depressed, reading books all day and letting herself become stout.

From an early age my mother lived by the adage she shared with her sister Gwenda: *It's not what happens to you that matters, it's what you make of it.*

Gwenda revered her older sister, seeking her advice with such devotion and trust that Rachel appeared to have assumed their mother's role. Their younger sister Githa had fallen off a horse at a tender age, and grew up rather dim and odd in manner. My mother said little of her, except that she disappeared when there was housework to be done.

The sisters were home-schooled by their mother before Rachel won a scholarship to attend boarding school in Gisborne. She convinced Gwenda to join her, and with Rachel's help she was accepted. Rachel was determined that Gwenda would not have to arrive at Gisborne Girls High School wearing a deceased aunt's clothes, thirty years out of fashion, as she had. Nor would Gwenda be embarrassed for not knowing how to launder an undergarment.

The latter item was a whalebone corset Rachel had inherited from said aunt. Figuring how to cinch it up was one thing, she said, but she hadn't a clue how to wash it. One day the headmistress appeared unannounced to inspect their rooms, and spotted her dingy, unwashed corset on top of an open drawer.

"Miss Williams," she snapped, "are you aware that proper personal hygiene includes cleaning one's corset?"

But Madame, I don't know how to clean it. I've never worn one before. Curious girls accumulated in the doorway, increasing her embarrassment.

"Well! Will someone please show Miss Williams how this is done, since apparently her mother has not taught her!"

An older student took Rachel into the laundry room and explained the process: soak the corset in soapy water, scrub it with a sturdy rag, rinse and wring it out, then let it dry on a towel draped over the back of the wooden desk chair in her room. New friends helped her replace her hand-me-down clothes with up-to-date skirts and blouses, most of which she sewed herself. Gradually she became adept at fitting in, and even became popular.

It's not what happens to you that matters, it's what you make of it.

Rachel made sure Gwenda was dressed properly, sewing most of her clothes. Nevertheless, Gwenda was terrified of boarding school, and went home during her first year. She would later describe it as having had a nervous breakdown. In the tennis socials Rachel orchestrated after she finished boarding school, Gwenda met and fell in love with Gordon Craig, a man who worked with his older brother Colin on Rauponga, the sheep station next to Mangaotawhito. Gwenda happily accepted Gordon's proposal of marriage. By all accounts he was charming and funny, but he drank heavily and tended to reduce everything to a joke. Gwenda began to suspect that Gordon's joking extended to his entire life and his future with her. She may have panicked at boarding school, but at marriage she did not intend to fail, and turned to Rachel for guidance.

My mother did an amusing imitation of Gwenda as a young woman, when she was first engaged and came to her with this problem.

Gwenda, you've got to think! Mom recalled saying, and mimicked how her sister made a terrible face, stomped her foot and shouted, "But I HATE to think!"

Doubtless with Rachel's input, Gwenda weighed her options and broke off with Gordon. Decades later, relatives told me that Gordon took it harder than anyone had expected, leaving the area and not marrying until late in life. Gordon's older brother Colin— who'd been engaged to a beautiful American woman who'd left him without warning to return to the States—remained at Rauponga, and began appearing regularly at the tennis socials.

Both on the rebound, Gwenda and Colin paired up. Colin had charm of his own and a legendary sense of humor. He was known as an honest stock agent, trusted equally by station owners and the buyers of sheep and cattle. The older Craig brother seemed a more mature and stable version of the younger. The drinking that distorted Gordon's life had not yet overtaken Colin's, though it was a customary facilitator of stock deals. He was Gwenda's best hope of marriage before the abyss of spinsterhood.

An old photograph shows the petite bride with a huge wedding bouquet, flanked by her groom and grim-faced mother. Holding onto her stylish hat to keep it from blowing off in the wind, Rachel stands apart from her mother, buffered by her father and Colin's best man. To the left of Colin's parents stands Rachel's beloved Aunt Anne, her father's widowed sister, next to Githa, her face in shadow. To me, my mother appears subtly in charge of the situation, protective and proud. She had sewn her own gown and Gwenda's silk wedding dress, perhaps even their mother's unusual early version of a floral pantsuit.

When they were past middle age, Gwenda wrote that if Rachel had not prepared her for adulthood, no one else would have.

After Gwenda's death, her son Grahame found a smudged, much handled document among her effects, and mailed it to me. Gwenda had stored it in an envelope marked "Keep! Advice Rachel wrote out for me long ago when she left New Zealand – I've tried to follow it!"

In a firm, youthful hand my mother had inscribed:

> *Never make a bad job worse.*
> *Reasonableness is one of the highest of all virtues.*
> *Be reasonable, be practical, be sane.*
> *Remember that a chain is only as strong as its weakest link. Your weak points are those that will let you down.*

Never try to influence another person except through the widening of their understanding & knowledge of fresh aspects of a case.
The individual is full of latent possibilities for good & will make sound decisions where he can see straight.
One's own standard is never high enough. Attempt no sort of reform that doesn't begin with oneself.
Never be satisfied with things as they are but always to work for the vision of what they might be.
Never accept anything as true unless after due investigation it agrees with one's reason.
Never leave ill alone.
Reason first, act afterwards.
Remember that the measure of love is in what it is worth for good will to those one loves.
There is no true love without service.
The love that will not suffer to hold another to the highest & truest in them is not real love.
Never expect another to travel where one will not lead oneself.

Rachel had penned these maxims on a piece of thick quality paper salvaged from some other document. They seemed tailored for an impulsive younger sister who, despite hating to think, had to forge a life with a husband she would find she hardly knew well enough. Somehow Rachel had invoked the gravitas of a sage, such that Gwenda read and reread these precepts and—against daunting odds—adhered to them.

My mother mentioned to me once that her childhood best friend was a Maori princess who died of tuberculosis. As a farewell gift, the dying girl had given her a priceless Maori ceremonial cape, handwoven and decorated with alternating rows of black and white feathers. For years Mom kept it in a box in her closet, which she opened briefly once to show me. Not until my trip to New Zealand after her death did I learn that some relatives had conjectured that my father's fatal accident and my mother's series of troubled marriages might have resulted from a Maori curse attached to that precious cape, if it were ever taken out of Maori country. A Maori researcher in Gisborne assured me that a gift given in such a loving way would never bear a curse. My mother brought the cape back to New Zealand on her first trip back, and her family donated it to a museum of the Maori heritage.

CHAPTER FIVE

Botched Proposals

Being the dutiful younger son of a British father whose life was spent mostly at his law office or private club, Douglas Elliott stayed home with his invalid mother while his older brother joined their father's profession. Mrs. Elliott, being a Christian Scientist, refused to receive medical attention for her undiagnosed illness. Douglas may have told his mother about Rachel Williams when she was hired at Duncan & Davies, but may not have realized that his growing interest in her posed a threat to his mother.

One summer morning, when I'd come home from graduate school, I surprised my mother by serving her breakfast in bed— her favorite: oatmeal cooked with raisins and walnuts and a cup of cold milk on the side. (She preferred not to pour milk onto hot cereal, rendering it soggy and chilled.) Mom smiled, dipping a spoonful daintily into the milk, and asked me about my social life.

In brief, I was dating a smart, funny guy previously well-known for womanizing, though I preferred the company of some-one smarter and funnier, who suffered from spells of depression and warned me not to become attached.

Oh well, sweetie-pie. In lieu of advice, Mom used the occasion to elaborate on the historic episode that ended her four-year horticultural romance with Douglas. She described him as painfully shy, the last person to realize that he loved her. Yet one day he stunned her with an invitation to tea at his home, a stately house where, after years of working together, he'd never before taken her. *At last,* she recalled saying to herself.

They left Duncan & Davies together that afternoon, passing a row of graceful shade trees as they approached the Elliott residence. Douglas opened a side door and showed her into an elegant drawing room, where a servant brought in a silver tea service with a tray of tiny cucumber sandwiches. As they sat alone on brocaded high-backed chairs, she watched him take a deep breath, and knew *He was about to ask me to marry him.*

Rachel..., he began tenderly, but was interrupted by a furious shriek from a far room in the house, too far away to have heard anything he'd said.

Mom's face contorted as her soft voice strained to approximate the brutality of that outburst: *Get that woman out of my house! Now!*

I was speechless, unable to imagine anything more humiliating.

As her voice and features returned to normal, Mom wondered aloud whether Douglas's sickly mother had been telepathic, or had she simply intuited something that would diminish her power over him. I listened to Mom's account of this trauma with sad, helpless frustration. How could Mrs. Elliott intervene like that, if she loved her son? Was Mom indirectly warning me that loving a man with parental baggage was a recipe for heartache?

Sorry, dear, she said, handing back the breakfast tray. *It was very thoughtful of you, but I can't finish it.* Her oatmeal was barely touched. *Don't expect the boys you meet in college to be reliable. You'll have time enough to meet more mature men.*

Mom left out what happened after that wicked shriek. But since I already knew that she'd quit Duncan & Davies and moved away immediately afterward, I had to assume that Douglas had shamefully ushered his beloved guest out the door, with or without an unacceptable, spineless apology.

After Mom died I would discover that Douglas had been smitten since the moment he met her. Knowing this, I surmised that Mrs. Elliott's disapproval of her, though they'd never met, may have also resulted from class prejudice. Had what my mother perceived as Douglas's cluelessness arisen from his mother's pressure not to get involved with a woman of Welsh descent who was beneath them socially? How different would their lives have been, had his mother not thrown acid on his intentions?

I also wondered whether the humiliation she'd suffered in the Elliott residence had contributed—when she and Douglas were eventually betrothed and his mother could no longer obstruct their marriage—to Mom's decision to marry my father.

After leaving Duncan & Davies, she accepted a position as nurse companion to a wealthy older woman with emotional problems. Archdeacon Cole's wife had two rivalrous daughters near Miss Williams' age, but Rachel got along with them and was included in the family's social gatherings and events. She found their subtle means of class identification edifying, and felt duty bound to explain to me that if you were *one of us, my dear* you would know that the aristocratic surname Chalmonderly was pronounced *CHUMly*. Likewise, the family name St. John had to be mumbled *SINjun*, but not of course when referring to a saint named John.

With a glint in her eye my mother described meeting a would-be member of New Zealand's upper crust: a Mrs. Sidebottom, who insisted that her name be pronounced *sid-ee-bo-TAHM*, making unconvincingly clear that she was *one of us, my dear*. Mom had informed me at an early age that the English elite thought poorly of the Irish, but she failed to acknowledge that they also looked down upon the Welsh. She did explain, however, that by the late 19th century Wales had no remaining nobility, only the landed gentry to which our forebears belonged. Her family's status as gentry, however, became less clear once they'd emigrated to New Zealand, because their ancestral land near Cardiff had been undermined—literally—by the coal industry, making it too unstable to graze sheep.

In the Coles' social circle my mother met a rich, handsome, gifted artist named Geoff Whisker, who asked if he could sketch her. He appreciated her candor and perceptivity, and did not think less of her for being a nurse companion of Welsh descent. She respected his talent and character, despite his too-good looks and inherited wealth. They fell in love, and there was no parental interference when Geoff asked her to marry him.

Whisker. An unfortunate surname for such a fine looking man, my mother once mused. On Geoff's arm she made a triumphant return to Palmerston North, introducing her dashing new fiancé to the staff at Duncan & Davies—including Douglas, who wrote something about it later.

With no need to earn a living, Geoff had shown hardly anyone his drawings, doubted his talent, and wondered if he was just a dilettante. Mom said she encouraged him to put together a portfolio and apply to the Sydney School of Art—the pinnacle of artistic training Down Under. Their wedding plans were postponed when Geoff got the exhilarating news that he'd been accepted. Even if it meant delaying their marriage, she wanted him to have the satisfaction of proving himself as an artist.

Geoff may not have lacked the courage to marry a woman outside his social circle, but he lacked something else. Things had never got too physical with Douglas, Mom said delicately, but nowadays Geoff might be described as highly sexed. She suspected that he, being rich and handsome, had no problem taking advantage of women, when less privileged men of the time were expected to practice so-called middle class morality.

In my day, women of good breeding did not engage in such things. Society people, very few excepted, were quite ignorant and clumsy. Perhaps it was better that way.

"So nobody did much?" I asked.

Perhaps Mom had not seen her own birth certificate, a copy of which a relative sent me after her death. It showed that she was born six months after her parents' marriage.

Not if they wanted to avoid disaster. It was all I could do to hold Geoff off. He would say please, and press against me until it hurt, and I'd tell him we'd be married soon. She looked at me sympathetically. *Boys today put girls under similar pressure, but marriage is hardly ever on the table. Be thankful no one's bothering you yet, Beck.*

Geoff respected her wishes, she added, and gave her a large diamond engagement ring. But the matter wasn't settled. *He was used to getting what he wanted, and probably had his way with more than a few before he met me.* She was delighted when he was accepted at the Sydney School of Art. *Off he went with my blessing*, she sighed, though it meant he'd be away from her a formidable length of time.

There were a few days of heady excitement after his arrival. Geoff sent her a photo of himself beaming with one of his toff pals on George Street, Sydney's main thoroughfare. His physical magnetism and swagger seemed timeless. Next to it, in a former chocolate box where Mom had stored her New Zealand mementos, was a faded clipping from the Gisborne Sun:

March 10, 1937.

Miss Rachel Williams, has interrupted her study of horticulture in Palmerston North to spend a few weeks in Poverty Bay with her parents, Mr. and Mrs. D. Morgan Williams, Ruatoria East Coast, and to assist in the prepa.ations for the marriage of her sister, Gwenda, to Mr. Colin Craig, of Raglan, (whose father is Dr. Craig of Morrinsville), which takes place this month. At a later date she will be preparing for her own wedding, for she is engaged to Mr. Geoff Whisker, of Bulls, though as yet no definite date has been f.xed for the tying of the knot.

—D. Low.

For a few weeks she didn't hear from Geoff. Then one afternoon, while relaxing with a cup of tea, wearing his engagement ring and imagining him sketching live models in Sydney, she skimmed through the paper's society pages, and found herself reading an announcement of her fiancé's recent marriage!

Horrified, devastated, she removed Geoff's ring.

Days passed under a cloud of betrayal. Then Geoff materialized before her, falling on his knees, sobbing and begging forgiveness. *He told me that a blond woman had pursued him on the ship crossing to Australia, and in a moment of weakness he'd slept with her.* He'd forgotten all about it, he swore, after he arrived in Sydney, but after a few weeks the woman appeared in the art school and accusing him of getting her pregnant. Her father, she claimed, was a judge who could ruin him if he didn't marry her, and the poor booby fell for it. He returned to New Zealand as fast as he could, mortified that his beloved Rachel would read about his marriage, announced to the paper by his efficient instant bride.

Geoff swore he didn't even like the woman. Tears poured down his cheeks, Mom recalled, as he asked how he was going to live without her. *I had to forgive him,* she said, as though referring to a wayward child, and advised him to keep his dignity even in a loveless marriage. He should make the most of his artistic training, and treat his wife decently until he could see his way clear—unlikely then in high society—to a divorce. She never heard from him again.

As I saw it, the first man my mother loved lacked courage, and the second lacked moral boundaries. If she felt jinxed, she never expressed it. Perhaps I felt it for us both.

At one point I asked Mom why she'd stuck it out in the States. Looking into the distance, she replied, *I always knew that if worse came to worst I could always go back to Douglas. But I had to think about you kids.*

CHAPTER SIX

"Those are the eyes!"

I never questioned my mother's story about being stuck in North America in the summer of 1939. She'd regaled me with indelible tales of society people she'd encountered en route to British Columbia. I was entranced by her experiences traveling first class on an ocean liner from Wellington to Victoria, B.C., as the guest of Mrs. Cole and her two daughters. Her accounts of the vain, bickering Cole girls, and the irony of class distinctions, were all too real.

Each of the daughters, Mom had been awestruck to observe, brought *five* steamer trunks full of fashionable clothes, and scores of gowns for the ship's nightly dinner dances. They were greatly peeved when their mother's nurse—who alternated two simple gowns she'd sewn and accessorized with two different silk corsages in lieu of fine jewelry—was constantly invited onto the dance floor. The Cole sisters, who remained wallflowers, assumed that men were drawn to Rachel for what she was wearing. They began to fight over which of them got to wear the gown and corsage that Rachel would not be wearing each evening.

By the time the liner docked in Victoria, Mrs. Cole's nerves had snarled, frayed by her squabbling daughters. As if putting paid to her girls' obsession with clothes, she sprinted naked from her stateroom, past the posh and the hoi polloi, and tore down the gangplank, ship stewards in stunned pursuit. After an unseemly skirmish on the dock, Mom said, her patient was wrapped in a sheet and whisked away to *an elite private loony bin*.

Fortunately, her nurse was already booked in Victoria's fine Glenshiel Hotel, for a well-earned vacation, and given a generous bonus. At 31, Rachel found herself alone in North America, with a war starting up in Europe that did not seem real except for the fears of her fiancé in London. She proceeded to call upon the list of people for whom she'd been given letters of introduction by members of the Coles' circle.

Since he lived farther away in Washington State, Roger Painter was last on her list. For reasons then unknown to her, one of the Coles' richer friends had been keen on her meeting him. This strange but friendly woman had urged her to make his acquaintance, because he'd helped her enormously on an earlier trip to Canada, when they'd conferred on a matter of great importance to her. At that time he'd been part of a Theosophist enclave in British Columbia, an American who'd somehow liberated Mrs. Coles' friend from a lifetime of anxiety.

According to my mother, my father, a.k.a. Brother Nine, had been second in command to a man called Brother Twelve, who'd founded the commune. Brother Twelve, the story went, took a shine to Brother Nine's girlfriend and absconded with her, along with all the commune's funds, which were pooled in the leader's bank account. Bereft and betrayed, Roger refused to become the group's new leader, and advised them to go forth and find their individual paths, as he planned to do. In recurring dreams, he'd been inspired by visions of a pair of eyes, and the premonition that they belonged to the woman destined to be his true mate for the rest of his life.

Roger and two other Theosophists, a retired mathematician named Alfred Barley and his wife Annie, eventually acquired an abandoned 80-acre farm near Lake Stevens, Washington. It contained over 40 acres of forest incised by logging trucks, a small brook, and a few acres cleared for cultivation near the roadside. It might have been my father's idea to grow raspberries and strawberries, as the property was eventually named Painter's Berry Farm. None of them, however, had any experience growing berries. They assumed they could hire people to do the farming while they pursued the higher dimensions of Theosophy.

At the farm's entrance stood a white frame house whose front lawn was forever being disrupted by molehills that no amount of slivered glass or poison could eradicate. New unsightly mounds of dirt appeared so routinely that no one bothered to establish a path to the front door, let alone a paved walkway across the ruined lawn toward the unused porch that faced it. Instead, everyone entered through the back entrance near the kitchen. The driveway past the house became a wide turnaround for cars, tractors, and trucks, on whose other side stood a barn where tools, equipment, and stacks of berry flats were stored. A narrow fork of the driveway went up a shallow incline—remembered in my toddler's perspective as a hill—to a well-designed log house where Papa lived until after he married Mom, while my brother Johnny was a baby. When I was born they exchanged residences with Mrs. Barley, by then a widow, to give our family the larger home.

Papa, in pith helmet, and my mother, in shorts, in front of the log house. Mrs. Barley is center right. Wayne Trubshaw stands far left; an unidentified visitor far right.

The real business of the farm was not to grow and sell berries but to provide a back-to-nature Theosophical modus vivendi for my father and the Barleys—and a destination for those who wanted to consult with Brother Nine and attend his talks.

The farm barely made ends meet. As a small child I heard Mummy worrying that we might not have enough cash to pay all the pickers. Many of them seemed too old or infirm to be climbing into our rickety former school bus for a ride home after the long workday. Mom wanted to pay them a penny or two more per flat of twelve boxes than the miniscule rate at other farms, but could not afford to.

I thought of a brilliant cost-saving measure and tugged at my mother's sleeve, beaming in eagerness to solve the problem.

"Mummy, why don't you pay them with checks?"

Now that's an idea, she answered, lifting an eyebrow. Soon she was sharing my financial advice with others, and Johnny suggested gleefully that we use checks to buy a new tractor, another pickup truck, and so on. It took me awhile to understand the hilarity.

Mom had her hands full with the berry pickers, a motley assortment of gray-faced migrants in tattered clothing, locals with sullen stares, and rowdy teenagers who worked just enough for summer pocket change. Many pickers took just the berries within easy reach, topping off boxes of mostly unripe berries with ripe ones. Few would reach for the ripe, less accessible berries, but they had to be picked. That was left to my mother and whoever would help her. When I was barely old enough to do this, I turned up in the rows one day, when I was supposed to be with Annie Barley and Johnny.

Why Becky, what brings you here?

Thinking it through a moment, I answered, "Partly to be useful, partly to earn some money, and partly to be with you." As I got older she reminded me of this occasion, saying she'd been struck by how truthful I'd been for such a young child, stating my reasons so carefully. Even so, not to trouble her, I'd left out a fourth motive: to find refuge from Annie and the pact she seemed to have made against me with my brother.

The one blessing Mom secured for the berry farm was to successfully persuade the Lake Stevens Public Library to have its bookmobile make a regular stop in our driveway. It became the most exciting part of our week. Johnny and I would load up on picture books and children's primers that had us reading long before we entered elementary school.

Uncle Wayne took this picture of us in front of the bookmobile, whose license plate says 1949. It was probably in the summer, when I was two and a half, Johnny four. He was reading by then. By my sad expression, I was not yet able to.

Mental integrity—the quality that my father claimed was seldom found in women—hardly accounted for my mother's range of interests. Grandfather Williams had been an avid supporter of the Labour party in New Zealand. The nearest thing to Labour in the States had a pinko tinge in the McCarthy era. My mother read everything from supermarket tabloids to political weeklies, local and national newspapers, and women's magazines at the beauty parlor. Though an intellectual by American standards, she saw nothing déclassé in perusing The Reader's Digest, never failing to ace the vocabulary quiz in its Word Power feature.

Some anonymous neighbors resented my mother's presence on the farm and tipped off the authorities that she might be a commie. Their complaints culminated in a visit one afternoon from agents of the Federal Bureau of Investigation. They were curious about her background, her immigrant status, and whether she might have Communist sympathies. Mom recalled greeting the agents and inviting them into the living room, serving them tea, and acting flattered by their interest. As they rifled through the publications on the coffee table, she explained that she was new to this country, and tried to read as widely as possible in order to understand American culture and politics. Her father, she admitted, had supported Labour in New Zealand, but she doubted whether its views of social justice were the same as what Americans feared in socialism and communism. The FBI agents left, thanking her for a stimulating conversation, and did not trouble her again.

Other neighbors were more supportive. One was a Greek immigrant, George Pappas, who ran a prosperous dairy farm. Mr. Pappas spoke little English, and returned to the old country to bring back a Greek wife chosen by his elders. His bride was unhappy being driven around in the shiny new Cadillac George had bought to impress her, so he sought my father's advice. Papa asked George if his wife liked riding in any kind of vehicle, and George said she enjoyed sitting up in his old pickup truck. Papa suggested he get her a new pickup, and teach her to drive. The next time we saw them together, Mr. Pappas drove in with his Cadillac, followed by his wife, looking happy and driving a shiny

37

new pickup. George told my father he had no use for the Cadillac, and wanted to leave it with him, but Papa refused to take it without paying for it. Mr. Pappas said he'd accept ten dollars for it, no more, no less. Papa pulled out a ten, George took it, smiled, shook his hand, and thanked him. Then he stepped into his wife's new pickup and they drove off.

One day my brother and I learned that Papa had a family of grown children my mother's age and older, in Florida. That was when Frank Painter, the youngest son of his first marriage, arrived at the berry farm, having traveled all the way from Florida with a bad limp and a foul-smelling leg wound, and begged Papa to take him in.

Frank was our only American relative we got to know. He entered our lives in desperation, an alcoholic unable to keep a job or stay in his marriage. Mom gently asked why he was lame. Frank was ashamed, but since she was a trained nurse he let her look at the wound. When drunk, he'd either stumbled into or caused a fire that burnt the side of his leg. He hadn't taken care of it, so it stank and would not heal.

Mom cleaned and properly dressed the wound. She was kind and gracious to Frank, and Papa was proud of her nursing skills. Johnny and I enjoyed the interest our half-brother took in us. With the well-balanced meals Mom fixed and no liquor around to tempt him, Frank regained his health and spirit.

Wanting to earn his keep, Frank asked Papa to put him in charge of building a large chicken coop for a hatchery big enough for 2,000 white leghorn chickens. Frank had participated in the family poultry business in Florida, and figured that selling fresh eggs would boost the farm's bottom line. In no time he became an important presence in our family. I was too young to perceive that he'd fallen in love with my mother.

This did not occur to me until I was in graduate school, when Mom offered a strange comment out of almost nowhere. By then Frank had spent years trying to locate our family, stymied by my mother's changing married names, and finally caught up with us. He called me in New York and invited me to attend a

Painter family reunion in Jacksonville, Florida. The night before I left, Mom called. *In case anyone suggests otherwise, you should know that you are your father's child, not Frank's.*

"How's that?" —Not what I'd expected as advice for a trip to meet my half-siblings and their offspring in Florida. Mom underplayed it, saying something to the tune of while Frank was on the berry farm he'd developed some very appreciative feelings for her, and his family in Florida may have jumped to the wrong conclusion. I was too stunned to imagine whether Frank might have contributed to that conjecture, or to wonder whether it had been a real possibility.

Once Frank had regained his health and was no longer drinking, Mom mentioned, he'd been reluctant to return to his wife in Florida. *I told him to go back to her and do his best to be a caring, responsible husband.*

Evidently he'd done so. At the reunion Frank and Louise gave every indication of being content in their marriage. Perhaps, through me, Frank wanted to prove his fealty to my mother. After I returned from Florida, Mom wrote that when Frank first called her he'd made a point of saying "I still love you, gal!"

After so many years, I chose to interpret it as Platonic love.

It seems she'd given him my number and suggested I go to the reunion in Florida rather than her, perhaps to avoid rekindling an unwanted flame.

When Papa died, Johnny was five and I was three and a half. At 63 our father looked older than his years, though until the accident he'd been in good health. Egalitarian by nature, he paid the farmhands fairly, did not talk down to them, and obviously did not suspect that his orders would not be carried out promptly.

The berry farm had a barn with a loft on either side used for storage. A thick plank, bolted down on either side, spanned the lofts high above the barn's dirt floor, so one could cross from one loft to the other without having to climb down and up the side ladders. The old plank was rotting, so my father ordered a new one from the lumberyard. Days after he'd told the workers to remove the old plank and install the new, Papa went up to one of the lofts and decided he needed something from the other. The new plank was in place, so he stepped onto it and took a step or two out. Until the unbolted board bowed under his weight, slipped off the loft's rim and plunged with my father onto the hard dirt floor. The injuries he sustained in this fall led to his death.

I was not taken to see him at the hospital when he was dying, but Mom told me she could hear him screaming "Rachel! Rachel!" as she drove into the visitors parking lot. The day he died, she and Uncle Wayne returned from the hospital and found Boy, Papa's loyal detrained war dog, dead on the ground under the driver's seat of Papa's pickup truck. We all loved Boy, but clearly that animal had lived only for his master. There was something so charismatic and otherworldly about Papa, no one was surprised that his dog would die on the same day, perhaps at the same time.

Likewise, it was too bad but no surprise that he hadn't considered anything so mundane as a life insurance policy for his much younger wife.

Papa shortly before the accident, communing
with two ducks and a chicken.

My only memory of my father is of him lying on the living room sofa, injured but barking orders and waving an arm toward where work had to be done. Uncle Wayne, who'd been protective of me since I was an infant, bequeathed to me another memory. In a gruff but sympathetic tone, he asked if I remembered an occasion when my father was speaking to a group of people who'd come for one of his talks. I ran up to hug Papa's knees as he sat in his easy chair in the living room, probably to say goodnight before I went to bed. Papa shoved me away so hard, Wayne said, that I landed flat on my back. Then, as if he'd simply swatted away a fly, he resumed whatever he'd been saying and left it to Wayne or my mother to pick me up and take me away. I suppose my mind had obliterated the memory to protect me. But the fact that an old family friend, without quite saying so, had been distressed at the way my father had dealt with me so harshly in front of others, touched me, so that the scene he described became as vivid as a clip from a horror film. It convinced me of what my mother had once confided, that when she married Papa he did not want her to have children. Though a photo survives of him smiling as he crouches between Johnny and me, I view it as a mere pose for the camera. He may have liked having a young son, but my presence in his life was probably a nettlesome distraction from the attention he valued from others.

CHAPTER SEVEN

Desertion and Voices

Within a year after Papa's death, my mother married the man she'd hired to help manage the berry farm. Ray Draine's name, it turned out, was eerily apt. Sandy-haired, blue-eyed, lean and capable of solid work, his good character seemed verified by his warmhearted, well-married sister, who invited us to visit her family in their fine home in Seattle. However, as Mom saw it, Ray had assumed that marrying her would make him either full or half owner of the berry farm. When he found this not to be the case, he began to disappear on hunting trips, a.k.a. drinking binges, taking the farm's available cash.

Before his final departure, late at night when my brother was asleep, I heard Ray's voice through the wall separating the master bedroom from the one Johnny and I shared. My bed being much closer to that wall than my brother's, I could hear Ray's muffled words growing louder and harsher, then a thud. The only words I could make out were my mother's: *O Ray, don't!* – in a tone of helpless dread unlike anything I'd heard before or since.

After Ray left, Mom seemed to step away from herself. She believed that Ray had made a genuine commitment to her, the farm had to be managed, work had to be done, and she could not oversee it all. So to honor her side of the commitment she had to find him. But no one knew where he'd gone. It was a time when one of my father's adages she used to quote seemed apt: *When the spirit of reason goes out, the spirit of insanity steps in.* Ray's rage and series of desertions, despite her attempts to reason with him, reduced my mother to such a state that she began to experience strange phenomena.

I learned much later that, in answer to her pleas for help from the Unseen, my mother said she heard a voice who told her its name was "E." It instructed her to drive to a small logging town she'd never seen, where Ray would be in a tavern that "E" specified by name. She was to go inside past the bar and knock on a green door, behind which Ray would be waiting. Mom drove off alone to that town, and the tavern and green door turned out to be real. But when she knocked the door and called for Ray to come out, no one answered. The door was locked; nobody had seen or heard of Ray. "E" had been so accurate about everything else, Mom suspected they were trying to fool her. She shouted and pounded on the door until the police removed her for disturbing the peace.

All I retain from that time is a wild ride Johnny and I took with Mom, a few days before she set off to find Ray. As we tore down unfamiliar roads away from the berry farm, she ordered us to huddle in the back seat below the window so no one could see us, in case *people try to take you kids away from me.* This fear turned out to be justified, for at some point after she'd driven off to fetch Ray, people arrived at the farm and took Johnny and me away. Numb with shock, we were afraid to ask where they'd taken our mother.

Some memories disappear mercifully from the mind. Days may have passed while Johnny and I were alone on the farm. I dimly recall being escorted into a strange house, where I was handed a towel and a change of clothes, and shown where I could (should, smelled so bad I had to?) take a shower. One image remains vivid. In the shower I stooped to wash my feet and was amazed to see my heels caked with dirt as black as pitch. I'd never seen them like that and could not imagine how they got that way. As I scrubbed away the grime, it never occurred to me that I had not bathed for some time.

Nor can I be sure whether my brother and I were put in the same foster home. I remember only that at the new school I told them my name was Miriam, my middle name. I wanted to keep my real identity separate, saving my first name for the person I actually was, at the school where I belonged. Then against my will they began calling me Becky. The only person who could have blown my cover was Johnny, so if he hadn't lived in the same house with me he must have gone to the same school.

What I cannot forget was how sorely I yearned for the warmth and timbre of my mother's voice. The rare times when I heard a woman speak in a faintly similar tone, every cell of my being sprang to alert. I whirled around looking for her, shouting "Mummy!" – only to have to reabsorb the pain of her not being there.

Just once I was brought to visit her. She was sitting up in a metal bed, in a long room with other beds separated by white curtains. She acted strangely formal, with a cool reserve that was almost worse than not seeing her at all. What I longed for most— that she would hold me and promise we'd be back together soon— she did not do. My only solace was seeing her alive, though the mother I'd known did not seem present in the person I'd been allowed so briefly to visit.

Eventually my mother shared a memory that had helped her survive that ordeal. After the police had hauled her out of the tavern, she was put into a jail cell with a narrow cot beneath a high barred window. She climbed up on the cot to look out the window, crying out "Ray! Ray!" incessantly. This annoyed the officer in charge, who ordered his subordinate to get her down off the bed and make her be quiet. To my mother's lasting gratitude, the junior officer replied, "No, sir. That woman's a lady. I'm not going to touch her." So they let her yell herself hoarse, until she lay down exhausted. Whereupon the police arranged for her to be hospitalized and treated kindly.

Reflecting on this episode, my mother admitted that, in her panic after Ray left, she had not actually prayed for God's help, but had called out to any spirit in the Unseen who would guide her. Without saying, she might have been influenced by my father's fascination with the Unseen, and his reluctance to believe in a personal God.

Long after her breakdown, I noticed that Mom had brought home a tabloid from the supermarket with a headline about paranormal phenomena. "Oh, that piece on telepathy looks interesting," I said, reaching for the paper.

She snatched it away. *I didn't buy this for the piece on telepathy. I wanted to catch up on Elizabeth Taylor and read the article on reincarnation.* Waving the paper in front of me, she said, *Whatever you do, Becky, stay away from the psychic world. There are entities out there that do real harm.*

I accepted the warning, needing no reminder of the psychic episode that landed my brother and me in a foster home and her on a psycho ward. It seemed wise not to mention that a month or two after we'd returned to the farm, a strange car pulled into the driveway. No one was in the house and I was sitting by myself on the front porch. The driver rolled down his side window, leaned his head out, and called to me in a slurry way. I was his favorite. He'd made a special trip to get me, and I'd have a better life if I let him take me with him. His hand gestured to the empty seat beside him.

"I don't like you," I shouted. "You hurt Mummy. You were mean to Johnny. Go away!" For a second I stared into his reddish eyes, then bolted to the back of the house where he couldn't see me. My heart thumped in fear until the crunch of his tires against the gravel told me Ray was pulling out, never to return.

On another occasion, Mom confided that before Ray left he threw at her a stinging question. At times when they'd been arguing, she'd been too depressed to get out of bed, and hardly cared whether she went on living. What snapped her out of it, she said, was Ray snarling at her, "If you just lie in bed and die, who's going to look after those goddamn kids?"

She did not elaborate on the extent of her malaise, or whether it bore some relation to his leaving her. Whether or not she should have told me about his parting shot, it was bracing.

CHAPTER EIGHT

A Polite Marriage

Verne McCormick, the farm manager who replaced Ray, told my mother that a divorce on grounds of desertion would be processed quickly. This proved correct. Unlike Ray, Verne was frank about his alcoholism. He assured Mom he'd been on the wagon many years, and he appreciated being entrusted with a responsible position on her farm. It was good to see her being treated with respect, but his manner hardly seemed romantic.

His prematurely silver hair was combed straight back with a sheen of pomade, unusual among farmers. His gray eyes peered out over a straight, thin nose, facial lines fixed in an expression of wary suspicion. He looked presentable, but at seven my take was that he lacked warmth. Mom began to invite him to join us for dinner, and seemed grateful to be treated with almost British reserve. Verne knew better than to order her around like Ray, but his manner was oddly distant. He told us he'd been discharged from the army for having too high an I.Q.

Becky, what would you think if I married Verne? It was the first really adult question Mom had ever asked me. As I turned eight, she was putting our lives back together and seemed to have recovered from her breakdown. But I feared her rushing into another marriage, especially with him. I took awhile to respond, hoping she'd be as moved now as when I'd told her why I'd come to help her pick berries.

"Mummy, I don't think you should marry him. I don't believe Verne will make you happy. There's something strange about him. Johnny and I don't like him and he doesn't seem to like us." I could not explain why. There was something hidden about him, though his manners were almost proper to a fault.

She gave me a pensive look, said nothing, and married him anyway.

Perhaps, as with Ray, Mom might have been moved by the man's welcoming family. His older brother, Ernest, was a distinguished looking retired naval officer with a kind, outgoing wife, Irene. His younger sister Esther had married a gentle fellow named Vern without the final "e" who everyone called Vernie. Verne's younger brother, Beryl, was rotund, odd and childlike, and lived with a loquatious aunt who was glad for his company, since her husband was nearly deaf. Except for the cautious Beryl, they all seemed relieved that Verne was marrying such a hospitable, sensible woman, and said nothing to us about his previous life. All we knew was what he'd told us: he hadn't had a drink in 20 years and had been honorably discharged from the Army for being too intelligent.

Time would prove, however, that in his case I hadn't been a bad judge of character. Verne did not openly dislike Johnny and me. He tolerated our presence with stoic restraint. In ways that Mom revealed later, he could not have made her happy. But the jobs he held helped us survive after we lost the farm.

CHAPTER NINE

Brother or Nemesis

The seat next to me was empty on my flight to Seattle, in the autumn of 1996. Through the window I watched the plane's ghostly shadow tracking us across the clouds, and wondered if my brother's spirit was tracking me. Fourteen years had passed since our mother's greatest sorrow, outliving her favorite child. In a parallel universe—if we'd been closer, and he in a stabler marriage—Johnny might have taken the seat next to me. I suspected Mom would have preferred his company, though she'd want me around to cook and tidy things up. But here I sat, the surviving sibling, longing to convince her at last of my love for her, and solve the riddle why she hadn't acknowledged this truth since I was a young girl. Perhaps Johnny, along with other supportive souls in the Unseen, would be able to help us both.

There's a family photograph of Johnny and me when he'd started school while I remained in kindergarten. It was taken professionally, where we were seated together in front of a white curtain. The photographer, unaware of the boy's revulsion toward me, told my brother to put his arm around my waist. For a second, Johnny obeyed gingerly, pulling away as soon as the shutter snapped. That he would do so even fleetingly made me glow with happiness. My plump face beams in the photo, but you'd be hard put to see a wisp of feeling in the uneasy little guy's face. I loved the picture. Why didn't Mummy display it in a nice frame? Perhaps for Johnny's sake.

After he'd learned to play the clarinet and became popular in school, my brother's life became a mix of hidden hard work, risk-taking in the face of authority, unspoken personal honor, and cocky self-indulgence. Seeds for the latter trait, I believe, had been sown by Annie Barley, widow of the berry farm's co-owner. Johnny and I were often put in Annie's care while our mother tried to manage the berry pickers. Annie had real affection for Johnny, but zero interest in me. Most likely she tolerated me only because of Papa.

Painter's Berry Farm was in northwestern Washington, near Granite Falls and Lake Stevens. In the late 1940s there were still glorious forests to be plundered, and our farm's swath of old growth trees was its most valuable asset. Logging trucks hauling enormous fragrant trunks, or swinging long empty flatbeds behind them, roared down the unpaved road in front of our house. Annie used to hold Johnny's hand and walk carefully with him on the road's slim shoulder, toward a service station that sold candy less than a mile from the farm. The first time I sensed personal danger and no one looking out for me was when I was three or four, waddling yards behind them, trying to keep up.

Once, after we'd left the farm, Mom admitted that sometimes she would look up from the rows of berries and see me trundling far behind Annie and Johnny on the dusty road past the farm. *All I could do was pray no truck would hit you.* I was taken aback to learn that she'd seen me in danger without running to get me, but did not think to ask if she'd ever expressed her concern to Papa or Annie. My childhood impression was that the pickers could have continued without her for awhile, but maybe some sense of having to stay helping Papa had held her back.

After this confession, my mother stared into her tea and muttered, *I'm afraid Annie may have turned your brother against you.* She confided her suspicion that Annie had expected Papa to marry her after Mr. Barley died, and may have favored Johnny because she associated the boy with his father. She thought Annie's disregard of me might have stemmed from the mother-daughter connection. *Annie,* Mom added, *wasn't the only woman who resented me for depriving them of Roger's, shall we say, personal attention.*

I didn't blame Johnny for enjoying Annie's coddling when Mom was busy with the farm. But without Annie's influence, I believe my brother and I would have had a better chance to be pals. To my surprise, people who knew us on the farm remembered me as a bubbly, inventive child who made up games and toys to entertain my brother. But after Papa died Annie moved off the farm, leaving behind a drop of poison in my brother's heart.

With Annie gone, Johnny could no longer bask in her favoritism. Ray Draine, our first stepfather, called Johnny a sissy and a spoiled brat, and my brother would complain to Mom that Ray did not criticize me equally.

Johnny went off to school two years before me, though he was just 18 months older. He quickly made friends with other boys and was reluctant to let me join their games when they came to the farm. By the time I got to school I'd become shy and wary of being excluded. Perhaps for that reason I often was.

Confident of being accepted, Johnny became impish in a deadpan way. When his fourth grade class was encouraged to bring their pets to school for a show-and-tell contest, he and his friend Buddy Kukle decided to upend the event. Having no respect for anyone who would encage birds or hamsters, or drag in the family dog or cat, Johnny hatched a plan. He asked Mom for a large Mason jar, and he and Buddy disappeared into the woods on our property. When they returned, the jar was lined with plump, slimy, black-speckled brown slugs common in the Northwest, their undersides luridly exposed against the clear glass.

"Want to see our pets?" Johnny asked the girls, pokerfaced.

This happened when we both attended Getchell School, formerly a church, where grades 1-3 were in one room and 4-6 in the other. I was not in the room that hosted the pet contest, but heard the girls shriek when they saw the slugs. The next morning a photo of the two Getchell boys appeared on the front page of the *Marysville Globe*, solemnly holding their jar of slugs. An equally deadpan caption stated their names as entrants in Getchell School's pet contest.

There being no little girls nearby for me to play with, I tried to join Johnny and his friends. Sometimes he'd let me, since I could help build a tree house, play catch, leap into the neighbor barn's hayloft, or dig snow tunnels as well as a boy. Johnny's friends were ready to accept me if he did, and there were moments when I felt we were all pals. Other times they took off without me as though we were strangers, or worse, from my brother's perspective.

The only reference I heard our mother make to the problem was an anecdote that never failed to amuse others. In it, Mom described the time Babs O'Neal, one of the berry farm's favorite customers, stopped by to pick up a dozen eggs, when Johnny and I were *in the midst of a sibling row*. As the story went, Mom was flustered when she answered the door, and Babs apologized for catching her at a bad time. *Oh Babs*, she replied, *if you only knew how helpless I feel. My son hates his sister!* To my mother's dismay, Babs burst out laughing, saying, "Good Lord, Rachel! Be thankful you don't have my problem!" At this point my mother would raise her eyebrows, change her tone and widen her eyes to imitate Babs, who confided plaintively, "My son likes his sister too much!!"

Everyone thought this was hilarious. Except me, who thought a boy who liked his sister too much sounded far better than hating her. I came to sense that in some cases people laugh at things to spare themselves the burden of compassion.

Johnny and I did have some sort of bond. Through early childhood we shared a bedroom, and at night he'd ask me to tell him a story to put him to sleep. I made them as fantasmagoric as possible, and at the peak moment I'd call out, "Johnny, are you listening?" He was never awake enough to answer, but I'd finish every story in case some part of him was listening, and to hear myself how it ended.

His greatest fear was bees, which roamed all over the farm. More than a few times he ran toward me, ghostly pale, crying "Becky! Becky! A bee!" He would hide behind me while I stood very still, watching the bee until it flew away. Instinct told me that sudden movements caused a bee to feel threatened and sting. When I learned that some people can die from a bee sting, I wondered whether Johnny's own instincts had made him so terrified of being stung. I like to imagine that I might have saved his life, but I'll never know.

Our mother had a legendary experience with Johnny before I was born. She was hesitant to call it a miracle, but at the very least it indicated a mysterious connection between intense human will and supernatural occurrences. As Mom told it, before Johnny learned to walk he used to crawl around the kitchen floor while she was cooking. One day she turned away from the stove for a moment and did not see him move toward it, where she'd prepared a pan full of sizzling hot fat. Out of the corner of her eye she saw a little hand reach up and tug on the pan's handle, and in the instant before it all capsized over him, she shouted NO! with all the force of her being. She watched the contents splash over him, hot enough to fry his skin. To her amazement, Johnny just sat there and smiled at her as though nothing much had happened. He blinked a few times, and was covered with grease, but his skin was hardly pink! If it wasn't a miracle, she said, it was the nearest she'd ever seen.

When Verne was helping her manage the farm, Mom spent all she could afford to buy my brother a good violin, thinking he'd be thrilled to play it. After a brief attempt, Johnny screamed "I hate this!" and pitched it across the living room, where it shattered against a wall. Mom was horrified, and furious at his ingratitude. When he begged her to get him a clarinet, she went to a pawnshop in Everett and bought the cheapest one there. It was dented, scratched, and appeared to be made of tin, but Johnny did not complain. He liked its reedy tone, and Flavia, our family friend, got him started with lessons at no charge.

Johnny got up early each morning to practice before school, struggling to produce a decent sound out of that tin tube, and soaking his reeds in a glass overnight. As his lung capacity increased, his own voice became stronger and fuller. As he mastered the fingering and learned to play simple pieces, his confidence grew. One morning I awoke to hear "Frosty the Snowman," note perfect for the first time, at a steady jaunty tempo. My brother's joy at this achievement uplifted the melody and made my heart swell. When he no longer lived with us, hearing that silly tune at Christmas time brought tears to my eyes.

CHAPTER TEN

Monaco Beach and Beyond

Among old-time farmers in Washington State, a mention of the freeze of 1955 brought grim nods of understanding. Its frigid cold killed the roots of our berry plants, so there would be no new crop in the summer. Thanks to Frank Painter's efforts, the farm's egg business thrived, but chickens alone could not keep us afloat. We did not go bankrupt because Mom sold the farm to pay off its debts. We had to move on, but where?

Verne may have had other skills, but he was silent about his previous work history. Without a license in the States, nursing was not an option for my mother, and her knowledge of sheep ranching Down Under was hardly applicable to this part of the world. Too little was left from the sale of the farm to put money down on another home. We were close to becoming transients like many berry pickers we used to hire.

Then Mom saw an ad in the Help Wanted section of the Everett Herald for a working couple at a saltwater resort on Puget Sound, housing provided. She called the number and spoke with the owner, Mildred Stromley Ruff, who must have been impressed with her plummy accent. *We had a pleasant chat*, Mom said afterward, with a slight nod. She and Verne were hired without having to go there in person. The next thing we knew, Johnny and I were riding in the back seat of the Cadillac, heading for a place called Monaco Beach on Camano Island.

Our move to this remote shore on Puget Sound boiled down to a deal between two women of similar backgrounds. Mrs. Ruff was also the daughter of a self-made man who lacked a son. Both she and my mother had learned to hold their own among dominant men. Each had married a man they'd hired to help manage a property they'd inherited. Verne and Rachel McCormick may not have fit her profile for the resort's boatman and cleaning woman, but Mildred hired them sight unseen. It didn't hurt that the Ruffs had two children, the younger daughter my age. It might have crossed Mildred's mind that Johnny and I might give her girls, Suzanne and Kate, a bit of company.

Monaco Beach had been hewn by Mildred's father, Mr. Stromley, from a tract of dense forest he'd bought for a song on the southwest shore of then sparsely populated Camano Island, a quasi-peninsula between Whidbey Island and the mainland. Stromley probably purchased this expanse during the Great Depression, removing just enough trees to build resort cabins near the shore, with a narrow access road that wound down through the forest to reach them. The woods he left uncut seemed to go on for miles.

We followed a map to Stanwood, crossed a stubby little bridge over the mud flat that turned Camano into an island at high tide, passed a few farms and isolated homes, and drove into a shadowy stretch of wilderness. Anyone searching for the entrance to Monaco Beach found themselves driving indefinitely under a canopy rarely pierced by sunlight. Peering through the Cadillac's dusty windows for signs of habitation, we wondered how such an endless forest could make room for a beach resort. Then a small gap appeared in the trees, marked by a handpainted sign: MONACO BEACH – Private Property – Registered Guests Only. Verne steered our stalwart old boat down a sliver of packed earth and gravel, through hairpin turns lined with stately pines. He hit the brakes hard when the trail opened out onto a breathtaking view of Puget Sound across to Whidbey Island. Another sharp turn put us at the resort's entrance.

Whitecaps were rolling that day between Camano and Whidbey Islands. A low cement bulkhead was all that separated us from the gray pebbled, driftwood-lined beach that sloped quickly into cold seawater. Stepping out of the car to the sound of waves pulsing on the shore, Mummy took a deep breath and sighed, *Ah, salt sea air.* It did not occur to me that she'd grown up within a horseback ride from such air on the other side of the Pacific. I got a whiff of seaweed rotting on the beach and reserved judgment. It was way different from the farm's dry aroma of loam and dust.

We must have been a sight, arriving homeless in a vehicle finer than our employers'. Verne told them our Caddy was a relic of times past. Though the Ruffs did not treat us as inferiors, working and living there was hardly a charitable arrangement. Verne interacted with the public more, renting boats to the guests and offering advice from his reservoir of fishing lore. Mom, however, became the resort's nearly invisible custodian, scrubbing cabin floors, changing linens, tidying the social hall after guests had left. It was hard on her back and hands, and potentially humiliating, given her upbringing.

Somehow she'd let us know that in British society a charwoman was viewed as one of the lowest of the low. *I'm glad this is America, where people don't care so much about class distinctions.* She cared, though. One could sense a struggle for dignity in her avoidance of discussing the drudgery of her job, refusing to harbor bitterness or self-pity. Without mentioning it, she adhered to the advice she'd once given her sister: *It's not what happens to you that matters, it's what you make of it.* Her example could not have been lost on Aunt Gwenda, whose husband would lose his job, and eventually his sanity, to alcoholism. With three children and no particular training, Gwenda considered herself lucky to find steady work on the custodial staff of a local hospital. She held this job until retirement, long after she'd successfully raised a family. Perhaps Gwenda was better able to ignore the social stigma of being a charwoman because her revered older sister had labored as one before her.

The Ruffs' roomy split-log house stood aside the entrance to Monaco Beach. A back entrance connected with the resort's small convenience store and registration office, with a side entry to the social hall. While Mom and Verne discussed the terms of their employment with Mildred and Viktor Ruff, Johnny and I explored the enormous lounge with its rustic furniture, dance floor, and walls of knotted pine, lined with fading photos of grinning men holding up very large dead fish. Off-season, the space seemed to recall and anticipate livelier times. We'd never been to a resort nor taken a vacation, so the idea of a vast room framed by easy chairs where people did nothing but relax or step onto the dance floor seemed unreal. Slowly it sunk in that better-off folks did this sort of thing regularly. Mom and Verne were there to work; guests were there not to.

Monaco Beach was booked mostly by returning clientele, who referred new guests, so there was no need to advertise. Set back from the other side of the entrance stood two rows of small cottages facing the beach. Overlooking them from higher up the bank were larger bungalows at the edge of the woods. Gravel crunched beneath the wheels of the Cadillac as Verne drove us past a cement tennis court enclosed by high walls of metal mesh, past the boathouse with row upon row of rental boats stacked bottom-up, to the Boatman's Cottage, where we parked to stay. Our new home was a simple wood structure with no yard other than gravel. It was small for a family of four, heated by a wood-burning stove in the kitchen. Johnny and I slept on either side of a low-ceiling loft, up a narrow wooden staircase. Mom and Verne's bedroom was adjacent to the kitchen, behind a small living room-dining area whose window looked across the dark water toward Whidbey. On clear days we could see Mount Rainier, a view that might have been my mother's only consolation.

The high point of Mom's workday after cleaning the cabins was freshening up the lounge and social hall in late afternoon. Mrs. Ruff would emerge from the resort's mini-store and offer her tea. The two of them shared a break, chatting about their children, news of the world, who was who among the guests, and whatever else. I doubt Mildred would have made their teatime a regular occurrence if she hadn't thought my mother interesting. Considering that some exceptional people had already found her company inspiring—not realizing how isolated she and Mildred were, and in need of thoughtful companionship—I thought it strange that Mom set such store by those cups of tea.

Viktor Ruff was taciturn, from recent immigrant stock, and acted more like Mildred's subordinate than her husband. She decided whom to hire, which guests to accept, and who deserved special privileges. Tall and big-boned like Viktor, Mildred never wore make-up, and her best feature—wavy, natural auburn hair—was crudely cut. Maybe it was once a love match, but Mom had her doubts.

Other women might have been stymied having to cook on a woodburning stove, but it was uncanny how easily my mother finessed lighting and stoking its fire, priming the skillet, rotating baked dishes to balance the oven's lopsided heat, always producing tasty meals. She did this without complaint, and with too scant praise. She'd had an electric range on the berry farm, but no one considered that she may have mastered cooking on a wood-burning stove in her youth at Mangaotawhito.

Flavia took this photo of Mom with Benjamin, her blue Persian cat—
the runt of a litter whose fur wasn't thick enough for cat shows—by
the woodpile next to the Boatman's Cottage, off camera to the right.
Suzanne and I sit atop the Cadillac, next to Flavia's car, while Johnny
holds up a baseball bat on the hood of the Hillman Minx that Mom
got for better mileage. The boathouse is visible left of the cars.

Mom and I both needed company at Monaco Beach. If I got
too lonely I would drop in while she was cleaning cabins. Though
pleased to see me, she continued sweeping and scrubbing and
would only let me help her make the beds with hospital corners. I
became an avid beachcomber, filling jars with translucent agates,
lining our windowsills with rare spiraled shells and ringed stones
signaling good luck. In lieu of a lawn, driftwood I'd collected
made a decorative border around our cottage. Mom was so taken
with one piece that she had Verne make it into a lamp.

One of the resort's preferred guests was Dr. MacLaine, a
physician who struck up a conversation with my mother while
she was cleaning the bungalow next to his. He asked about her
accent, and soon found himself in a meeting of minds. Like Mom,
he was well read, with insights into health issues that were ahead
of the times. He respected her knowledge and shared her regret

that medical schools did not offer training in nutrition, which both of them believed essential for wellness and disease prevention. Dr. MacLaine visited with us every summer, reporting that, among other things our mother had suggested, he was sprinkling wheat germ on his breakfast cereal, and giving his wife tablets of desiccated calves' liver to cure her anemia.

Best of all, he taught Johnny and me to play tennis. Kind, firm, with a steady banter of encouragement, Dr. MacLaine showed us the essentials of a strong game. He insisted I hit the ball as hard as I could to keep my brother on his toes, and persuaded the Ruffs to install a backboard at one end of the resort's tennis court. He said it would allow the guests to practice their strokes, knowing that the cleaning lady's kids would use it the most. At the backboard Dr. MacLaine demonstrated how to punch forehands, backhands and volleys. He saved a basket of used balls for us to practice our serves, and gave each of us a racquet he said he no longer used. Johnny began to pick up games with some of the guests.

Though it was decades after our mother played in boarding school, tennis was still considered a sport of the privileged. She was glad to have a skilled player teaching us, as she had no time or energy to do so. Dr. MacLaine was impressed that she'd won tournaments in New Zealand, where she'd also been a nurse. He encouraged her to enter a nurses training program in the States, even if circumstances prevented her from becoming a Registered Nurse, as she would have been in New Zealand. Whenever they discussed medical topics they seemed to exude a mixture of reserved joy and mutual regard that I did not see when Mom was with anyone else.

It would not have been proper for Dr. MacLaine to invite us to his bungalow, but he enjoyed dropping by the Boatman's Cottage on Mom and Verne's day off. Mrs. MacLaine did not join him. She kept to herself, and seemed not to enjoy vacationing at Monaco Beach. Verne and Mom surmised that the MacLaines were not happily married. At one point, when they were discussing the MacLaines, I overheard the word divorce. I was about nine, and what little I knew about divorce struck me as a sensible choice for the kindly doctor and his aloof wife.

The following summer Mrs. Ruff alerted us when the MacLaines would be returning. She'd booked them in the best bungalow and had Mom leave a welcome basket of fruit on their table. Soon after they arrived Dr. MacLaine strolled by to ask how things had gone for us since the previous summer. We were delighted to see him, and he seemed to glow as he chatted with us.

The next day I spotted Mrs. MacLaine sitting alone on the bulkhead, staring sullenly at the waves. I greeted her, then plunged headlong into a cringe-inducing exchange that Mom would repeat for the amusement of others for years:

"Hi, Mrs. MacLaine! I hear you and Dr. MacLaine are getting a divorce."

"No, I haven't heard about it," she replied softly. "Not yet."

That ended my mother's horrific anecdote, which she used to illustrate my talent for rudeness. However, I recall that after I'd dropped that bomb, Mrs. MacLaine looked only mildly surprised, took a long drag on her cigarette, and stared out to sea as if it was not something she was unaware of.

"Oh, I'm so sorry," I stammered. "Please excuse me. I must have heard that about someone else. I hope you enjoy your stay here." She nodded indulgently. I trudged away mortified, in search of my mother's cleaning cart.

Becky, Mom insisted, *you must NEVER be the one to say anything personal about someone unless they bring up the topic FIRST. And ONLY if they seem ready to discuss it. And then with UTMOST discretion—which at your age you do not possess!*

All I knew about divorce was that it had freed my mother from Ray Draine. As a result I'd been terribly indiscreet with Mrs. MacLaine. Most of all, I feared Dr. MacLaine would no longer visit us and offer Johnny and me his tennis tips.

Amazingly, Dr. MacLaine remained warm and gracious as ever, never mentioning what Uncle Wayne called my *fox's paw.* Maybe his wife hadn't mentioned it to him. Or if she had, he might have sympathized with me for blurting out a possibility that kindness and decency would not permit him to act upon.

Truth be told, Johnny and I liked Dr. MacLaine far better than Verne. We were sorry to lose touch with him when we left Monaco Beach, but kept his memory alive in our tennis game.

Mom used my gaffe with Mrs. MacLaine as a prime example of my tendency *to slap the truth in someone's face like a wet dishrag.* Though she could not accuse me of ruining a valued family friendship, she used it to cement in me a lifelong fear of tactlessness. In coining this unforgettable simile, she doubtless had in mind a foul-smelling dishrag, the kind she would soak in a bowl of hot water and bleach. Alas, their stench would vanish for awhile, only to return. For her sake, I've tried waiting for others to utter the truth first. Unfortunately, bluntness tends to reemerge no matter what kind of bleach I soak it in.

The most shameful communication of my middle school years, however, was nonverbal. On a weekend afternoon I was walking past the tennis court on my way to the Boatman's Cottage, when I caught sight of Suzanne—who'd shown no interest in tennis until Johnny and I started playing—receiving a lesson from a professional tennis instructor. She'd already copied my practice of beachcombing for driftwood, agates and shells, and did likewise when she saw me checking out stacks of books from the Stanwood Public Library. Her behavior struck me as strangely oppressive, a reaction unhelped by my mother's repeated adage: *Imitation is the sincerest form of flattery.* Willing the gravel not to crunch under my feet, I tried to slip past the court unnoticed, and almost succeeded, when Suzanne called out, "Becky, look! I've got a new racquet!!"

Burning with resentment, I found myself for the first and only time in my life making the shameful gesture from which the word *snooty* is derived. Glancing back at her, I could not stop my nose from jerking skyward and my chin from jutting out in defiance. Then a wave of remorse pushed me past the court toward the Boatman's Cottage. I was ashamed of myself for reacting this way to Suzanne's innocent enthusiasm—even more than for jabbering about divorce to Mrs. MacLaine. But I was so mortified by the ugliness of my response that I could not bring myself to turn back and pretend to admire Suzanne's racquet.

Given the ridicule I'd received for my tactlessness with Mrs. MacLaine, I waited till after supper. Washing the dishes, I mentioned to Mom that Suzanne had offered to show me her new racquet and I couldn't think what to say to her.

Well dear, it's not the racquet that makes the player. You've made such progress with the one Dr. MacLaine gave you. Why would you need a new one?

While we lived at Monaco Beach I had a medical problem too embarrassing to bring up with Dr. MacLaine, though he might have brought it to an end sooner. Night after night I had vivid, lifelike dreams of getting up and going to the bathroom, safely sitting on the toilet—only to wake up in horror as hot urine soaked through my pajamas and into the sheets, quickly turning cold and smelly.

"Mama!" I'd cry out in distress. Every time she'd appear as swift as an angel, always comforting, never angry or exasperated that I could not control my bladder. Night after night, year after year, she changed my sheets, washed me with a warm soapy cloth, dried me with a towel, and put me into clean pajamas. Throughout this long, humiliating affliction I feared my mother's kindness would turn into blame and disgust. But it never wavered. For this I would always bless her.

I was finally diagnosed for a chronic kidney infection, and given sulpha drugs. Overnight the bedwetting ceased.

As our third summer at Monaco Beach came to an end, Mom was closing up the last of the cabins when a disoriented motorist barreled through the resort's entrance, braking inches before the seawall. As my mother told it, the driver, a youngish man, saw her pushing her cleaning cart nearby and rolled down this window. "What place is this?" he shouted.

"Monaco Beach," my mother said wearily. Hadn't he read the sign?

Taking note of her work clothes and cart, the man replied jauntily, "Princess Grace, I presume?"

Mom insisted she'd answered with a straight face: *Well, someone has to look after Prince Rainier.*

They both laughed, but Mom was so amused that she had to compose herself before she could direct him toward his destination.

I imagined him being impressed at the inner elegance of this cleaning lady with a quick wit and plummy New Zealand accent. The way he smiled and thanked her, my mother concluded, was *in the manner of true friends.*

Mom loved telling this story and I loved hearing it. It was liberating for her to find hilarity in her frowsy exterior, to relish her role in an impromptu skit in which she'd bested a smart-mouthed motorist. To me it signified her genuine regality of character, a worthy stand-in for the former Grace Kelly, with a cartful of cleaning regalia at the entrance to a New World Monaco. It marked the onset of her joke-telling expertise. From someone who'd routinely botch a punch line, Mom progressed into an effortless raconteur who could make people laugh even as she lay dying.

Down the road past Monaco Beach, the Camano Island State Park posted an opening for an assistant ranger. Verne got the job, but the park provided a residence for the head ranger only. A neighboring resort needed a caretaker over the winter months, so we stayed there while Verne finished his training. Chances are Mrs. Ruff made that connection for us. She may have tipped Verne off about the state park position as well. By early summer Mom had found us a house with a gate made of two historic wagon wheels brought there by early settlers. From the dinner table of our new home we had a loftier view of Puget Sound, and Mom could cook on an electric range in a spacious kitchen.

Flavia took this photo of Mom in front of a row of shrubs she'd planted, looking gratified to have a lawn and a house of her own.

After we'd moved into our new home on Camano, Mildred called to ask how we were doing. Mom, looking flattered, chatted with her as though they'd never been boss and employee. Mildred was impressed that Johnny and I were getting such good grades at school, Mom reported. She'd heard about my drum playing and Johnny's skill with the clarinet, and said that I'd been a good influence on Suzanne, who took her studies more seriously to keep up with me. Mom mentioned that she'd bought me a piano that I was learning to play, a sturdy old upright with real ivory keys, but not that she'd paid almost nothing for it at a garage sale. She told Mildred that Johnny and I were receiving music lessons in Everett, not that a family friend was teaching us for free.

Though Mildred reached out to her after we left Monaco Beach, my mother made no effort to continue the relationship. She could laugh at herself in the role of Princess Grace, but showed little desire to revisit the charwoman associations attached to it.

While Verne was training to be a state park ranger, Mom enrolled in classes to be licensed as a practical nurse. She scored at the top of her class on her final exam. Frankly, a score of 98 was something my brother and I would have expected her to receive—and frequently got ourselves. We either forgot or hadn't known when her commencement ceremony would take place, but one Sunday afternoon we found ourselves in the back seat of the old Cadillac with Verne pokerfaced at the wheel.

The convocation passed in a blur. Sadly, Mom focused on a classmate who had not graduated with distinction: *Did you notice how proud that woman's children were of their mother, giving her a mug saying World's Best Mom? Why is it I can place at the top of my class and you kids take it for granted?* Plunging the knife in further, she noted that the mug those kids gave their mother was an affordable gift.

"But Mummy," I protested, "we *are* proud of you...but how would we get into town to buy you something like that?" Verne could have taken us, but he stayed out of the discussion.

She was in tears. *Well, you are both clever enough. You could have spent a few minutes making me a card.*

Johnny got himself off the hook with a comment about dorky mugs being for people who had a hard time passing. This won him a wan smile and left me the burden of guilt. Not to further dampen her spirits, I left unsaid my fierce belief that, given her nursing experience in New Zealand, she deserved to be a Registered Nurse. I was sorry she could only afford a Practical Nurse's training. The pain of Mom's disappointment that we hadn't given her a graduation gift persisted after all the other memories of this milestone had dissolved.

How many other disappointments had she buried that would resurface later?

CHAPTER ELEVEN

An Open Mind, or The X-File

Verne had no degrees, but he had a skill other men envied: a genius for fly fishing. He could choose a spot on a river or on Puget Sound, a stone's throw away from anglers who'd been fishing for days without catching anything. Within an hour or two his basket would be filled with a large catch, sometimes so many he would share them with the luckless anglers.

Verne met Burt Kruger while fishing. A wiry, silver-haired former Navy pilot, Burt wasn't bothered that Verne caught more fish. He preferred to learn from a master of flies, lures, tackle and casting techniques. Verne invited him to join us for dinner at our new home on Camano Island—the only friend he ever had us meet. At this dinner Burt discovered that his friend's wife, besides cooking a fine meal, was informed on many subjects and had a sense of humor keener than Verne's.

As I cleared away the dinner dishes, Burt mentioned that he used to live on a bluff on Washington's coast, with nothing west of him but the Pacific. Then he hesitated, and asked if we'd promise to keep secret what he was about to tell us. He didn't want to be written off as a nut case, especially by his old Navy buddies. Nor did he want the Feds coming after him for knowing something about things they didn't want anyone but them to know. Verne, Johnny and I took our cue from Mom, who smiled indulgently, saying *Of course.*

A few years back, he explained, he had trouble sleeping since his missus had recently died. None of his neighbor friends stayed up late, so he spent most nights out on his deck scanning the sky with Navy-issued night binoculars, getting familiar with lesser-known constellations and spotting the occasional comet. One night, he said, he noticed an unusually bright object near the horizon, throwing off way too much light to be an airliner or any kind of military plane. What's more, the damn thing seemed to be moving steadily toward him. As it drew closer he made out its slightly oval shape, almost flat, like an egg fried sunny side up.

His eyes scanned us for hints of skepticism, but we were all there for him.

Burt said he watched the object grow ever more distinct as it approached the coast. Somebody else had to be seeing this, he thought, he couldn't be the only one. As soon as this thought entered his mind, he insisted—eyes widening as he leaned over the table—the vessel's underside went pitch black, while the top half stayed lit up! It felt like that sucker was reading his mind! If you hadn't been tracking it for some time from a vantage point like his, he swore, it could have damn well hidden itself from all detection.

Halfway down the coastal bluff in front of his house, Burt went on, there was an inaccessible grassy shelf that protruded above the shore. The craft blacked out its underside light and moved directly toward this spot. In no time he could hear and feel the vibration of its hum as it landed on the isolated ledge, where no one could disturb it. When the humming stopped, Burt felt an uncanny certainty that he was the only earthling who knew it was there. Damned if he was going to stroll over to the edge of the bluff for a closer look, though. We should understand that he was not above being terrified by an encounter with extraterrestrials. But in this case he felt that the occupants of the vessel were communicating clearly that they had no intention of troubling him. He was so convinced of their wordless, invisible message that he went to bed, calm as you please, and got the best night's sleep he'd had in years.

When he awoke the next morning Burt knew the spacecraft had gone. He had no qualms walking over to the edge of the bluff to look down at the grassy ledge, where plain as day he saw the imprint it had made on the wild grass where it landed—a precise oval of blackened stubble. He assured us he was not dumb enough to fetch his camera and record the image for posterity. The irony was, when he was a Navy pilot he used to scoff at sightings of so-called unidentified flying objects. Now he believed that at least some UFOs were as real as you and me, operated by beings with finer intelligence and technological mastery than anything known to man. But he couldn't share this belief with anyone—ourselves excepted—without being labeled certifiable. To avoid any repeat visits from this craft, he sold his house and moved inland to Puget Sound, where he could look out over the same salt water, but not the ocean.

My mother spoke first. *Well, Burt, you can be thankful you weren't abducted. I've read some frightful accounts of that type of thing.*

Burt shook his head with relief. "That's for damn sure."

Verne gave Mom a blank look. Her acquaintance with this subject matter was news to him. He seemed unaware that she kept abreast of supermarket tabloids like the National Enquirer, but did not bring them home.

Verne and Mom assured Burt that his secret would be safe with us. He thanked us for hearing him out. *On the contrary, Burt,* my mother insisted, *we're grateful that you trusted us with such a momentous experience.* Burt seemed grateful, too, to be freed from his burden of secrecy.

The way my mother responded to Kruger's account had a lasting influence on me. From that point on I hesitated to dismiss anyone's far-out story, no matter how unearthly.

I wished we'd stayed in touch with Burt, but soon after his visit Verne got promoted and transferred to Millersylvania State Park. It was too far south for friends from Camano to visit, and too distant for me to continue my piano lessons with Flavia. Only Uncle Wayne made the long drive from Marysville to see us on weekends.

That dinner with Burt was probably our happiest moment as a family with Verne. We were in our own home, comfortable and enjoying a fascinating visit from Verne's only known friend— before the troubles began between my mother and me.

CHAPTER TWELVE

Cursed by Her Favorite Patient

My mother's first nursing job in this country was on the night shift at Northern State Mental Hospital, a long commute upstate to Sedro-Woolley. Returning to Camano Island one morning, Mom was less than a mile from home when she fell asleep at the wheel. Her foot relaxed on the accelerator, sending her tiny Hillman Minx off the road and into a tree. Someone heard the crash and called for an ambulance, which took over 30 minutes to arrive from Stanwood. My mother's head had burst through the driver's side window, her right hand thrust into the windshield. Her nose was crushed and she'd lost a lot of blood. The medics said she would not have survived another hour.

After she recovered from the accident, Mom joked that her reconstructed nose was far more becoming than the original. Shards of glass, however, had cut into her right hand. When healed, that hand's finger joints were twice as large as those of her left, and could not bend easily. This did not prevent her from returning to her job at Northern State, where her skills had been noticed and she'd been put in charge of an entire ward—a rare promotion for an LPN. The patients could be unusually difficult, but she treated them with kindly patience, capably handling a responsible position for which only RNs were considered qualified.

Besides being very proud of my mother's promotion, and amazed that she'd recovered from a serious accident in such good spirits, I hold onto one memory from her job at Northern State. When she told me about it, I had a bone-deep intuition that the episode would hold great significance for me. It soon receded into my subconscious, and did not resurface for decades—until I was an adjunct professor at Marymount Manhattan College and found myself in the proverbial class from hell.

Half the students in this benighted group—a freshman introductory course on writing and literature—had not purchased the required books. In this era before laptop computers, several did not bother to bring the essential notebooks or writing implements. More than a few expected to be entertained. They looked askance at those who brought their books and took the class seriously. Early in the term I handed back some writing assignments to which I'd given provisional marks, pending revisions I hoped they'd make before their work was given permanent grades. No one asked any questions, so I began to introduce the next assignment. My focus was disrupted, however, by angry taps of a pen on a desk occupied by my oldest student, a redfaced woman of retirement age.

When I asked if she had something to say before we moved on, she berated me for daring to suggest in my written comments that she take advantage of the college's free tutorials on sentence structure and ways to develop a paragraph. Furious to receive such elementary advice at her age, and ill at ease in a classroom among students young enough to be her grandchildren, the intensity of her bitterness moved even the do-nothing students.

Before I could respond she stormed out, and my class sat frozen in silence. I knew quite well that such an outburst could be perceived as an affront to my dignity as a professor, and I might lose the respect of the few students who'd responded to my efforts up to then. But from the recesses of my mind came a surge of inspiration, and I began to tell them about my mother's favorite mental patient.

This woman, I explained, had been so friendly and appreciative of my mother's nursing skills that my mom had made a point of looking in on her at the beginning of her shift, so she could start the job with a warm, encouraging reception. This time she arrived on the ward hearing frenzied shouts coming from her favorite patient's room. From the doorway she saw this normally congenial woman wrestling with two muscular male nurses' aides, who were forcing her into a straightjacket. Spotting my mother, the patient began to curse at her, shrieking a blue streak of insults. It was quite a shock to my mother, who'd shown her nothing but kindness—for which, till then, the patient had shown nothing but appreciation.

Mom looked dazed when she came home, as if she'd received a body blow worse than her actual car crash. "Verbal abuse can do that, as some of you might already know," I said to the class, looking around to make eye contact.

The next day, I continued, my mother passed this patient's room cautiously, noting that she appeared calm and was no longer in a straightjacket. So my mom stood in the doorway and asked the woman why she'd shouted all those terrible names and cursed her the day before.

At this point my whole class was paying attention, possibly aware that real knowledge might be at stake. I advised the ones "who tend to be kind and gentle, like my mother," to listen carefully to this patient's frank response to her favorite nurse. She'd said: *Because I knew you wouldn't hurt me.*

Some of them sat expressionless; others looked perplexed. A sophomore who'd transferred from another college said the patient was probably furious about whatever got her institutionalized in the first place, not my mother. A beefy young man opined that the patient had to know that, if she cussed out the aides, they could have roughed her up bad with impunity. Others agreed that she was safer blowing off steam at a nurse she knew would not retaliate. Others just listened, perhaps reflecting on moments of rage in their own lives. The discussion seemed to increase the students' sympathy for their older classmate—whose anger might have stemmed from fear of failing to fulfill her long deferred dream of a college degree.

A colleague took this undated photo of my mother on break, the only one of her in her nurse's uniform.

My oldest student cut the next two classes, and earned a C+ for the course. During her absence, I learned, she'd gone to see a writing tutor. Though she never apologized for exploding at me, she left a comment on her anonymous teacher evaluation form (which I identified by her handwriting) that I'd helped improve her writing skills. I've shared my mother's account with more than one traumatized friend, and used it as an example in an interdisciplinary humanities course I called Trauma and Transcendence. Unfortunately, I did not make the connection earlier with how my mother came to speak against me.

CHAPTER THIRTEEN

"If I die it will be your fault."

Family life got stranger after Verne completed his apprenticeship at Camano Island State Park. He was made assistant ranger at Millersylvania, a large state park ten miles outside of Olympia, the state capitol. Housing was provided, but the assistant ranger's place was shabby, isolated and viewless. Though hardly new, it showed signs of having been hastily built, a far cry from our sturdy home overlooking Puget Sound that Mom had found and beautified for us. Now all we looked upon were a few scraggly trees and the remains of a gravel pit. There were no neighbors to visit, no young people to hang out with. Our house was hidden on a turnaround about a mile from the park's entrance, where the head ranger's well-kept residence stood. The head ranger and his family did not socialize with us, so my brother and I never saw its interior. Johnny didn't mind, because he found a summer job as a car hop at a fancy restaurant, where he earned generous tips, met lots of people, and became more independent. I was often alone, but could still practice piano and drums, read books, and look forward to starting high school.

Our only visitor, Uncle Wayne, paid no attention to our Spartan quarters. Our front step was a cinder block next to a sagging wooden porch, and our front door opened onto a dingy kitchen-dining area with a narrow, uninviting living room off to the right. Left of the kitchen was a laundry room, bathroom, and corridor leading to two bedrooms that faced the driveway. The drafty storage area behind the laundry room, facing a few thin trees, became Johnny's bedroom, where he slept on a cot in an Army-surplus sleeping bag.

When we moved in, the floor of the laundry room was unfinished wood, with a motley assortment of linoleum tiles stacked in one corner for us to install or not, if we chose. My mother rifled through the tiles, shrugged, and asked if I could find any pattern to put them in. Amazed to be entrusted with an artistic challenge, I did not realize how discouraged she was. I dove into the project, arranging the tiles in a quirky but workable zigzag design. Mom looked at the layout, smiled wanly, and said, *Why not?* I was thrilled to have my plan accepted, but sensed she had little enthusiasm.

Years later I discovered a prayerful note she'd tucked into a Bible during our Millersylvania days: *I will live in a comfortable house that I own, with a view overlooking the water and a garden, in a place where I am known and accepted. I will be of independent means, able to socialize with people I enjoy being with and who appreciate me.* It took a long while before I noticed that she'd made no mention of Verne.

Millersylvania fell within the school district of a tiny town, Tenino. Mom took one look at its forlorn little high school and decided I would not be attending. She discovered that the farthest stop on the school bus route to the newly opened Tumwater High was two miles up the road from us. She'd be asleep after working the swing shift when I'd have to catch it, so Verne was appointed to drive me there each morning. The road to Millersylvania was lined with woods and—except in the summer—had almost no traffic. Tumwater's nearest school bus stop was so deserted that I had to wait in the car with Verne until the bus's yellow outline arose on a distant hill. He and I had little to say to one another. Our silent ritual of watching for the bus was an endurance test for me, but perhaps it meant more to him.

Freshly built, Tumwater High was modern but not nearly as large and impressive as the stately Olympia High. Everyone knew that the new school was built to absorb Olympia High's overflow, but the excluded students were determined to make something special out of not being able to attend the more prestigious school. It helped that the town of Tumwater was home to the Olympia Brewing Company—a readymade claim to fame. At football and basketball games Tumwater High's cheerleaders gleefully chanted "It's the water! It's the water!" – the slogan of Olympia Beer.

As a new student, I had to audition for the band, where no one expected to see a girl drummer. To the boy drummers' dismay, I was made leader of the percussion section. And thanks to Dr. MacLaine's coaching and many hours slugging balls with Johnny at Monaco Beach, my tennis game was stronger than the other girls, so I placed first in singles on the girls' team. When it came to tennis, drums, and coursework, I thrived on self-motivated practice and study. But I remained awkward talking to kids my age, and lived too far out of town to form after-school friendships.

Other than her few colleagues at American Lake Veterans Hospital, my mother was also isolated at Millersylvania. Flavia lived much farther away, phone calls to her cost more, and she rarely visited us. The head ranger and his wife were our only neighbors, and they kept their distance.

At Millersylvania I entered puberty—a messy process that did nothing for my looks or self-confidence. I was still pudgy, and accustomed to hearing only adult—i.e. far-out and esoteric—conversation. Therefore I was clueless what people my age talked about. I did pretty well in class, but heard sneers like piggy or fatso in the hallways between classes. My mother and I had been confidantes for as long as I'd been able to speak intelligibly. Of course she knew that since my days in Getchell School I'd been mocked for being overweight, and found it difficult making friends. I was sure she understood that as a new student at Tumwater High I would feel strange and isolated. When I confided these rather predictable experiences to her, she did not put things into a more mature perspective, as I might have expected from her.

In the past, she might have pointed out that the boys in the drum section were quite likely to resent me—and the girls on the tennis team to keep their distance—not only because I was new, but also because I'd placed first in both groups because I played better than the rest of them. Mom might have offered me her usual wisdom, encouraging me to take the long view and keep doing my best. I was profoundly taken aback when my typical candor about these difficulties led to serious trouble.

On Camano Island Mom had expected me to get straight to my homework after I'd cleared and washed the supper dishes. She took it for granted that I'd practice on my drum pad and on the fine old piano she'd found for me. But at Millersylvania my normal routine began to meet with bewildering resistance. If I mentioned any problems I had at school—which were not so terrible, as I was adapting fairly well to my classes and activities—she no longer offered kind and practical advice. She began to begrudge the time I spent studying and practicing music, and fixated on my *attitude*. Her concern with my lack of tact changed into a perplexing claim that my relationship with her was my *Achilles heel*, the root of all my problems.

This accusation seemed beyond my capacity either to defend myself or translate it into manageable improvements in my actions. I was the same person, albeit in a new environment. I had not become a rebellious adolescent, grown rude, disrespectful, slovenly or wild. I was cautious by nature and uninterested in waywardness. Given my earlier humiliations, I tried hard to steer my forthright nature toward the shores of tact and diplomacy. My mother did not seem willing or able to acknowledge this about me.

In time, I won tennis matches for Tumwater High, led the band's drum section in a series of well-received concerts, and won recognition for the school at Northwest national music competitions, placing first in drum solos and ensemble percussion performances. Classmates began to accept me, though I lived too far away to hang out with any of them. I began to pay more attention to clothes and accessories. Mom and I had different tastes, but we each appreciated the quality bargains at our Favorite Shopping Center, the Goodwill store in Olympia.

I loved and admired my mother as much as ever. But now, if I mentioned any tensions with or snubs from other students, it became grounds for nearly endless, ultimately traumatic "lectures." I couldn't think of a better word for these intense but meandering one-way talks that could last for hours. They consisted of a collection of truisms and vague illustrations of *principles* that she insisted I give my undivided attention, putting aside my studies and music practice. Out of respect, I listened, trying to reduce her stated principles into doable changes in my behavior.

In this surreal lecture mode, she was no longer the mother who'd given the younger me succinct, practical advice. At Millersylvania she didn't seem to care if I finished my homework, which I managed only by staying up late and losing sleep.

It is impossible to convey the change that came over her in these lectures. Without raising her velvety voice, she spoke with fierce intensity, for hours, often becoming hoarse. Because they were never loud, one could not call these talks tirades or diatribes. Yet she was relentless, repeating platitudes that she described as *ideas and principles* so often as to render them in singsong. The examples she used to illustrate her points—such as the Good Samaritan who stopped to help a wounded man on the roadside—sounded commendable but were not very applicable to my circumstances. Her accusations of selfishness and an overall *attitude* problem seemed to boil down to character traits that most mothers would have been pleased to see in their daughters: being a serious student and faithfully practicing her musical instruments, after washing the dinner dishes and doing her share of household chores every week. So why was she so fixated on my *attitude*? Why was she now so dissatisfied with me?

At the time I did not have this perspective, but there had to be something going on with my mother that I had no knowledge of. All I could do was stick to reason and honesty. Though she accused me of being selfish, she stopped short of saying I studied too much, which seemed to be more the issue. I'd never tried to avoid doing my share of housework, nor did I buy things beyond my budget, though I had a weakness for costume jewelry when I wasn't buying books. Did that make me a bad person or selfish? It felt absurd to defend myself and insist that I loved her—though I tried, to no avail. I was too ignorant to understand that the problem went far beyond me.

None of her lectures were ever directed at my brother. Johnny had his driver's license by the time we arrived at Millersylvania. Over the summer he bought a vintage Plymouth with the tips he made carhopping at an upscale restaurant. With wheels of his own, he was able to attend Olympia High, and spend less and less time at home. Unlike Johnny, I was not taught to drive right away, so if I didn't have after-school band events or tennis matches, home was where I stayed. On Camano Island I could stroll safely on the beach, but the unlit, shoulderless road past our driveway at Millersylvania made long walks risky. When I returned from school it was impossible to escape my mother's scrutiny. At any moment one of her lectures could envelop us in a suffocating cloud. If I was practicing the piano, she would lean over the keyboard and declare in a cynical tone, *You probably won't be interested in this, but if you could spare a moment to listen to your mother…* So I would stop to hear her out, and the rest of the evening would be lost to a depleting soliloquy that no effort of mine could convert into a genuine conversation.

I tried every honest response I could think of—agreeing with whatever seemed fair, defending myself when accused of things I did not do or feel. Hokey as it sounds, I hated injustice and loved her. Even if I'd had the stomach to lie, my mother had no desire to be placated or to cut short her fulminations. So I began to endure her lectures in silence. Stoic perhaps in demeanor, it took all my strength to survive in a Jekyll and Hyde situation that threatened to destroy whatever was true in our bond of love.

My mother's softspoken rants felt worse than being blasted with threats, insults, or obscenities. The spirit that came over my mother did not care whether the hours she held me hostage were exhausting and demoralizing. Where was the kind, angelic woman who'd rushed to comfort me every night when I wet the bed? She remained an excellent nurse, always there for others. But in lecture mode she was driven by a force impervious to give and take. To my adolescent heart, her accusations felt unfair and—most frightening and difficult to acknowledge—unloving. I dreaded her lectures more than any other form of suffering.

Though I promised to give whatever points she was trying to make my sincere consideration, and asked what I could correct in my behavior, she did not seem able to reduce anything to a doable request. After much time had passed, if I asked what point she was trying to make, she would sigh, and answer in an exasperated singsong: *My point is, those who bring sunshine into the lives of others cannot keep it from themselves.* The only one of her basic principles I remember.

No question, it had the ring of truth. But something else had to be at stake. I was unable to produce the sunshine, or consistently cheerful disposition, that my mother seemed to be looking for. I was no longer the bubbly little girl on the berry farm—before Annie Barley turned my brother against me, before Mom's breakdown and my time in foster care, before she married Verne. I never thought to ask why she couldn't forgive my failure to bring sunshine into people's lives, like she'd forgiven my bedwetting. Maybe her strange, intense, meandering lectures arose from an unfulfilled longing for someone to bring sunshine into her life, which somehow got funneled into a bitter, unending dissatisfaction with my *attitude*. There was a sad irony underneath it all. My dread of—and trauma having to endure—her lectures robbed me of the cheerfulness that would have come naturally. In its place came a quiet determination to get through whatever difficulties as best I could, even if I couldn't please her.

One night when I was fourteen, Mom interrupted my studies after dinner, and held forth in lecture mode in my bedroom until well past midnight. I got so tired that I put on my pajamas and crawled into bed, pleading that we both needed sleep. She leaned against my bedroom door, hoarse but unable to refute this fact. Reluctant to end her fulminations before she felt like it, she opened my bedroom door and took half a step out. Before closing it, she turned back toward me and hissed, *If I die it will be your fault!*

The curse pierced me like a poisoned arrow. After she'd bitterly shut my door, a gentle, inner voice reasoned that my mother was nowhere near dying, and that anyone who would lay that kind of blame on a child was not driven by good will. For reasons I could not fathom, my mother was undermining the trust we'd shared until this final stage of my childhood. When I was younger she'd valued my honesty, and though she'd warned against and mocked my tendency to be tactless, she'd expressed zero doubt about my love for her. No more. Annie Barley had provided my first taste of personal malice, but my mother's accusations against me dealt a much deeper blow—because she was my beloved mother, who went to her grave without rescinding them.

I can't deny that, in the immediate aftermath of my mother's monologues I turned inward, unable to show affection for her until the high-stress atmosphere of those sessions had dissipated. To protect my sense of integrity, I became more guarded, less spontaneous in showing my feelings. I took pains to avoid causing her to accuse me of being unappreciative and selfish. Regardless, the lectures continued, and eventually I protected myself with a shield of silence rather than trying to defend myself. I associated being selfish with wanting things for myself that ought to be left to or shared with others. In truth, I enjoyed helping others whenever possible. If I'd been as witty and charming as Johnny, I'd have been eager to bring sunshine into people's lives. Somehow my mother's accusatory ramblings never seemed to focus on my actual circumstances and character.

From that time forward it became the primary challenge and ordeal of my life, to have such a wise and gracious mother, who seemed driven by a force bent on destroying my identity as a good person. The first time she declared that I did not love her, it struck me as no mere rhetorical flourish, but something very grave and wrong. She carried the authority of being my mother. Up to this point in my childhood she had experienced my spontaneous expressions of love and affection. Her implicit denial of my sincerity as a loving daughter made the injustice of this ongoing judgment all the more severe. Through the decades until her death, if I mentioned some obvious example of a loving act on my part, she would brush it off as done *out of duty*.

It was a painful paradox that the truest thing I knew about myself was that I loved my mother, and deeply appreciated her wisdom and her other wonderful qualities. To be accused of not loving her put me into a Cordelia-like role, with my mother as a relentless Lear. There was something indescribably devious, if not willfully dishonest, about her unrevoked judgment that I did not love her. In some way it felt as though we became opponents in a supernatural power struggle over my true character.

What helped me to survive were the moments when my mother's own loving nature reemerged, between the dark spells of her lectures. At those times we reverted to being confidantes who could easily banter and express our affection for each other, and I could learn from her selfless wisdom. I could describe how the boys in the drum section resented when I had to correct them, or that my tennis teammates sniggered about my chunky legs, and Mom would draw upon the Bard for a longer view: *Thrice armed is he who hath his quarrel just... Judge not the play until the play is o'er. Its scenes have many changes. The last act crowns the play.*

Hamlet's advice raised goose bumps on my arms. Who knew how our lives would turn out, if we kept trying our best? It gave me courage to board the school bus in the morning.

No one saw my mother in lecture mode except Verne and Uncle Wayne, but neither of them witnessed the extremity of the sessions when she had me to herself. When Mom was holding forth on other issues, Verne would sit at the table smoking, swilling coffee, hardly listening. Years passed before I drew some connection between her relationship with Verne and the hellish lectures that began as I entered puberty.

Verne on duty at Millersylvania State Park, 1960.
Photo by Flavia Van Dyke

At Millersylvania Verne had more contact with the public than on Camano Island or the berry farm. I was puzzled when Mom muttered something about him in a tone that implied an obscure meaning. *Some men act as though Verne is one of them. They seem to know their own kind.* For fear of triggering another lecture, I nodded and did not ask her to explain.

Verne's opinions—at the dinner table or conversing with Uncle Wayne, whether the topic was politics, work, human nature or the supernatural—struck me as cynical and overly pessimistic. He found little merit in anyone else's thoughts, though he'd acquiesce to points Mom raised. I had no reason to change the opinion I'd expressed when I was eight: that she should not have married him. I did not disagree when Mom remarked, on more than a few occasions, *There's no love lost between you and Verne.*

In Uncle Wayne, though, I had an ally. There were many Saturdays on Camano Island when Wayne took Johnny and me to a rollerskating rink in Burlington. In the afternoon we'd take skate dance classes, and stick around for the evening social. Since I'd become a fairly good skater, rollerskating was the one social activity I felt comfortable doing. By the time we'd moved to Millersylvania, my brother had lost interest in skating. Seeing I had no one else to do things with on the weekends, Uncle Wayne checked the Yellow Pages and found a rink within driving distance south of Olympia. That Saturday night I met a friendly, nice-looking guy about my age, who skated with me most of the evening. Tumwater High's prom was approaching and I had no one to go with, so I asked if he had a car. He said yes, so I took a chance and asked if he'd like to take me to the Tumwater prom. He grinned, nodded, and took my number.

A few weeks passed, and for reasons beyond my control I could not make it back to the rink to reconnect with him. Two days before prom night, he phoned to say he wasn't sure he'd be able to come. I took this as meaning he was unsure how to find where I lived. Verne was sitting near the phone, so I relayed his precise directions how to get to our place, and his assurance that it would be easy. Perhaps the boy mumbled something I did not catch, implying that he still might not make it. Exactly how the call ended was a blur. But we'd enjoyed skating together so I chose to think positive.

Early on prom night I opened a package of quality nylons purchased for the occasion, pulling them up carefully so as not to start a run, and stepped into the beautiful gown my mother had sewn from a remnant of lavender silk brocade she'd found at a fabric sale. Unfamiliar with makeup other than lipstick, I patted on some of Mom's face powder, daubed at my lashes with a wand of mascara recently acquired at Woolworth's, combed out my pincurls and spritzed them with Mom's hairspray. Listening for the sound of my date's car in the drive, I sat waiting at the kitchen table. Never having been to a prom, I failed to consider that this boy would have had to rent or borrow a tuxedo, buy a corsage, and go on a serious date with a girl he'd met only once.

Mom hovered nervously at the kitchen sink, washing stray dishes. Verne sat Sphinx-like at the table with his ever-present cigarettes and coffee. Across from him, Uncle Wayne stared at the clock. When my date was an hour late, he stood up and growled, "Let's go, Becky. That sonofabitch will never show up." Sliding the weekend paper toward me, he said, "Pick a movie. We'll go see it."

Blinking away tears, I scanned the movie ads, pointed to one, and withdrew to change out of my prom dress, replaying every fading word of my date's phone call. Why hadn't I pinned him down whether he was really coming? As I hung up the fine-ly-sewn gown, I regretted that no one would see my mother's exquisite choice of fabric, her workmanship, and me on the arm of a presentable young man.

It hurt too much to ponder openly, but a dark possibility hovered over the whole episode. Was I was doomed to such rejections because my mother no longer believed that I loved her?

I washed off the makeup, put on jeans, an old sweater, socks, sneakers, and my winter coat, and climbed into Uncle Wayne's new Dodge Dart. Knowing I was susceptible to the cold, he had the heater running. From the doorway Mom gave him a grateful wave as we drove off.

In those days I hardly ever got to go to the movies, so I took this chance to see "To Kill a Mockingbird." Within seconds the silver screen's magic dispelled the ache of humiliation, and immersed me in the small-town Southern childhood of a plucky tomboy and her brother. I drew courage from the kinship I felt with Scout, uplifted by Gregory Peck's performance as her attorney father, Atticus Finch. Deeper still was my bond with Boo Radley, the reclusive neighbor boy, whose shy attempts to communicate with Scout and her brother resonated with my failed attempt to find a date for the prom. My helpless terror at my mother's lectures did not seem too different from how Tom, the innocent black man, felt when he was accused of rape. When

Boo turned out to be the one who'd sprung forth in the dark of night to save Scout and her brother from a life-threatening attack, a message came to me. It warned me not to expect anyone else to save me from my own threatening circumstances. The Boo in me would have to save myself.

CHAPTER FOURTEEN

Frosty the Snowman

In grade school, my brother's face seemed narrow in relation to the width of his ears, but he could make people laugh. By the time he entered high school, the face-to-ear ratio had improved, he proved himself a top student, capable athlete and accomplished clarinetist. Johnny's quick ironic wit, while protecting his sensitive side, made him cool to other guys and intriguing to girls. So effortless was his popularity that he was voted junior class president shortly after his arrival.

Olympia High possessed an Olympic size pool with a swim and diving team Johnny could try out for. He'd been taught to dive by lifeguards at Monaco Beach and Millersylvania State Park, and easily qualified. Thanks to Dr. MacLaine's coaching, countless hours at the backboard, and rallying with his sister, Johnny also earned a spot on the tennis team. Flavia's early lessons plus years of daily practice won him the first chair clarinet position in their prizewinning concert band—comparable to concertmaster in a symphony orchestra.

With our own bedrooms, Johnny no longer asked me for stories to put him to sleep. Since we now attended different high schools, we had no shared teachers to talk about, like in Stanwood when we took the school bus together from Camano Island. On rare occasions, Mom would ask Johnny to pick me up after my tennis or band practice on his way back from Olympia. He did so without complaint, but on the ride back to Millersylvania neither of us knew what to say. I had a helpless feeling that what little closeness we had felt was slipping away. I was proud of him and longed for his approval, but he was handsome, confident and successful in a prestigious school, while I was plain, chubby, solitary, and awkward with others. My grades weren't bad, and I was doing well as a drummer and on Tumwater's tennis team, but my school was smaller and unknown compared to Johnny's.

Most kids my age were thinner. In those days an extra 15 pounds could make any girl an object of ridicule—especially if she was a newcomer and clueless how to talk with people her age. I wondered why my brother couldn't be more of an ally. It felt as though he'd worked all summer to buy a car and drive himself to Olympia High, mainly to distance himself from the sister who'd rallied with him for hours on the cement court at Monaco Beach, and protected him from bee stings on the berry farm. Did he have to keep calling me Piggy?

When I heard Johnny shouting at Mom "I hate Becky!" through the thin walls of his bedroom, I couldn't figure out what I'd done wrong. They were discussing something with the door closed, that neither of them wanted me to hear. I couldn't tell whether her muffled tones were conciliatory or—unthinkable for me at that age—if she sympathized with his hostility toward me. She may have tried to reason with him privately, but there was never an open discussion of my brother's grievances. Nor did she ever suggest, to my knowledge, that Johnny see me as a loyal would-be friend rather than his adversary.

Verne taught us the basics of poker, perhaps at Mom's suggestion, to give Johnny and me something to play at home together. Our first real game was with nickel bets. It was great fun until I won the jackpot, about $2.45. My brother was so enraged that Mom intervened, making me give back what he'd lost, though at that point in his life he did not lack for pocket change. It was only a game, I protested, and Verne vouched that I'd won fair and square. But in my brother's heart there was no such thing as a friendly game with me. I never played poker again.

In his senior year Johnny met a quick-witted brunette from a well-off family. Slim and athletic, with warm brown eyes, she was as unpretentious as she was lovely, and looked more like my brother's sister than I did. Her name, Michael, was unusual for a girl, and everyone called her Mike. I knew Johnny was smitten when he arranged for me—whom he normally avoided—to meet her. When Mike and I came to one of his tennis matches, he introduced her to me as if she were a long-lost member of our family. He didn't mind at all when she teased him and I laughed with her. For a timeless moment I felt part of a natural, happy threesome, and hoped our new friendship would flourish. But that did not happen. Johnny was a frequent guest in Mike's home, but he never brought her to Millersylvania.

Spending so much time with Mike took a toll on his grades. Unlike Mike, Johnny did not apply to prestigious colleges. When she got accepted at Stanford I was impressed, but sad that she'd be moving into more elite circles at a top university, and my brother would soon lose the girl I believed would have been his best partner in life. It was a mixed blessing that he'd heard about the Coast Guard Academy in New London, Connecticut. Unlike other military academies, its cadets were chosen by a competitive examination, which Johnny took and scored well enough to be accepted. It was a tribute to his practicality and pluck, and a relief to Mom, since she and Verne could not afford to help pay for his education. Now he had a chance to earn an engineering degree, become an officer, and have a guaranteed career.

My brother during his first year at the Academy. Though movie-
star handsome, to my eyes there was something fatalistic in
his expression. Was it because he'd lost his beloved Mike?

It saddened me that I'd never wake up again to the sound of
Johnny practicing his clarinet. Rarely would I get to play tennis
with him. I'd lost some of his heart when Annie took him under
her wing, then lost his company when he attended Olympia High,
and the rest of him when he left for the Academy. But by then, at
least, he'd stopped yelling at Mom that he hated me.

Johnny made the Coast Guard's diving team, and played dou-
bles on its tennis team. No surprise, he cut a fine figure around
town, dating several young women at a time. I was taken aback
when I saw in his class yearbook that his nickname was "Sleazy."
Did it refer to his way with the ladies? Or was it a tribute to his
efforts to bypass the Guard's grooming requirements concerning
hair length?

I didn't blame him for rebelling against the Academy's razing
of new cadets, who were called "Plebes." First year cadets, for
example, were woken at 2 a.m. by upperclassmen and ordered to

spit-polish their toes—applying bootblack and saliva, followed by rigorous buffing. At other ungodly hours they were roused to perform "butts and muzzles," an exhausting drill snapping heavy M-1 rifles forward and back above their heads. Cadets in Johnny's day were forbidden to take odd jobs to supplement their princely salary of $24 a month. This did not cover the cost of illicit hamburgers and pizzas that he and his classmates had delivered to their dorms surreptitiously, to supplement the scraps left by upperclassmen who got to serve themselves first at mess.

Mom was curious when Johnny asked her to send him a barber's kit, which she did, only to discover that he'd started a lucrative business customizing his classmates' haircuts to look trim below their cadets' caps, while more luxurious locks appeared when the caps came off. One day she got a call from a man who identified himself as Commandant of the Coast Guard Academy. Ensign Painter, he informed her, had accumulated an extraordinary number of demerits. Evidently Johnny's barbering business hadn't been sufficiently clandestine. Mom confessed that she was an unwitting accessory, having provided her son's barber kit. Hearing her genuine surprise that her son had done something illicit, perhaps laced with quaint British expressions of horrified dismay, it seemed the Commandant relaxed a bit. After her initial shock, Mom reported, they had an *enjoyable and amusing* conversation. He assured her that with no further entrepreneurial infractions, her son's career in the Guard would not suffer.

Johnny's fleeting joys beating the system were outweighed by deep disappointments. When he asked if he could play clarinet in the Coast Guard Band, he was turned down because the illustrious group accepted only enlisted men, and cadets were officers in training. He was permitted to sit in once with the Band, but protocol barred him from a wonderful opportunity to share with skilled musicians the artistry he'd so diligently acquired. When Mom told me about this, tears welled up like they did when I heard "Frosty the Snowman."

CHAPTER FIFTEEN

Illahee - A Call to Ingenuity

Two years as Millersylvania's assistant state park ranger qualified Verne for a park of his own. When we heard of his new assignment, no one could imagine what a little jewel he'd been given. Illahee State Park was on the Kitsap Peninsula, near Bremerton, an important Naval shipyard, and an hour's ferry ride across Puget Sound to Seattle. It offered a small, pebbled beach for swimmers like me who tolerated the Sound's bone-chilling water, and a very long dock for fishermen like Verne. A few picnic tables and barbecue grills sat close to the shore under a canopy of evergreens. A small number of campsites nestled in the woods up a steep drive from the beach. The park could be managed by one fulltime ranger, whose spacious, well-designed residence overlooked the entrance.

Mom loved its wood-paneled living room with a modern circular fireplace in the center. In no time, she'd planted an array of flowering shrubs around the house that framed the upward slope of its lawn. She was pleased and proud to live there. The road to Illahee from Bremerton was on the school bus route to East High School, so I no longer needed Verne to drive me to the bus stop. We were six non-scary miles from a bustling mid-size town, living in a comfortable, attractive home.

When I transferred to East High as a junior, my brother was in his first year at the Coast Guard Academy, so I had to finish high school alone. Once again I was the only girl drummer to audition for the band, and was put in charge of the percussion section. Likewise I tried out for the girls tennis team and ranked first in singles. By then I was more inured to disgruntled boy drummers and resentful girls who lacked the rigor of Dr. MacLaine's coaching. Among East's more studious types I had a better chance of being accepted.

Verne quickly figured out how to oversee the compact park and manage its upkeep. Perhaps it didn't pose enough of a challenge. Maybe he missed having a fulltime colleague to work with. A week before it happened, I found myself alone with him after school. He'd never shown any real warmth toward me, but this once he seemed vaguely friendly.

"Becky, there's something I want to discuss with you," he announced coolly. "Why don't we go over to the couch?"

I wondered why he couldn't say whatever he had to say from his habitual seat at the table, coffee mug and ashtray at the ready. But he seemed to have something serious in mind, so I did as directed. There was an easy chair nearby, but Verne sat next to me on the sofa. It felt unreal when the next thing he did was place his hand on my knee, saying, "You may not believe this, Becky, but I've always found you attractive."

He was right about my not believing him. His declaration was so incredible that it triggered suspicion. To the teenage ears of a girl who'd learned to anticipate being mocked and bullied at school, Verne's words struck me as some weird, cynical form of derision. Stunned, I stared expressionless at the hand on my knee—a bizarre move, coming from someone so undemonstrative. Verne was watchful and passive, waiting for me to react. The ghost of a smile faded back into his poker face. It felt like some sort of mind game he'd cooked up in a moment of boredom to embarrass me. Determined not to be played by the man I felt justified for having warned my mother not to marry, I kept calm. He seemed sober, and supposedly had a high I.Q., but I wasn't an idiot.

"What's that noise?" I asked, turning toward a nonexistent sound outside the window. Verne's head jerked in that direction as he took his hand off my knee and listened. Providentially, the telephone rang in the kitchen, and I jumped up to answer it. To my relief, it was a classmate asking about homework. I did my best to prolong the conversation until Verne got up and left the house. Presumably he busied himself in the park until evening, when I was studying in my room with the door locked. Instinct—and the shock of what happened a few days later—kept me from reporting this incident to my mother.

I was at school when Verne lost patience at the prospect of driving the park truck down through the switchback turns he'd been routinely negotiating in his daily descent through the woods to inspect Illahee's beach area. Crazily, he floorboarded the accelerator and drove straight down, but the trees were in no mood to make way for him. The truck was totaled, but Verne—in the days before seatbelts— emerged from it with hardly a scratch.

He'd lost consciousness, or sanity, or both. No one knew. I did wonder, silently, whether there was some connection between his freak accident and our strange aborted conference on the sofa. The police who came to the scene were astounded that my stepfather had survived intact. Afterward, Verne confessed that he'd kept several prescriptions for tranquilizers at different pharmacies in town. Unbeknownst to anyone, he'd also resumed drinking, after many years—vodka, because it left no odor on his breath.

Mom explained that combining liquor and tranquilizers could cause momentary insanity or even death, and a famous actor had recently committed suicide this way. She offered no insights on Verne's behavior or motivation. Nor did she express any bitterness that he had disrupted our family's better quality of life at Illahee, as if spurning our more comfortable standard of living by getting himself fired. Dazed and short of words, she said the State Park Service had been gracious to give us as much time as we needed to find another home. It went without saying that we'd have to live in a place she could afford on her LPN's salary.

After Verne's truck rampage he was assigned to a psychiatric ward at American Lake Veterans Hospital, near Tacoma, where he remained over two years. After one of my mother's first visits to his ward, she reported that Verne's idea of a happy life had been not having to work, being free to sit and read the paper all day, with an unlimited supply of coffee and cigarettes. At the V.A. hospital he got exactly that. Ironically, his only responsibility was to make the coffee for his ward, perhaps because he consumed most of it. Tax-free cigarettes were plentiful, too, at the hospital's store. It did not seem to concern him that Mom was now our family's sole provider.

In a stroke of luck, she found a modest rental unit three blocks from East High. From there I could walk to class, to the tennis courts, and to marching band practice on the football field. No need to take the school bus, or get rides home at night after school concerts or games. Given Mom's three-to-eleven p.m. shift at American Lake Hospital, she'd be asleep when I set off to class and I'd be asleep when she got home. On her workdays we communicated on a spiral steno pad she left on the kitchen counter. Typical entries were: *Heat up the meatloaf, dear, for supper… Good luck at the tennis match.* …"Wish you could have heard the concert, Mummy… Is there anything we're running out of?" … *Thanks for picking up that carton of brown eggs, Beck. I see you checked that none were cracked.* Eventually the smudged pages would contain wisecracks from Johnny on leave from the Academy, and almost illegible scratchings by Uncle Wayne on his visits. After I left for college Mom packed the notepad away, and brought it out years later to attest that *we really did have a family life of sorts.*

I was unaware that we were living hand to mouth. Years later, my mother very nearly bragged about how she'd juggled our bills, holding some till just before she'd have to pay a late fee and lose her credit, budgeting her small salary to the last dime. *Unlike most people*, she asserted, *I actually enjoy paying bills.* As her circumstances improved, she admitted to savoring the comfortable feeling that there was enough in her checking account to cover them. She was grateful to be spared the shame of kiting checks.

For my mother, a tight budget was not so much a hardship as a call to ingenuity. She was a champion bargain finder, able to spot finely made garments for pennies at the Goodwill store. Having sewn her own and some of her sister's clothes in New Zealand, she could make faultless alterations, and complete ambitious sewing projects that others had abandoned and donated to the charity. I recall that she'd finished sewing the linings of two tweed suits, one for each of us. For the nights when I wore a long black skirt and matching blouse to play tympani for the Bremerton Symphony, the same treasure trove provided me with an elegant, many-gored skirt and vintage ruffled top. There Mom obtained my first evening bag—a black ostrich-skin clutch lined in satin. Arching an eyebrow, my mother pointed to the label inside—Saks Fifth Avenue—and an exquisite tiny beveled mirror, tucked into its own pocket within the lining.

Bremerton's Goodwill was rather small, so it was a special thrill to accompany my mother to Everett's cavernous store. There we browsed beneath lofty ceilings with huge slow-rotating wooden fans and high windows, among endless rows of blouses, slacks, and skirts in mint condition, neatly sorted by color and size. All anyone needed was taste and a modest amount of cash. No matter how pinched things got at home, Mom would bring home an occasional choice item to lift our spirits. In a conspiratorial tone, she referred to the source as *Our Favorite Shopping Center*.

There was no space in our rental home's living room for my upright piano, so it took up a wall in my bedroom. Mom could afford piano lessons if they were every other week. In The Yellow Pages, she found a teacher across the bridge in West Bremerton who would accept me on that basis. Tall and birdlike, Mrs. Mjelde could dive like a kingfisher to catch errors on the keyboard, and make my spirits soar like a heron on the wings of her encouragement. I was her last student every other Friday evening. Before either of us thought to look at the clock, our one-hour lesson had stretched to two, and she'd have given me all I could possibly handle for the next two weeks. There were scales and arpeggios to strengthen my fingers, and pieces by "The Three B's" (Bach, Beethoven and Brahms), Mozart, Schubert, Chopin, and the occasional modern composer.

By the end of my senior year Mrs. Mjelde had prepared me to perform an entire recital from memory, and scheduled me to play before the State's music examination board, which happened to convene that year in her living room. After the panel of adjudicators heard me play a selection of pieces, they recommended that I audition for a conservatory. I listened as though they were speaking to someone else. I'd practiced diligently and loved music, but the piano was not something my mother took seriously for my future. I have no memory of her reaction when I told her about the board's recommendation, so she probably hadn't been encouraging. Without her support, a career performing or teaching music did not seem real.

A few weeks before my senior recital, I was practicing a Beethoven sonata when my mother, who had the day off, came into my bedroom to berate me for not doing enough housework. This was news, since I routinely handled quite a few chores and planned to do several after my piano practice. Irritated at this sweeping accusation (no pun unintended, but the shoe fits), I asked her to make a list of all the tasks needing to be done that weekend. I offered to do all of them if she'd allow me to finish practicing. She declined, insisting that she only wanted me to do my share. But what was my share? I urged her to write down all the tasks she expected of me and to add a few more so the issue would not have to come up again. Unwilling to settle the matter, she demurred, as though determined to see me occupied with something other than Beethoven. Frustrated, I vacuumed the rugs, so the noise would decrease my odds of being lectured.

By then I was earning straight A's, winning tennis matches and northwest national music competitions as a drummer. My pocket money came from giving drum lessons to a handful of grade school boys who'd been referred to me by the music director at East High. My mother rendered suspect all I was doing, insisting that my *Achilles heel* was my attitude toward her. She pronounced this—to me and no telling how many others—with such finality that she seemed convinced of her right to judge my character as seriously flawed. I was far from alone in esteeming her exceptional wisdom and kindness, but my behavior—and by that I mean manner of speaking, as there were no physical actions at issue, except housework—though at times blunt, had never been recognizably rude, nor ungrateful. Except for the cloak of silence I wore to survive her lectures, I remained respectful, if not as spontaneously affectionate as I'd been before the onset of her obsessive lectures.

It was deeply confusing.

CHAPTER SIXTEEN

The F Daughter

Fed up with being called fatso for my stubborn layer of baby fat, I spent the summer before my senior year at East High on my approximation of a diet. It featured carrots, celery, iceberg lettuce, cottage cheese, hardboiled eggs, smaller portions at meals prepared by my mother, fruit for dessert, and between meals more carrots. My skin had acquired a rather orange tinge from so much carotine, when I returned to school two sizes smaller. Gone were the sniggers and catcalls. I began to get some social traction, even a friend or two.

After a couple months of eyeing me across the room, a smart, mild-mannered classmate got up his nerve to ask if I'd see a movie with him. I hadn't been to a movie since "To Kill a Mockingbird" with Uncle Wayne, on Tumwater High's prom night. I tried not to show how thrilled I was to be asked out on my first real date. A few weeks later, I found myself with something previously unimaginable for me: a steady boyfriend. At last I had someone to sit with at football and basketball games, someone in the audience to watch me play at concerts. To my surprise, my mother liked him, with no caveats or criticism.

Bruce didn't play tennis or an instrument, but he was determined to make straight A's, not to be outdone by his girlfriend. In addition to Saturday night dates, he'd come over some weekday evenings to study with me. Mom suggested that I invite Bruce to dinner with us, where she displayed considerable wit and charm. Afterward she'd excuse herself and retire to her bedroom, leaving us to cuddle on the sofa. Our affection was real but not unlimited. It was 1964 in Bremerton, where the swinging sixties would not arrive for another decade, if ever. What mattered was, for the first time in my life, I had a reliable beau who found me attractive. Only in hindsight did I notice that he never invited me to dine with his family.

As graduation drew near, my classmates secured their companions for the much-anticipated senior cruise—an all-day trip to a fancy resort near Seattle. Never doubting that Bruce and I would go together, I enthused about the fun we were going to have ice-skating, which I was eager to try with him since I was a fairly good roller skater. For some time he listened without responding. Then, avoiding my eyes, he told me he'd promised to go on the senior trip with Lenny, his longtime friend—who may have extracted this promise in return for tolerating my presence in Bruce's life.

The problem was, Bruce had not told me until everyone we knew considered us a steady couple. At the eleventh hour, if I tried to tag along with other friends, they would wonder why I wasn't with Bruce. I begged him to ask Lenny if I could join the two of them. "I've already asked," he shot back. His friend said "No way." I'd already signed up for the trip and did not want to miss it, so I hoped against hope that Bruce and Lenny would relent, out of basic kindness.

East High's senior cruise has sunk into a void, except for one scene. I was leaning against the rail surrounding the ice rink, watching clumps of people skate by, too dejected to brave the ice alone. In the corner of one eye I glimpsed Bruce and Lenny approaching in the distance, and observed the exact moment when they recognized me and pretended they hadn't. My eyes locked onto them as they strolled past the rink, looking everywhere except at me. Lenny sauntered past with a triumphant air, while Bruce maintained a prairie gaze of scrupulous innocence.

As they receded into the crowd, I silently begged my so-called boyfriend to turn around, meet my gaze, and save me from my isolation. But the same clean-cut young man who'd studied, cuddled, and gone out with me every weekend for six months trod into the distance like a pod person.

Bruce and Lenny, I resolved, deserved each other. The laws of karma would reward them with some future experience of being ignored by someone they cared for, on an equally significant occasion. When that happened, I hoped they'd think of me. That night I waited up for Mom to come home, and poured out the whole humiliating story. But she defended Bruce!

They've been friends since childhood, sweetie-pie. Bruce probably agreed to go with Lenny before you arrived on the scene. Couldn't you have gone with a girlfriend?

"Mom, you know very well that Bruce and I were going steady. He didn't leave me any time to find anyone else." She made no reply, except that we both needed to sleep. In the days that followed, Bruce did not so much as admit that he noticed me on the senior trip. In our last phone conversation he was so evasive that I told him not to call again and slammed down the receiver. Forgiveness in the absence of contrition, I decided, was unjustified.

The following summer, home on break from college, I was dumbfounded when Mom mentioned casually that Bruce had called her several times during the year, and that they remained on friendly terms. *I rather enjoy hearing from him. He always asks how you're doing.* A storm erupted in my mind, from which one lucid thought emerged. They'd both betrayed me. What's more, my mother seemed to enjoy informing me of her continuing contact with Bruce, as though gloating over a win in some weird, spiteful competition.

Counterposed in my memory of Bruce's abandonment and my mother's defense of him, is Mom's reaction to the injustice I experienced at the biggest tennis tournament of my high school career. I'd beaten the other first-ranked girls in Kitsap County's high school tennis league, and advanced to the regional championship that drew top players from neighboring counties. By luck of the draw, I was scheduled to play the highest ranked girl from a larger league, a six-foot Amazon from a much stronger team. The winner of that match would play, for the championship, a girl I'd consistently beaten.

In 1965 the rules for girls' tennis tournaments were not codified, and were decided ad hoc by the coaches' consensus. After a long, grueling match, I defeated the Amazon, 12-10, 9-7. Drenched with sweat, muscles twitching with exhaustion, I was given 20 minutes to rest before the championship match. For unknown reasons of the draw, the other finalist had done nothing but wait to play the winner of my match. My coach asked to reschedule the final match so both players could be fresh, but my opponent's coach liked the odds favoring his girl, and insisted we play. Our first set was 4-1 in my favor when a fierce leg cramp forced me to default. Miserable and bitter, I brought home the second place trophy. Never again would I subject myself to the inequities of tournament tennis.

Sweetie pie, it was only a tennis match, not Armageddon.

"But Mom! I was cheated out of the championship! I don't want the lousy second place trophy."

Well dear, I'd be glad to keep it if you don't want it. Second place is not so bad, especially if you deserved to be first. Her words did not console me, but the trophy sat atop the chest of drawers next to my mother's bed for 31 years, until her death.

If it had not been for East High's career counselor, Gordon Berry, the tennis tournament would have felt more like a bad omen. A former athlete stricken by polio, Mr. Berry had changed his career plans from coaching to counseling. He'd noticed my arrival at East, and seemed to understand my isolation as a serious student. One day, making his way on crutches to his office, he noticed me in the hallway, and invited me in for a chat. Seated across from him, my eyes focused on the objects on his desk.

"Becky," he said kindly, "you seem to find it difficult to look someone straight in the eye." It was a habit I'd developed to withstand my mother's lectures and avoid her manic gaze. "It's natural to be shy. But people tend not to trust anyone who avoids eye contact. You don't want people to think you're afraid of them, do you, especially in an interview, for a job, or college…?"

I didn't have the nerve to say that some people found it disconcerting when someone they did not know well stared at them boldly. Wasn't it better to show a modest, dignified reserve? I asked my mother later.

What a fine man, that Mr. Berry! He's perfectly right, and I'm glad he told you, because if it came from me you'd brush it off like everything else I tell you.

Before Mr. Berry mentioned the possibility, Mom had not been keen on my going to college. I could not understand her lack of encouragement, when so many of my classmates' parents had pushed them to excel. Was it because college had not been an option for her? In the 1920s, when she'd left home to be trained as a nurse, there were no scholarships for women to attend university in New Zealand, if women were even admitted then.

My dream was to attend Radcliffe, the historic women's college next door to Harvard, whose classes they could attend. Mr. Berry advised against it. In those days there were no student stand-by flights at lower fares. He estimated that my family could afford for me to come home only in the summer, and I'd have to earn my airfare back to Boston in the fall. During the Christmas and Easter breaks I'd have to stay in Cambridge, where the dormitories would be deserted except for a few foreign students.

"Your mother needs your company," Mr. Berry said. "It would be hard on her and lonely for you. Why don't you consider an equally fine but less famous college on the West Coast?" Reaching into a drawer, he pulled out an application form he'd requested for me from Scripps College in Claremont, California. Nobody at East had applied there before. I took it with me, wondering if I had even a chance.

Mr. Berry was not the only counselor at East High. There was another, who dealt with problem students. Without telling me, during my senior year my mother called the latter and made an appointment for me, claiming that my intense focus on studies was causing problems in our family life. When the counselor asked if I had any difficulties with my mother, I was grateful for the chance to talk with a professional about the endless criticism I'd received for not being radiant enough to bring sunshine into the lives of others. My mother's long critical lectures, I confessed, were difficult to bear, and to withstand them I retreated into silence, which only seemed to infuriate her and prolong the agony.

The counselor concluded that my mother had given him a biased account of our situation. He was convinced that I was well-meaning, and willing to do my share of the housework that she'd accused me of neglecting. He told me he planned to call her as soon as I left, to suggest that she ease up on her demands and be more supportive, since I seemed mature for my age and was a top student.

Mom was seething when I got home. *I see you've convinced him that I'm the problem,* she sneered, implying that I'd deliberately deceived the counselor. Glaring at me, she took a deep breath and exhaled with venom: *You may be an A student, but you're an F daughter!*

Diesel fuel in those days was much cheaper than gasoline. On a supermarket bulletin board Mom spotted a postcard offering a second-hand diesel Mercedes Benz for an amazingly low price. The owner touted the car's fuel economy, repair-free history, and sturdy traction. Mom grabbed the bargain and soon may have discovered the reason for it. Taking the car to visit Verne at the Veterans Hospital, she found that by the time she'd parked and got up to his ward, the World War II vets had the shakes. Her car's engine, they said, sounded just like a German tank. After all, Mercedes Benz had made both. That car became my high school graduation gift.

CHAPTER SEVENTEEN

Parcels

Judge not the play until the play is o'er.
Its scenes have many changes. The last act
crowns the play.

On particular occasions my mother intoned these lines from
Hamlet. When I came home in grade school, frantic because
someone had stolen my homework; when a boy I liked in eighth
grade called me Pigface; and after everyone in my high school honors lit. course was invited to a classmate's birthday party, except
me. At such moments my mother resorted to the Bard's wisdom.

In various dark scenes preceding my graduation from East
High, I'd been cheated out of a tennis championship, abandoned
by my boyfriend on the senior trip, and declared an F daughter
after earning straight A's. Nevertheless, and perhaps contrary to
my mother's wishes, the ambivalent Dane's words rang true for
my graduation. In the last act, I received a fat embossed envelope
in the mail.

I'd been accepted at Scripps, an elite private women's college renowned for its humanities core curriculum. And, unlike
the University of Washington, Scripps offered me a manageable financial aid package. No one at East High had heard of it
except Mr. Berry, its vigilant career counselor. The college nei-

ther advertised nor sent recruiters—at least not to Bremerton. My mother agreed to let me go because Mr. Berry recommended it, and because Scripps offered more generous terms than U. of W., which would have required me to take out a much larger loan. But she had doubts.

I hope you won't be wasting your time, Becky. You'd probably do better to start as a secretary and work your way up in the business world. She brought home a teach-yourself-to-type manual, and a sturdy old Remington from Our Favorite Shopping Center. *Playing the piano should make typing easy for you,* she predicted correctly.

Hard experience eventually proved her right on the other point as well. But I had no interest in the business world. I longed to pursue what Scripps called "the life of the mind." College felt like my only path to a better future—and respite from her lectures.

Despite my limited popularity, the high-school senior class voted me Most Likely To Succeed. The election felt absurd, even scary, since few students knew me. What if I didn't succeed at Scripps? Mr. Berry brushed aside my fears, saying he'd be happy if I earned a C average at such a tough college. "Please call me if you do," he said with a reassuring smile. "Don't forget."

Though my mother was pleased to have her daughter accepted at a prestigious college, there were conflicting undercurrents. As she mustered our meager resources for my move, she noted that Southern California's warm weather made clothing more casual and less expensive. She sewed two short-sleeved, cotton A-line dresses, took me shopping for summery blouses and slacks at Our Favorite Shopping Center, and purchased new underwear, sandals, and a light jacket for me at J.C. Penney's.

I also needed a scale to watch my weight. One day Mom brought home a lovely new bathroom scale, rosy pink and oval, with a matching pink fluffy surface to step on with bare feet. Delighted by her thoughtfulness, I praised its beautiful shape and color, kissed and thanked her, and was about to place the new scale in one of the packing boxes we'd foraged from the grocery store, when my mother stiffened and drew back. With stinging coldness she asked, *What makes you think I got that for you? Can't you be satisfied with the old one?*

I was shocked, cut down by her sullen, spiteful tone. Then came a slow, sorrowful realization that my mother felt no joy or pride in my life-changing opportunity. This hard-won fruit of countless hours of study, music practice and tennis workouts, she had probably resented more often than not. Tears rolled down my face.

"Mummy, I can't believe you want those rich girls to see me with our rusty old scale! But I'll take it if you want to have the new one."

She considered this a moment. *Oh, go ahead,* she said in a martyred tone, as though vindicated by proof that I was bone selfish. *Take it, since you've convinced yourself it was meant for you.*

Thereafter the scale had no beauty in my eyes. My suite-mates at Scripps occasionally used it, but I could not bring myself to step on the soft roseate surface that bore my mother's bitter accusation. Half a century later, it sat unused under my chest of drawers, its pink top faded but still fluffy. And a new thought arose. If Mom had wanted to treat herself to a pretty new scale without embarrassing me, she could have got one after I'd left. Why bring one home while I was packing for college? It joined the ranks of other unanswerable questions, though hardly the most troubling.

Such incidents drained the happiness out of my good fortune at being accepted at such a fine college. Lacking any enthusiasm from my mother, all I could manage was hope and determination to survive there.

The day finally came for my flight to Los Angeles, from where I would complete my journey to the Claremont cluster of colleges that included Scripps. Mom drove me to the Seattle-Tacoma airport. *At least you'll get to fly in an airplane. A far cry from riding three days in a stagecoach to go to boarding school.* She waited somberly for my flight, as I watched the giant silver lozenges taxi to and from their docking ramps. Barges of baggage rolled by on the tarmac, under the serene gaze of Mount Rainier, as I tried to spot the luggage she'd got for me on sale at Sears. *You and I both have come a long way from the berry farm,* Mom declared. She voiced no particular hope that either of us would go further, but I filled that in for her, in my thoughts.

When the loudspeaker announced my flight, I hugged my dear sad Mummy, and told her I loved her, would miss her, and was grateful for all she'd done for me. She pressed her lips tight and held back tears, unwilling to acknowledge my love even then. My heart ached, but I told myself that tears had prevented her from saying what I longed to hear. When I turned to wave before boarding the plane, she looked grim but gave me a wave. During takeoff I prayed for us both.

Aloft, I stared in awe at the Olympic and Cascade Mountains with their aura of dignity and power. The lakes below appeared as drops of blue wax. Towns and cities peeping out from green swaths of forests in the Northwest gradually morphed into the parched landscape of Southern California, where a vast gray-brown haze blurred the outline of Los Angeles. So that's what they call smog, I thought. In those days Seattle and Tacoma had nothing like it. Alas, not much longer.

My stomach surged as we landed, not from the plane's jolt but from the impact of hope mixed with terror. Praying not to get lost in the enormous airport, I sighed with relief at signs pointing toward the baggage claim and street transportation. An hour's bus ride to Claremont left me at the Scripps College entrance gate on Columbia Avenue—perhaps more than a coincidence, as I would eventually attend the university of that name.

When my eyes swept across the jewel of Scripps' Southern Missionary-style campus, I felt as if I'd stepped into a fairytale. The adobe buildings had a cozy elegance, nestled among velvety green lawns and columns of stately elms. The residence halls had interior courtyards with fountains encircled by museum-quality frescoes. In the fall of 1965, Scripps' student body consisted of about 400 women, largely from well-to-do families. Most of my classmates had been raised with every advantage. They seemed mildly pleased—rather than flabbergasted, like me—to have access to a cutting garden whose sole purpose was to provide them with roses for their rooms.

Classes were luxuriously small, led by professors who thrived on the exchange of ideas and treated us as younger colleagues. No one was mocked or shunned for being studious or withdrawn, and least of all for loving books, literature, philosophy, or science. "Gracious living" at Scripps was like an ermine cape worn over a monk's homespun habit of scholarly rigor. In the first of countless collect phone calls, Mom downplayed my awestruck description of the college, and warned me not to be overwhelmed.

Each dorm had its own character and history, and its own dining hall. Breakfast and lunch were served buffet style, but we were expected to dress for sit-down dinners by candlelight. Dinner conversations tended to be substantive and rather formal, with newer students keen to pick up pearls of wisdom dropped by their elders. It was a dream world of deference and gentility to which I hoped to belong—before reality intruded.

Assignments were demanding, with extensive recommended readings beyond the required texts "for those interested." That phrase, dear to the astute scholarly faculty, began to sound almost cruel. I was beyond interested, yearning to immerse myself in the extra reading, but for me there was scarcely time to get through the essential coursework and survive.

All Scripps students were selected on a need-blind basis. Those who could not afford the tuition were given financial aid packages consisting of partial scholarships, loans, and part-time campus jobs. To acclimate themselves to the demands of a challenging curriculum, the freshmen on financial aid were not given campus jobs. In my case, however, the Financial Aid Office had overestimated the amount my mother could contribute to my tuition, so she was unable to provide for my incidental expenses as well. When I explained this to the financial aid director, he told me there were no remaining funds available for financial aid. All he could do for me was waive the prohibition on freshmen work-study jobs.

So in the second semester of my first year I began work as a waitress at dinner, setting and clearing the tables, and serving food. In the evening, after I returned from my dorm's dining hall, I was anxious to study, but tired and unable to concentrate well. Burning the candle at both ends, I fought fatigue with quarts of coffee. I could not spare the time or the necessary energy to play tennis or drums, nor even to spend an hour now and then for a dip in the college's fine swimming pool.

More than a few Scrippsies whose dishes I cleared at dinner wore real pearls with their evening dresses, set off by the tans they'd acquired at the pool I never could visit. They took their time returning to their rooms to study. On the occasional evenings when I could join my dorm sisters at the candlelit dinners, my presence as an off-duty waitress seemed to alert the regulars that I was not *one of us, my dear.* My mother's account of British high society resonated anew. I had a keener sense of how she must have felt not to be welcomed by Douglas Elliott's parents into their son's life.

In some way my years at Scripps resembled my mother's stint as the cleaning lady at Monaco Beach. My nonworking dinners struck me as oddly similar to the times Mildred Ruff used to join my mother for afternoon tea. I remembered how, after Mom had finished cleaning cabins for the day at Monaco Beach, she stopped by the tennis court, where I was practicing at the backboard. She asked to borrow my racquet to hit a few balls, to see if she could still hit a decent serve. The way she tossed the ball up and took a firm graceful swing, it was clear she'd once played well—but life had given her no chance to return to the sport. At Scripps it was my turn to walk wistfully past the courts, lacking energy and opportunity to keep up my game.

If I accomplished little else, I was determined to win the approval of the legendary Professor Philip Merlan. He'd emigrated from Germany during WW2 and founded the comparative literature program at Scripps—possibly the only program in the country that considered literature in a wider context of the history of ideas, philosophy, and other humanities disciplines, rather than simply comparing works of literature written in different languages. I was fascinated by all aspects of the humanities and wanted to study literature in the broadest perspective. With no personal connections in the academic world, I would need an influential mentor to open doors for me to attend graduate school and secure a scholarly career.

Professor Merlan's dignified reserve could be intimidating. Seeing him seated alone at teatime in the Scripps Commons, I mustered the nerve to introduce myself. He surprised me by summarizing his academic credentials, as if he had to prove to some unknown peer—surely not me—that he was worthy of respect. Hearing that he'd earned two doctorates and could read twelve and speak five languages, I was so humbled that all I could manage was a wan smile. To my dismay, the great scholar reacted as if I was expressing polite skepticism. "No! It's true!" he protested with childlike vulnerability, looking up at me, who was standing because I hadn't dared sit with him without being invited. Totally flummoxed, I spluttered words to the effect that of course I believed him, whereupon he waved at an empty chair across from him. Incredible, that someone of his erudition and European sophistication could feel defensive with a naive American girl from a berry farm! That moment inspired me to major in Dr. Merlan's program.

His comparative literature course was so substantial that he offered it in four different semester-length sections. To take all four I was willing to forego tennis, drums, plays, swimming and much else. But I could not give up the piano. In the second semester of my freshman year, Scripps created the position of Artist-in-Residence for Alice Shapiro, a concert pianist better known in Europe, who'd played regularly on the BBC in London. The college was abuzz with anticipation, and I was scared but eager to audition for her.

Born and raised in New York, Miss Shapiro had an I've-seen-everything-so-don't-mess-with-me expression, which melted in response to any form of wit, even goofy puns. She put me into a master class with two classmates who were majoring in music, and we played for her and each other every week. Beginning my junior year, Miss Shapiro urged me to start preparing a program I could use to audition at the Juilliard School in New York, where she'd studied with the great Russian pianist Rosina Lhévinne. I'd heard of Juilliard—the conservatory Johnny could've attended with a clarinet scholarship offered by the president of Selmer Instruments. It didn't seem wise to tell her that he'd turned down that chance in favor of the Coast Guard Academy.

To my mother, who had a sense of rhythm but could not carry a tune, the idea of a career in music was most impractical. She accepted that a college degree could lead to a steady job like public school teaching, but made no secret of thinking I'd do better to work my way up in the business world. Not that Mom knew personally any young woman who'd done this, nor was she aware of what came to be called the glass ceiling.

Even if Mom had supported my learning to play the piano, I was not sure she believed in my musical talent. I was not confident of my chances, for some of Miss Shapiro's students had started playing the piano at four or five, whereas I'd begun at twelve, after years of playing drums. I'd drilled on the rudiments of drumming so thoroughly that I was secure in my technique, memorized pieces easily, and played solos for others with confidence. None of these skills could I transfer to the piano. Nerves plagued me at recitals, even during lessons.

Only my love of music, and what I heard inside as its potential for expression, kept me going. Any technical competence had to be fought for, and the fear of unforeseen mistakes loomed over my every performance on the piano. Miss Shapiro assured me that artists with determination could overcome their nerves and have concert careers. I could not bear to disappoint her, so I set a goal to prepare a full-length senior recital as well as fulfilling the requirements for a degree in comparative literature.

"Collect call from Becky," the long distance operator would announce. "Will you accept the call?" Countless times I waited on edge, afraid my mother might say no. I always chose the phone booth at the far end of my hall in the dorm—after looking to make sure no one heard me say I was calling collect. Long-distance rates were too high for me to call often, but to my relief Mom always answered yes. My heart would soar at the warmth of her voice, and I'd forget what I was planning to say.

Not that she ever said she was glad to hear from me, but my mother drew from whatever experience she found relevant to address my problems. The latter boiled down to loneliness, lack of sleep, and falling short of the goals I'd set for myself. She too had spent time away from home at boarding school, but unlike me she'd won a full scholarship, had time to do award-winning work, and became very popular.

One conversation endures in my memory. It went something like this:

Operator: "Long distance calling. Will you accept the charges for Becky?"

Of course! Hello, dear.

"Oh, Mummy, it's so good to hear your voice. What's happening in Bremerton?"

Well, I'm actually rather proud of myself. I was on my break, walking past the newborn nursery, looking through the glass at all those babies, when I noticed that two of them were a frightful shade of blue. I had to move fast, but I managed to get both of them breathing again. The nurse in charge had stepped away for a few minutes. That's all it takes for newborns to choke on something and stop breathing. I dare say they were lucky I was passing by.

"Wow, Mom! What a miracle of timing. You saved their lives!"

Probably. I'm quite a celebrity now at the Naval Hospital. I did my best to convince the charge nurse that it was just a fluke that cast no reflection on her.

"At least one of us is doing great things. This week I was a complete dunce. I took the creative option for the Humanities final, instead of the straight Q and A version of the exam. Dumb move."

Wasn't the creative option more challenging?

"Maybe too challenging. I tried to create a dialogue among muses representing history, philosophy, religion, and literature, and their contributions to the medieval era and early Renaissance. Finding suitable names for those silly muses cost me 45 precious minutes. With only three hours to write, I'd barely got into the historical and philosophical aspects when I had to hand in the wretched thing. The clever girls looked at both exams and chose the Q & A because it was much easier."

Didn't you get credit for trying something original?

"They said I got off to a promising start, but since I hadn't covered much ground they couldn't give me more than a B. I had an A average before, but the final brought my final grade down to B+. Humanities being a double course, that B+ counts twice and really lowers my GPA. I've studied so hard, Mummy. You wouldn't believe how many girls asked to borrow my notes to prepare for the exam. Now they're getting A's while I'm stuck with a B+."

Sweetie-pie, why do you torment yourself so much with grades? Do you really think that B+ means anything compared to the knowledge and understanding you got from all that study?

"You save lives, something that really matters in this world. What can I do?"

Judge not the play until the play is o'er. There are other ways to save lives. Who knows what you can do with the knowledge you're acquiring? But right now I need to save myself from bankruptcy by ending this call. Try to get more sleep. Take the vitamins I sent. And stop fretting about GRADES!

"I love you, Mom, and I'm very proud of you."

By the way, long before you were born your mother won a prize for an essay on Shakespeare. The prize was a book I seem to have lost, but I've never lost the Shakespeare. Bye bye, dear.

Every few months Mom would send me a parcel, compressed to the last cubic inch with useful personal items. Underwear from Penney's or Sears, blouses and skirts from our favorite shopping center, samples of perfume and lipstick from upscale department stores, bottles of vitamins, bars of scented soap, tubes of hand lotion, a jar of cold cream, cotton sun hat, miniature sewing kit, a collection of various sized safety pins. After I mentioned that there was going to be an all-college spring ball that everyone was excited about, she told me to watch for a package.

Just before the ball a box, wrapped in brown paper cut from recycled bags, was waiting for me at the front desk. Inside was a gold-colored brocade evening gown, trimmed around the neckline with white fur. Mom enclosed a note that Bremerton's elegant Dior dress shop was closing, and she'd snapped up the gown for next to nothing. My well-off suitemates were impressed. One of them volunteered to pin up my long hair, and brought along an eye-popping array of salon products to do my makeup. Another loaned me her pearls so that, as she put it, the gown wouldn't be wasted on me. As I left the dorm for the ball, the dorm matron said she could hardly recognize me. Neither did many of my classmates when I danced by.

Afterward I called Mom, to let her know that I'd thought of her as I whirled around the floor with a sequence of handsome men. A mere mist of years separated me from the girl in New Zealand who'd ridden her horse through a thunderstorm to attend that society ball in Ruatoria. Like her, I had no escort, but did not lack for dance partners. I did not have chicken pox, but I'd endangered my health with so little sleep. Though all I had to do was walk across campus to get to this dance, my survival at Scripps required facing other kinds of storms. What kept me going was hope for a better future—and my mother's parcels of love.

There were letters, too, from Verne and Uncle Wayne. Verne's bristled with accusations that I was selfish and not truly grateful to my mother, never a word of encouragement. I wondered why he bothered to write. It did not occur that his letters might have been collaborative efforts—perhaps to return to my mother's good graces after his spell as a mental case. It was puzzling.

Verne's harsh letters were counterbalanced by Uncle Wayne's odd but supportive epistles. He seemed well aware of Mom and

Verne's complaints about me, and offered a mix of esoterica and boosterism. I should hang in there and try to understand that my mother had "a lot to deal with." In his view, she was "driven by a compulsion to talk at excessive length." He seemed to suggest that my mother's case against me had little to do with how I behaved as her daughter. More puzzling.

I was a sophomore at Scripps when Verne decided he wanted out of the Veterans Hospital. He'd grown tired of what he once thought would be ideal circumstances: not having to work, drinking coffee and reading the paper all day. Diagnosed as psychotic, he had no need to concern himself with the outside world or cater to the whims of others. But after two years of toxic leisure, Verne convinced a V.A. psychiatrist that he'd regained his sanity and was ready to return to productive life. The doctor wrote to the Washington State Park Service, vouching that Verne had made a full recovery and should be given another chance.

The Park Service responded cautiously, offering Verne a position at Seabeck, an underdeveloped park far out on the Olympic Peninsula, several hours by car from Bremerton. The ranger's house there was shabby and poorly insulated, but Verne did not complain. Mom could only visit him on weekends, but wrote me that she was gratified when he said his chief reason for leaving the V.A. hospital was to enjoy her company again. He'd stopped smoking, replacing that source of nicotine with the occasional pinch of chewing tobacco. He still consumed endless cups of coffee, but how bad was that? A year later Verne was put in charge of Scenic Beach, a park closer to Bremerton, where Mom could live with him. The kitchen window looked upon dense woods, while the living room offered a breathtaking vista of Puget Sound.

On my sophomore Christmas break from college, I set out into the woods to find the perfect Christmas tree. My boots crunched into the glistening snow as I trudged beneath the frosted evergreens, trying to absorb the winter glories of nature while weeping in helpless frustration. Our dog Valla, my faithful companion, wanted to romp with me in the snow, but all I could do was give her a pat and plod along, miserable to be using what should have been a joyous errand to escape another dreaded lecture. With Verne better and me doing fairly well at Scripps, I failed to understand why Mom had to resume her torturous monologues about my *attitude* and how my relationship with her was my *Achilles heel*.

Her threat not to pay her small portion of my college tuition never failed to reduce me to abject tears and pleading. She would relent at the last minute, as though releasing a wounded animal. But once I was back on campus, the warmth of her voice on long-distance phone calls, and her lovingly packed parcels, sustained me. Until the next ordeal at home.

CHAPTER EIGHTEEN

What's the Alternative?

On leave from the Academy, my brother brought Mom a house-warming gift during our first winter at Scenic Beach. The ranger's house there was far more habitable and closer to civilization than Verne's Spartan residence at Seabeck. Scenic Beach would be the last place Johnny and I stayed under the same roof with Mom and Verne. My brother strung up his gift—a lifesize rubber replica of a plucked chicken—above the kitchen sink. Its head went off at a convincing angle indicating a broken neck. Its sickly white body looked for all the world like its blood had just drained into the sink below. As visitors passed by the kitchen, Johnny watched gleefully as they failed to suppress looks of revulsion. Then our mother would walk over to the sink, give the chicken's feet a tug, and smile as its body stretched down a few inches and rebounded into its previous shape.

A present from my son. Very tasteful, don't you think?

Hilarity all around. How I wished I could have that effect on her, instead of the low-volume unbearable rants she reserved for me. Still, I was glad one of us could amuse her, and laughed with relief like everyone else.

One frigid day I came upon Verne sitting alone in the kitchen, sipping his coffee and staring out the frosted window toward Hood's Canal. Muttering how tired he was of the cold, he announced defiantly, "Next year I want to live in a warm climate."

Taking him literally, I asked, "What about Mom? What would she do?"

Verne gazed at the icicles outside with no reply. Perhaps he hadn't included her in his plans.

The following December, 1968, a three-day blizzard swept across western Washington, shortly before I returned for Christmas my senior year at Scripps. The house at Scenic Beach was snowbound. During the storm, it seemed, Verne had placed a wad of chewing tobacco under his tongue, and the jolt of nicotine stopped his heart. My mother called for an ambulance, but it could not forge through the snow up the steep driveway to the ranger's house. By the time paramedics reached the house on foot and carried Verne on a stretcher down to the ambulance, he could not be revived.

The roads were mostly cleared and Verne's body was in a mortuary when I arrived. I drove Mom to the funeral home, where she faced the typical pressure of funeral directors, who all seem in cahoots to shamelessly gouge the bereaved. I accompanied her into the casket showroom, where the only affordable model was a pine coffin covered with a floral print fabric that had been allowed to fade and gather dust amidst a bounty of costly caskets of varnished walnut, cherry and mahogany, trimmed with gleaming chrome or brass. I locked arms with her and steered us past the rows of exorbitant sarcophagi.

"Mummy, Verne would be furious if you paid these outrageous prices!"

Do you really think so, dear? The only one we can afford looks so shabby.

"I can hear Verne now. He'd be saying, Don't let them take advantage of you for my sake! You think I give a damn about a fancy coffin?"

She meekly chose the cloth-covered pine box. At the funeral we were grateful that Verne had not been put in the faded showroom model, but one with new, brighter fabric, tastefully topped with a wreath of fresh flowers. The funeral director's wife, whose low-cut black dress was accessorized with ropes of gold chains and a diamond ring the size of an almond, whispered that she'd saved the flowers and some cookies and sandwiches from a previous reception. Coffee and tea were complimentary, so we were not charged their excessive fee for refreshments.

The blizzard had made driving difficult, so only a few came: Uncle Wayne, one or two state park personnel, and a couple of Mom's nurse friends. Once again, the Park Service gave my mother as much time as she needed to get her bearings and move out.

It was so cold that winter that we had to roll up rags and towels to stuff around the windows to stop icy blasts from whistling through the panes. In the gray, hollow days after the funeral we sat together in the only warm spot in the house, the kitchen, drinking tea and sipping hot soup. There were no more lectures.

All in all, Mom mused, *Verne's life was a success story.* He'd taken control of his alcoholism and abuse of tranquilizers, and done his best to overcome what the doctors said was his nature as an "addictive type." Most important, he'd told her that he'd left the Veterans Hospital and returned to the Park Service in order to be with her. His attention, she said, no longer drifted away whenever she talked. They'd been able to engage in real conversation. Their final year together, she assured me, had been harmonious.

I listened in sympathy, not mentioning Verne's pronouncement the previous winter about moving to a warm location. At the time I did not allow myself to consider that he might have known what he was doing when he put that bolus of chewing tobacco under his tongue.

After her glowing account of the last year of their marriage, Mom took a deep breath and pushed away her unfinished bowl of soup.

Becky, you're old enough to hear this. I haven't told anyone else.

She then stated calmly that in their thirteen years of marriage Verne had not made love to her. His public displays of affection—the occasional arm around her shoulder or peck on the cheek—

were all she'd ever received from him. Her face contorted briefly as she blurted, *In bed he would flinch away from me.* As soon as this was said she lifted her chin and looked away, as if to defy pity.

I stared at her with compassion but not disbelief. From the beginning I'd sensed there was something missing in Verne's demeanor toward her. I just hadn't imagined it went that far. Mom gazed stoically at the snow-laden shore and slow, ice-laden waves of Puget Sound. She was possibly awaiting my response, but I had none. I was certain she would not confide such a thing to anyone else, but I had no words for the magnitude of her confession. She was bereaved. Who was I to question the consolation she took in the success story she'd perceived in Verne's life, if it helped her feel validated as a woman? I reached across the table and squeezed her arm. She stood up, took our soup bowls to the sink, washed them, and never mentioned this again.

It was in no way gratifying to have my childhood intuition validated. I did not believe that Verne's self-orchestrated return to normal life made up for depriving my mother of a husband's full measure of love and affection. I pondered anew a comment of Verne's that Mom had quoted admiringly. Years before, when they'd been hesitating about some course of action to take in some forgotten weighty matter, he asked her, "What's the alternative?"

Marrying my mother may have been Verne's best alternative, but I could not accept it as hers. As I put away our clean soup dishes, I was reminded that this was another example of the motto my mother had first imparted to her sister Gwenda: *It's not what happens to you that matters, it's what you make of it.* Mom had made the best of this what's-the-alternative marriage.

CHAPTER NINETEEN

Schrödinger's Cat

I had chronic anemia during my last year at college, and struggled not to succumb to the quicksand of fatigue. I had to ask for extra time to complete coursework, and confided to Miss Shapiro that my waitressing job was draining. She pulled strings and got me a less strenuous job in the Scripps music library. With an ambitious glow in her eyes, she mentioned some wonderful, difficult pieces I might perform in a solo recital—ones she hoped I would use after graduation to audition for the Juilliard School, her alma mater. I was ashamed to admit that I lacked the stamina to tackle them. Her expression hardened.

I didn't blame her for feeling exasperated. That's how I felt about myself. But my heart bled when she accused me of being lazy. It was a bitter comedown in her esteem from the previous year, when the musicology professor—who'd heard me practicing Bach's Italian Concerto—asked me to perform it during his presentation for my third-year humanities class, to illustrate the sonata form. Miss Shapiro had sat proudly among the humanities faculty members in the back row of the recital hall, behind a hundred of my classmates. As far as anyone knew, no student had ever been asked to perform before an entire humanities class.

After a brief false start, I played the piece with my usual love of Bach, delighting in his rhythm and melodic genius. The applause felt genuine. However, as I walked back to my dorm afterward, I overheard a classmate describe my playing as "more technique than expression." Her remark struck me as catty, and unwittingly ironic. She did not know that technical skill had always been my weakest element. Expression and love of music was my only strength. At least Miss Shapiro was pleased.

But that was yesteryear. As a senior pushing through exhaustion, all I could offer were two pieces in Miss Shapiro's group recital. Though I played them well, nothing could assuage her disappointment that I had not prepared a full solo recital. My playing continued to improve, but she lowered my grade for the first time from an A to a B+. It broke my heart, and lowered my GPA.

After Verne's death, these painful details seemed too trivial to share with my mother. Nor did I tell her that toward the end of our last semester at Scripps Miss Shapiro invited the two other students in our weekly master class to dine with her, individually, at her home in Claremont. She did not invite me.

In my only photo of Miss Shapiro—taken nervously by Mom when I graduated in June 1969—she seems to pose dutifully, not quite masking her disappointment in me. She was polite but made no favorable comments about me that my mother might have taken to heart, and quickly excused herself to greet other graduates.

To my shock and immense disappointment, Professor Philip Merlan died suddenly during my last year at Scripps. His widow, Dr. Franciszka Merlan, a philosopher in her own right, took over his remaining classes in comparative literature. I had not met her when she called to ask if she could use my class notes to prepare her lectures. I felt honored that my revered professor might have mentioned me as one of his better students. She may have gotten my name, though, from the recommendation form for my application to Princeton University, which, she informed me sadly, was on top of the pile of paperwork her husband had planned to complete when he felt better.

When I no longer had a mentor, I learned the value of having a well-known one. Dr. Merlan had once been a scholar at Princeton's Institute for Advanced Studies, and might have paved my way into Princeton's top-notch comparative literature program. Mrs. Merlan promised to write my letters of recommendation on his behalf.

Earlier in the year Dr. Merlan had enthusiastically approved my senior thesis topic. I was eager to prove I could meet his standards, and focused all my intellectual energy on this project. When I'd finished and submitted my 50-page essay, I was elated, believing it to be significant, original, and publishable. But alas, Dr. Merlan was no longer alive to judge its merits and connect me with a publisher. Instead, my thesis was read by a professor with whom I'd never studied. My heart sank as I read his/her begrudging A- scrawled at the top, followed by the killer phrase, "Original but wrong-headed." The reader identified no errors in my reasoning or scholarship, so his/her verdict was based merely on a difference of personal interpretation. Unfortunately, this reader's response seemed to deter the second and third readers from judging the essay more favorably. I was so angry and disappointed that I threw away the manuscript, and to this day cannot recall the topic.

I graduated thirteenth in a class of 104. Not quite stellar, either in academic or musical performance. I was leery of excuses, but didn't see any way I could have studied harder, with the time and energy that remained after completing the college's work requirement for students on financial aid. The students who never seemed stressed out were those who didn't need scholarship support. In fairness, I had to consider that circumstances beyond my control contributed to my failure to prove to the world, and my mother, that I was capable of greatness, and worthy of her trust that I loved her.

Commencement came just half a year after Verne's death. In family solidarity, Verne's sister Esther, her husband Vernie, and Verne's sister-in-law Irene drove from their homes in California to attend the ceremony with my mother. I was very fond of Aunt Irene, widow of Verne's older brother Ernest, a Naval officer. She'd invited me to visit her in Cathedral City on two of my spring breaks. She was easygoing, glad of my company, and ready to laugh at herself. On her honeymoon, she told me, she'd forgot to pack her pajama bottoms, and Uncle Ernest teased her that she'd done so on purpose.

After the commencement ceremony I left Mom to have tea and socialize with Aunt Esther, Uncle Vernie and Aunt Irene, while I returned to my dorm to finish packing. Descending into the basement of Grace Scripps Hall to sort through the residue of four inspiring, bittersweet years, I found it remarkably free of dust and disarray. Even the storage area was a model of gracious living! In this unexpectedly pristine lower level, I'd hoped to be alone with the disappointment I'd concealed from my family. A few compartments away, though, was a former classmate who'd faced a different challenge.

The late sixties brought what was called the New Morality to many colleges. Judith had been among the first girls in my class to spend weekends off campus with her boyfriend, who was older and accustomed to a worldly lifestyle. When we'd been freshmen at Scripps we had to return to our dorms by 11:00 p.m. On weekends we could invite male visitors into our rooms but our doors had to be left open. If we spent a night or weekend away we had to leave sign-out sheets with addresses and phone numbers where we'd be staying. However, by our senior year the college's role *in loco parentis* had been abandoned in favor of personal freedom and sexual experimentation, often on a troubling if not dangerous scale. Judith became a loner in class, with only her boyfriend for company. Seeing me, she gave out a happy chirp of relief. Our conversation went something like this:

"Say, Becky, can you believe we're actually getting out of this place?"

"Judy! 'Haven't seen you since Hum. 3. Where've you been hiding?"

"With Chuck, of course. We're engaged now. I got a lot of nasty looks in the last couple years, so Scripps became just a place to finish my courses. The only people I still respect are some professors, and a few classmates like you."

I bent over a box of textbooks trying to decide which ones I could not bear to part with. "Why me? I didn't finish so well. Not getting an A in Humanities really brought down my average."

"Oh well, 'can't win 'em all. Do you remember that Nobel Prize physicist from Caltech? The one they brought in to explain relativity theory and quantum mechanics?"

"Yeah. He was pretty full of himself."

"Until you raised your hand in the Q&A."

"I did?"

"I can't believe you don't remember! It was the academic high point of the year for me—maybe the whole four years."

"Sorry. I'm pulling a blank."

"This guy was talking down his nose like we were a bunch of airheads. He said something about a cat in a box that by the laws of physics had to be either dead or alive for 25 years, but not until somebody opened the box to look. You were sitting off to the side, listening calmly, not petrified like the rest of us. When he asked for questions, up went your hand."

"I remember the gist of his lecture. Not much else."

"Becky, how could you forget that smug look on his face when he called on you, as though none of us were worthy of his genius? You asked whether the cat's either-or state was too limited, whether the poor creature might be in some other state of existence not covered by quantum theory. Well! His face fell, his whole vibe changed. 'Oh,' he said, 'That's what Einstein asked.' I think a lot of us wanted to cheer—Home run for the Scrippsies! On the team with Einstein!!"

Looking up from my packing boxes, I tilted my head to make eye contact. "I'm so glad you remembered this, Judy. I must have been too wiped out to retain it. Didn't get much sleep the whole four years. Really, thanks. I was feeling down and you pulled me out of it."

"Yeah, well, it's hard to leave such a gorgeous place. But I get to start a new life with Chuck, and I'm sure you'll be moving on to great things."

"No idea what I'll be doing. Super to see you, though. Best of luck in your marriage."

"Hey, not to worry. You just need the right opportunity. And thanks. Not just for your comment on the quantum cat. For not snubbing me."

Judith's recollection of my query about Schrödinger's cat became my best memory of Scripps.

CHAPTER TWENTY

Peripeteia

One ship sails East and the other West,
By the self-same winds that blow.
'Tis the set of the sails and not the gales
That determines the way they go.

(My mother's version of a poem
by Ella Wheeler Wilcox)

By the time I'd graduated from Scripps, Mom had moved into a modest home on North Wycoff Avenue in an older area of West Bremerton, where the Washington Narrows appeared in the distance like a shiny thread weaving into Puget Sound. Recently able to fill an opening at the Naval Hospital in Bremerton, she was free at last from tiring commutes. As ever, my mother was respected and taken into the confidence of doctors who normally kept aloof from the nurses. Still, at the end of her shift she returned to an empty home and widowhood. She hoped I could find a good job with my college degree and make a life with her in Bremerton. If I brought up the possibility of applying to graduate school, she would change the topic.

Without a degree in science, technology or business, jobs for new college grads were scarce in Washington State. The only position I could find was in the management training program at Sears & Roebuck in Seattle. To enter it, one had to pass the notorious "Sears battery," a four-hour written exam calculated to identify candidates with traits that would make them effective managers in a nationwide retail chain. My only association with Sears was Mom's regard for it as a source of reliable household appliances and underwear. I skimmed the exam questions before daring to answer any, and my gut decided that honesty would not work for me. When asked whether I'd rather to go to a museum, watch a football game, read a book, or work on a stamp collection, I checked the box for the football game rather than the museum or book. Sears obviously wanted sports fans, not reclusive intel-lectuals. Tailoring my answers to fit that profile, I passed—uncomfortably aware that others who took the test might have been eager to work at Sears, told the truth about themselves, and did not pass. Needing a job, I rationalized that my need to earn a living trumped four hours of insincere testimony.

To get to the training site, a cavernous old store on the out-skirts of Seattle, I drove 20 minutes from North Wycoff, parked near the ferry terminal, spent an hour on the boat to Seattle, and caught a bus that got me to Sears in 40 minutes. Buses and ferries were less frequent in the evening, so my workday could last 13-14 hours. I found myself reheating leftovers from suppers Mom had prepared for both of us hours before. She would sit at the table with me, sipping tea, and ask, *How was your day, dear?*

She hoped I could produce something interesting we could talk about, but all I'd gathered were mind-numbing merchandis-ing details, imparted by a dowdy old trainer in orthopedic shoes who eyed me with suspicion. I had nothing substantial to dis-cuss—except for a pamphlet we'd been given on how to remove spots from a broad spectrum of fabrics—a keeper. Afterward, Mom suggested that I practice the piano, but for me that required real energy, and by late evening I was running on fumes.

Becoming a sales manager at Sears was not what I'd endured the rigors of a top college for. I had nothing against well-trained department store managers, but a career at Sears had to be someone else's destiny. I still cherished the Scripps ideal of a life of the mind, hoping someday to be a college professor in the lineage of the great Philip Merlan—and, in time, a serious amateur pianist.

On the ferry going home I recognized a former classmate from East High, one of the insiders who'd never accepted me. Ronny Rutledge was handsome, self-assured and popular. How could I forget that he'd been on the committee that chose the seniors who'd be "dubbed"—the high point of East's commencement ceremony? East's basketball and football teams were called the Knights, so being dubbed was the school's greatest honor. Despite earning top grades and bringing recognition to the school in tennis tournaments and music competitions, I was not deemed worthy of dubbing by this committee. Rest assured, Ronny had not voted for me.

He blinked a few times when I took the window seat across from him on the observation deck. "Well, well, if it isn't Painter," he said, with a cool, snide edge. "What have *you* been up to since college?"

I answered frankly, about being a Sears management trainee, though it was far from a career goal. Ronny listened with a faint smirk, then let me know he was doing research in the law firm where his father was a partner, and would be attending law school at the University of Washington, his dad's alma mater. In the awkward silence that followed, I pondered the vast difference in our prospects.

"What do you do for fun?" he asked.

"Oh, reading, piano practice, some tennis now and then." Actually, I had no one to play tennis with, had hardly held a racquet in college, and my current schedule left me little energy to read or practice the piano.

Ronny expounded on his hobby, mountain climbing. He found it exhilarating to climb high above the rest of the world, surrounded by crystal white snow and breathtaking panoramas. "It takes real discipline," he boasted, "so only the best people do it. We don't talk about it much, but we know who we are."

"Well," I replied defensively, "playing the piano also requires discipline." He stared past me while I completed my thought. "Classical music has a beauty and altitude of its own." Ronny examined the passing shoreline of Bainbridge Island without comment.

After an awkward conversational hiatus, the ferry's engine cut off, and the boat began its silent glide into the Bremerton terminal. Perhaps we both sensed the fluke that our paths had crossed, that our parting words would probably be for the rest of our lives.

"Good luck in your law career. I'm sure you'll do well." I had no doubt Ronny would enjoy every possible advantage.

He gave a slight nod and mumbled something inaudible like "Right." Then Ronald R. Rutledge III strode briskly onto the exit ramp far ahead of me, as though destined to be the wheat and I the chaff.

When I got home my mother noticed something uncommunicative about me. She seemed ready to launch into one of her lectures when I cut her off. "How can you expect me to make myself happy and spread sunshine to others, when the deck is stacked?" It caught her unprepared. For once she did not ask me to examine my behavior for ways that I might have handled the situation better—her standard reproach since I was first bullied in elementary school.

Feeling unopposed for once, I proceeded to recount Ronny Rutledge's cushy summer job courtesy of his father, his guaranteed future in a top Seattle law firm, his loftier-than-thou hobby, and my firm suspicion that he'd voted against my being "dubbed" at East High. My mixture of anger, despair, and brute facts seemed to block Mom's dreaded shift into lecture mode. She muttered something vague about snobbery, paused, then wondered aloud whether this Ronny fellow was genuinely pleased with his life if he had to stoop to making others feel inferior.

In the silence that followed, my mother nodded slowly to herself as her scarred fingers strummed on the kitchen table.

Then, in a businesslike tone, she asked, *When is the deadline for you to apply to graduate school?* She'd shown zero interest before. The date was very near.

Amazed, I realized that I was witnessing what the Greek tragedians had called a *peripeteia*, a turnabout that makes possible the resolution of a drama. My mother had decided that the only way I could feel good about myself was to continue on the path of scholarship that had opened doors for me thus far, and might lead to a more suitable career than retail sales management.

She conceded that I'd done whatever I could to find suitable employment near home, but my return was not providing her the companionship, nor me the job opportunities, she'd hoped for. The practical, kindly mother of my early childhood had miraculously resurfaced. I could hardly believe—after so much trauma the past eight years—that we were back on the same page. It meant everything to me that she finally supported my setting forth in a more promising direction. Even though we would each have to proceed alone.

I hastily applied to three graduate programs in comparative literature. At Scripps, Mrs. Merlan was still using my notes for her late husband's comparative lit. courses, so I trusted that she and a few other professors would be supportive.

The University of Washington accepted me, offering no financial help other than a huge loan. So I was exhilarated to receive a telephone call from an admissions officer at my top choice, Princeton. A distant voice said I was being given serious consideration, but the university would accept me only if I could take an intensive course in a third language, preferably German, to fulfill the prerequisites for their doctoral program in comparative literature. In those days the only way to learn German fast was to hire a private tutor or fly to Germany for a total immersion course at the Goethe Institute. Neither of which could we afford. Explaining this to the Princeton official, I pleaded to be allowed to learn a third language at Princeton. Sorry, the voice replied, but their program was highly competitive and they had other applicants who'd already mastered more than three languages.

Mom watched as I hung up the phone, overwhelmed with disappointment. Had I not recently reminded her that the deck was stacked? If only Dr. Merlan had not died, he might have convinced Princeton to take a chance on me. Maybe his name on my application was the only reason they'd called.

That left Columbia, where I was offered a modest stipend, a tuition waiver, a smaller debt burden, and another work-study job. Mom would have preferred that I stay nearby in Seattle, but rolled her eyes at the enormous loan I'd need to attend U. of W. She agreed that Columbia, a more prestigious university, had made the better offer.

The day before I left for New York, Flavia rescheduled a block of piano lessons in order to drive down from Lake Stevens and present me with a farewell gift long in the making. Inside a blond, satin finished, velvet-lined wooden box, were eight place settings of Wallace stainless steel flatware in a simple, elegant design. Over the years, unbeknownst to me, she'd saved the coupons from countless boxes of the facial tissues used in her chiropractic practice, and redeemed all these items one by one. In addition to place settings there were several serving spoons and forks, two long-handled teaspoons for ice cream sodas, and a triangular spatula for serving slices of pie. I stared at the contents, tongue-tied at such incredible thoughtfulness.

Flavia smiled indulgently. "Stainless is so much more practical than silverware, Becky dear. You never have to polish it." She said she was relieved to have completed the collection in time for me to "set out for parts unknown." Thanking her did not seem enough, considering how long she'd persevered with this project, graciously preparing for my unknown future.

As she left, Flavia asked if I might walk her to her car, a new white classic Impala. Then my beloved first piano teacher and surrogate aunt unlocked the car door, urging me to write often and to call my "angel mother" as often as possible. "She will miss you greatly. I'll pray for you both not to be too lonely." Rolling down the driver's side window, she rested her finely manicured, articulate hands on the steering wheel and looked up at me somberly. "Be careful, my dear girl. Columbia University is beyond what I could imagine for you, and New York is…well, never having been there, I'm in no position to advise!"

Smiling and waving as she pulled away, Flavia tapped the horn twice, *presto pianissimo*, for my angel mother's ears. My heart ached to make her proud of me.

Flavia, Johnny and me on a visit to her home on Lake Stevens, one summer in the early sixties.

CHAPTER TWENTY-ONE

Postmarks

With a deft thud, the plane touched down on the runway at JFK in September of 1969, as if confirming that New York City would be my real home. On the approach I'd peered through the haze, incredulously identifying two or three famous skyscrapers. To me the atmosphere seemed less like smog and more like vapors of creative energy. During the flight I'd chatted with an Australian inventor, who insisted on hailing a cab for me after I'd collected my luggage. He knew his way around, found a taxi quickly, stuffed some bills into the cabbie's hand, and told him to give me a tour of Manhattan before dropping me off at 116th and Broadway. "Consider it a good-luck gift," he said, "for attending my alma mater—a capital way to start your new life." The driver fanned the wad of cash, nodded, and gestured for me to get in. The Aussie opened the door for me, closed it, and was gone before I could ask his name.

"Nice guy," said the cabbie. Relishing the role of guide to a newbie, he introduced me to the Triboro Bridge as we crossed it toward 125th Street, heart of dicey but vibrant Harlem. He turned down Park Avenue through the posh Upper East Side, and across artsy Greenwich Village, then toward midtown past the spires of the Empire State and Chrysler buildings, west to Broadway, past the newly built Lincoln Center. Farther up came the slightly seedy but hip Upper West Side, and the campus where I would settle into a narrow graduate dorm room in Columbia's Johnson Hall.

Besides the business at hand—learning the lay of the land, where to register, how to get to my classes—a nimbus of realization began to hover over me: that until then I'd spent my life in various stages of exile, and now I was entering the real world. On the sidewalks people were speaking unidentifiable languages, in all manner of clothing and quirks of self-presentation. I loved the city's ambient energy, that so many peoples' genius and striving had earned it the implicit status of world capitol. At Scripps, when Miss Shapiro still held great hope for me, she'd said I belonged in New York. I'd disappointed her by not auditioning at Juilliard, but I was here anyway, and knew she was still right.

Columbia's doctoral program in English and comparative literature had an impressive faculty and roster of intriguing courses. As at Scripps, my first few weeks were exhilarating. I wrote to Miss Shapiro about my arrival, and was thrilled when she wrote back, claiming that my happiness had leapt off the page—making her very happy. "I was so afraid that you had decided to stay in Washington and work for the Civil Service or something idiotic like that," she wrote, and recommended a few New York colleagues I might try for piano lessons.

Flavia wrote that she'd "perused in various lights" my letter to her, which enclosed a postcard with an aerial view of Columbia. "How wonderful you are realizing your dream of attending Columbia!" She said she'd absorbed as much information about my new environs as she possibly could, and mentioned having seen my mother several times since Wayne died. "This took her hard, but as usual she is being sensible, working hard, staying cheerful, but I know is oh, so lonesome."

My mother's letters posed practical questions like which of my books to ship and what I needed for my dorm room. She noted that she was beginning to struggle with an arthritic hip, getting overtired, trembly and weepy. Not recognizing the symptoms of a heart condition, her physician had told her to take two weeks off, prescribed strong painkillers, and advised her to avoid weight-bearing—nearly impossible for a practical nurse. As today, Western medicine had no cures for arthritis, so my mother tried alternative therapies: detoxification programs, exercise classes.

I imagined that the silence for her at home was interrupted only by occasional phone calls from Flavia, a nurse friend or two, and myself—buffered only slightly by evening television. Her only steady company was Valla, the gentle Norwegian elkhound who'd been my truest friend through adolescence. Mom described how she went to the door to let Valla out during a downpour, but the dog *stood still a few minutes barking at the weather in disgust, then ran to the side entrance hoping things might be better in that direction!*

While sorting through the college texts I'd asked her to send, Mom examined some of my marginal notes. At the end of Beowulf I'd penciled, "Why do we have to have heroes?" She thought I might have stumbled on something perceptive:

> *Don't know whether you were conscious of what you were opening up – But...there are vital implications in the vast field of symbology where heroes slay monsters and dragons and set out on voyages into the unknown. There are dragons everywhere —of loneliness, misconceptions, ignorance, lack of communication, you name it. ...I may not be exactly looking for "islands of the blest," but venturing into conditions such as widowhood and physical old age is a lot more pleasant if one invests it somewhat with glamour and importance!*

What a wonderful scholar my mother would have made, I thought, regretting that she no longer read serious literature, which she'd loved in her youth. Now all she found time for were newspapers, murder mysteries, and celebrity gossip magazines at the hairdresser's. Her letter continued:

> *I'm grateful for those who have slain dragons for me. Probably every beneficial condition I find myself in is the product of dragon slaying of one kind or another. ...In my own internal nature... there are plenty of monsters of fear, loneliness, of ignorance. And I don't care to play the role of a helpless villager waiting to be devoured. I'd rather be looking for points of view which might replace discouraging ones, and actions which identify me with heroes inside my own self!*

At 60 she could no longer sustain the wear and tear on her hips as an LPN. A local business school advised her to learn to type so she'd be able to work in a doctor's office. She'd inherited Uncle Wayne's electric typewriter, and took pains to type portions of her letters to me. I hoped she wouldn't have to take an office job, knowing how much that sort of work could sap one's energy.

Mom protested that letter writing was difficult and devoured her free time, yet her letters seemed to flow effortlessly, lightened by wit and attention to minute particulars. Her own *field of advanced study*, she claimed—a jab at my doctoral program?—was human nature. Her stated goal: the kind of relationship with her daughter that seemed possible but kept eluding her. Chatty as it seemed, this declaration gave the recipient a shiver of dread.

Columbia's terms of acceptance required me to start fulfilling its work-study requirement immediately. I was to assist the Dean of Students at Columbia Law School, a capable but overextended woman who deserved a fulltime assistant, but had to make do with one work-study grad student for a maximum of 20 hours a week. She needed all the time I could spend and more, and would not allow me to leave in the midst of a crisis—her office being one long traffic jam of student crises. No way could

I decompress from that job, attend all my classes, and do my best on coursework.

With academic survival at stake, I reverted to the risky practice of sacrificing sleep to study. To fend off late night drowsiness I guzzled coffee and put myself into yoga positions that were supposed to be more restful than sleep. Perhaps I didn't do them well enough, for they failed to lessen my craving for slumber. I consumed so much caffeine my hands began to shake—a warning sign easy to ignore since I rarely got access to a piano.

I lived for the rare, wonderful moments in Columbia's small literature seminars, when I'd managed to reflect on the readings and could offer something to stimulate the discussion. Perhaps due to my unconventional upbringing, the remarks I made in class seemed to come from somewhere beyond left field. The professors noticed my disregard for the usual grad student posturing, occasionally lobbing questions at me about problems they'd spent much of their careers trying to solve.

In one philosophy class I asked a question, now forgotten, that took a visiting German philosopher by surprise. He struggled in earnest to respond, but all I retain from our exchange was what happened afterward. As the classroom emptied, a bushy-haired young man walked out of Philosophy Hall with me as though we were buddies. Asking where I was from, he admitted in a droll deadpan that he hadn't expected someone who looked like a "shiksa farm girl" to say anything worth that professor's time.

Steve Devere, one of Columbia's top philosophy students, was the elder son of two Holocaust survivors. Would I be interested in meeting him at the Thalia—a legendary art house specializing in foreign films—to watch "Stolen Kisses" by François Truffaut? He didn't need the subtitles, being fluent in French and German. I fell for his combination of dry humor, salty skepticism, and self-deprecation. After a glorious night of philosophical jokes, followed by my first experience of gratifying sex, he did not call for several days. Though I had very little time for dating, I missed him. When I could no longer refrain from calling, he described himself as reclusive by nature, with chronic spells of depression. For a reliable companion, he warned, I should find someone else.

To get Steve off my mind, I began dating a law student who'd appeared at the Dean of Students' office, holding his head and begging for any painkiller we had on hand. Jaime was another charming young Jewish man, an immigrant from Cuba. His problem, however, was the opposite of Steve's: not reclusive enough, preferring to party rather than study. His Latino friends could not understand why he'd taken up with someone so book-ish, given his lothario reputation. I didn't know whether to be flattered or cynical when he confessed to being surprised at hav-ing no desire to cheat on me. Going out with Jaime did nothing for my lack of sleep.

My mother, referring to something she'd read about Native American culture, urged me to take better care of *little sister in the body*. Early in my second semester at Columbia, little sis-ter succumbed to what I'd thought was a nasty flu but could have been something worse. I was too ill to continue working in the Dean's Office. Mom sold the diesel Mercedes that had been my college graduation gift so I could live off the proceeds through June, and complete the master's degree that was prelim-inary to a doctorate from Columbia in English and comparative literature. My degree came with high honors—not because I'd had sufficient time to study there, but because I'd been able to use knowledge gained from Dr. Merlan's masterful courses at Scripps.

It took my last scrap of stamina to finish a master's essay on the nature of time in Emily Dickinson's poetry. When it was returned to me, I was delighted that the main reader had writ-ten "original and publishable" on top, and signed his name. He'd been one of my favorite professors at Columbia, but when I tried to contact him he'd already left for a tenured position in the Midwest.

Meantime, a financial aid advisor at Columbia informed me that the Nixon Administration had cut federal support for higher education in the liberal arts. Only a few privately funded fellow-ships were available for doctoral students in the humanities. With a dead-eye glance, he told me I might not be returning in the fall. Never had I felt more sorely the absence of my kind, resourceful high school counselor, Mr. Berry. I blamed myself later for not being more assertive, but the near certainty that I would lose my fellowship at Columbia deprived me of the nerve to write to the professor who'd read of my master's essay, to ask his help finding a publisher.

I phoned my mother with this distressing mix of good and bad news. She reflected further on it in a letter:

> When I left the telephone last night I remem-bered the type of doctor you should see. An endo-crinologist... In the meantime don't get disheart-ened, honey. Life is a series of challenges. Who knows the unseen benefits which are registered in those inner worlds where the patterns are formed for future history, whenever our energy goes...to solve our human problems?
> ...It is easy to be scared...and I get just as scared as anyone else. But after one has noted the condition the main emphasis has to go on "What to do" to improve, or cure?

I should keep my cool, she advised, and if it was lost, retrieve it. She congratulated me on finishing my master's essay, which she considered *the result of tenacity and persistence, plus an abil-ity factor that you can be proud of.* I deserved the A, she wrote, because it was not *earned at the expense of oneself as a daughter!* I puzzled over this as I walked across campus.

Her next sentence stopped me in my tracks: *In fact I think we can write that old "F" off the books forever.* Dazed, I sat down on the steps of Low Library to reread her words. It seemed that she'd remembered—well enough to retract—the curse of my senior year in high school: that I was an A student but an F daughter. She concluded:

> 'Think the move to New York was definitely the right one for you, even if you never bother to go through to a Ph.D. Especially as it was qualified, on the human side, by a willingness to stay here and help me out, if I felt I could not manage alone. Funny how often all that is needed of us is willingness.
>
> Fondest love,
> Mother

Wait. Had she threatened to stop paying her portion of my Scripps tuition because she wanted me to be willing to drop out and keep her company—when Verne was still with her—but instead I'd begged her to let me finish college? Was that what she'd meant by my being selfish? Had Verne sent me all those demoralizing letters at Scripps to support her accusations of selfishness? Would my offering to drop out have satisfied them both?

If nothing else, my mother's letter revealed that she'd remained fully aware of the F she'd given me as her daughter. It stood to reason that she was equally cognizant of—but unwilling to lift—her enduring judgment that I did not love her.

CHAPTER TWENTY-TWO

Two Farewells

She'd bought an older home in Bremerton, my mother explained, because it gave our dog Valla a freer environment than she'd have in a new rental unit. During my Christmas break from Columbia she asked me to construct a warm bed for Valla, who was not allowed to stay indoors at night, for her to sleep outside next to the house. With some remnants of carpeting and an old quilt I found in the garage, I chose a covered area nearby. I layered the carpeting and folded the quilt over a thick plastic tarp, so ground moisture would not seep into Valla's bedding. My beloved old pet padded closely around me, ducking her head and wagging her tail as I assured her that this cozy new lair would be hers alone. As soon as I finished she stepped onto the quilt, circled around her tail, plopped down and rolled onto her back for me to rub her tummy as I'd done since I was a girl. Stroking her tenderly, I wondered if she'd be there the next time I came home, and regretted that past winter when I'd been too miserable to romp in the snow with her as we searched for a Christmas tree.

When she was a puppy, I'd asked Mom if Valla could be my dog. To my sorrow, she would not answer. Still, I was the one who fed, groomed and trained Valla to respond to simple commands. But while I was away at college, then graduate school, I was glad Valla was there with Mom. After Verne's death she'd written: *I*

can almost cry, when I think how much I owe to the loyal com-
panionship and comfort of that dog, not only out at the park where
loneliness and isolation except for her were almost complete, but
here too, with not only Verne gone but Wayne also. Within a few
months at North Wycoff, Valla fell down a drainage culvert, and
was injured so badly that she had to be put to sleep.

Valla, tail no longer curled up on her back due to
age, in the snow on North Wycoff Avenue.

Uncle Wayne's visits had tapered off in his last months.
When he did make it to Bremerton, he'd stay a few nights downstairs in the area Mom was fixing up to be a rental unit. I imagine
these visits were among the happiest moments of his life. He'd
have been there when she got home from the Naval Hospital,
sitting at the kitchen table fulminating on his latest paranormal
theories while she fixed their meal. As they ate her simple tasty
suppers, he'd have been gratified to now be her sole companion

and object of her complete attention, having outlasted Verne and her previous husbands. She'd have been grateful for his company, as he listened to her insights on human nature, illustrated by happenings on her ward. It was almost as if they were an old married couple. Perhaps better. They were far removed from the berry farm, where his loyalty to my father's family had not yet been proven.

As Wayne's health worsened, he withdrew to his Spartan rental unit in Marysville. His landlord noticed that he had not left it for days, and looked in. Finding him desperately ill, he drove Wayne immediately to Everett General Hospital—where the examining doctor said he probably had cancer of the liver and should notify his next of kin. Mom sent me a postcard from the Kingston ferry on her return from Lake Stevens, where she'd joined Flavia for the drive to see Wayne in Everett. They were shocked at his appearance. Flavia could not stay long, so Mom stayed and listened to all his concerns. Besides his fear of dying, Uncle Wayne confessed he had no will. With no one else's name on his checking account, he was worried that no one could pay his bills, *"if I'm at the end of my string,"* as the poor darling put it. She offered to act for him and call for a lawyer to *tell what he wanted done and have everything legally taken care of.* He was grateful and identified an attorney in Marysville.

On Mom and Flavia's next visit he told them he was afraid and had lost hope. Mom reported that he seemed relieved to talk about it, and the three were able to speak freely and even laugh a few times. Before she left, Mom realized that her old friend, though in terrible pain, was refusing to take his pain medication for fear of dying in his sleep. Wayne had dismissed the idea of God and doubted there was an afterlife, though the possibility that he was destined for oblivion terrified him. Meridian etheric polarity action and his hodgepodge of arcane ideas had failed to instill the courage to release himself into the unknown.

Mom wrote that as she sat by his bedside in the hospital wondering how she could help him, a simple—and ancient—analogy occurred to her. Holding his hand, she reminded him that she'd taken the ferry from Bremerton to Seattle to be with him, and though she didn't know how ferries work, she'd driven her car onto it, trusting it would take her to Seattle as it had always done. She suggested that he think of leaving his present life as boarding a ferry that will carry him to his next form of existence. He could trust that whoever was operating that ferry was very experienced and knew how to get him there safely.

Wayne gave her a trusting look, she recalled, and accepted her offer to give him his pain medication. She left when he became drowsy. Minutes after she'd driven home from the Bremerton ferry terminal, the hospital called to notify her that Mr. Trubshaw had died in his sleep.

When Flavia referred to her as my angel mother, occasions like this came to mind.

CHAPTER TWENTY-THREE

Disease or Cure

Mom was so pleased that Columbia had given me a master's degree "with high honors" that she called Mr. Berry at East High. He phoned while I was still awaiting news of my only chance to continue at Columbia. In a voice more grandfatherly than I recalled, he gave almost the same advice as he'd offered for Scripps: "Consider yourself successful just to survive in such a place." Although I'd survived for one year, Mr. Berry was too tactful to mention that I would need more than survival skills to complete my Ph.D. at Columbia.

I thanked him for connecting me with Scripps, whose strong humanities program had opened the door for me at Columbia. But would it stay open? I tried to sound optimistic, but anxiety whispered that the deck was probably stacked. Even a master's with high honors would not put me in the running for a college teaching career unless I was on solid footing to finish the doctorate.

In 1970 federal support for the liberal arts had been sidelined by the war in Vietnam, and Columbia offered no fellowships in my field. How I wished they had someone like Mr. Berry, who could find a private source willing to help me! Fellowships were still available to minority students, but being poor and female didn't count. Columbia's financial aid office gave no guidance, just a bulletin board, where I saw posted a fellowship sponsored by the Leopold Schepp Foundation. It did not seem limited to minorities, so I applied.

Mom wrote that she hoped I'd get a favorable decision, *But I won't pray for anything but what will fill your greatest needs.* The Schepp Foundation, whose founder was Jewish, awarded their fellowship to a young Jewish man whose qualifications appeared no better than mine. Another stacked deck.

By then I'd already moved with my Columbia roommate to an apartment in Inwood, across from Fort Tryon Park on the northwestern tip of Manhattan. There, seated at a cheap card table we'd installed in the kitchen, I read the first letter Mom sent to my new address. Despite a cheery tone, her words seemed reminiscent of past lectures that began with questions like *Would you rather be part of the disease or part of the cure?*

April 18, 1970

Dearest Becky,

My friend the pheasant is back. So are the astronauts [from the near-disastrous Apollo 13 moon mission]. *I use the same words to make both statements. No wonder we are many times frustrated with their inadequacy. However I did not mean to digress when I made my opening remark. I was just making a simple statement of pleasure at hearing him honking under the cherry tree. When all's said and done life is made up of a succession of small things, for the most part, some pleasant and some otherwise.*

You said something in one of your letters about taking something in your stride, and you'll be able to do so, honey, if you have to, and things don't work out with the Schepp Foundation. Money alone doesn't add to a person's feelings of worth, and I'd like to feel that you were situated somewhere in a job in which you would be working with people who would be part of the cure instead of part of the disease, as it were.

I noted glumly that she assumed my next step would be a job, not doctoral studies. As I read it cynically, there was little chance of working with people who were part of a "cure," because my "disease" was lacking the connections to succeed in academe.

Then came her point about the inadequacy of words:

There is something about broadcasting into empty (?) space which is, to say the least, uninspiring. I am reminded of the nightmare monologues [my emphasis] *of the past in which either "Rachel"* [coming from Verne or Wayne] *or "Mother"* [presumably coming from me] *was talking on and on by the hour just because "Let's face it, she likes to talk." And nobody would comment either in disagreement or agreement, let alone think out alternatives to the policies and principles she was so painfully advocating, in situations where obviously something intelligent needed to be done!*

Of course the total picture now is vastly different, and I don't mean to convey the impression that I want you to be devoting yourself to longwinded written exchanges of abstract ideas with me…(not that it wouldn't be fun if there were more time).

Mother
XOXO

The first thing that struck me was her mistaken recollection that I'd ever called her "Mother," as I disliked the formality of that term and addressed her only as Mom, Mummy, or—when calling to her in great distress—Mama. Was she confusing me with how she used to address her own mother, with whom she reportedly did not always get along? I had never accused her of going on and on because she "liked to talk," as Uncle Wayne had opined in his letters to me. There was a difference, I felt, between liking to talk and being driven to speak obsessively until one's voice gives out.

The next stunner was my mother's apparent loss of memory that I had indeed commented—both to agree and disagree with her statements—and tried to respond as if in a normal conversation. I had begged for something actionable to emerge from her "policies and principles," and had in fact offered an "alternative view"—suggesting that I'd have a sunnier disposition if she did not spend hours berating me for lacking one. At least where I was concerned, she had hardly been a moral astronaut broadcasting into "empty space." Had she not realized that perhaps a billion people around the world had listened anxiously to every word coming from those astronauts on Apollo 13? Had she not noticed that I retreated into silence only after it became clear that taking issue with her did nothing but prolong the trauma of her rants?

I was awestruck, however, by her masterful turn of phrase. *Nightmare monologues* was infinitely more apt than my insipid schoolgirl term, *lectures*. Unfortunately, her choice of words managed to be both shockingly true and evasively unclear. Had she meant that the monologues were nightmarish only to her, who delivered them, or to me, their recipient, or to both of us? She now described our situation as "vastly different." But was she willing to acknowledge her will and agency in making those monologues nightmarish? I could not be sure that the force behind them—which I sensed was hostile rather than nurturing—would not find some other avenue of attack, such as accusing me of not loving her.

Thrice armed is he who hath his quarrel just. Of all my mother's Shakespearean armory, this verse clung to my heart. If, as her letter suggested, we'd had time to exchange abstract ideas, my older self would have asked what she thought of persons whose "quarrels" were constrained by unworkable options. Reasonable responses and queries from me had done nothing to stem the tide of her relentless, softspoken tirades, so I'd retreated into silence. Would she be willing to clarify why she had prolonged those verbal ordeals when they left us both depleted and miserable? The times I'd dared to defend myself, her rebuttal was an adage the Bard might have rejected as imprecise: *The road to hell is paved with good intentions.*

Only in the last days of her life was I inspired to refute this adage.

CHAPTER TWENTY-FOUR

"Same Old Becky"

My brother graduated from the Coast Guard Academy two years before I finished at Scripps, but by then he'd found himself in a long-term dilemma. Having impregnated one of the young women he'd been dating, he would have been dishonorably expelled from the Academy and made to repay the government what it had invested in his education, had he not married this girl immediately after graduation. In fact, to quell any misgivings on the part of her parents, she and my brother were secretly married a few months before he graduated. I'd lost contact with Johnny in college, and got only occasional updates about him from Mom. She mentioned that his sudden bride had not been his actual favorite, if circumstances had not made their marriage inevitable. Even so, Johnny had been so moved by the fact that he was going to be a father that he stopped competing on the Academy's diving team. He knew that his skull could be broken and he could be killed if his head hit the board on the way down.

Johnny was well into this marriage, possibly seeking a challenge and to defy fate, when he applied for flight training as a rescue pilot. He told Mom he needed to find something that demanded his complete attention. Learning to fly a helicopter, he wrote Mom, was literally a matter of life or death. "Missing

153

one detail of training could kill you." Soon his letters, some of which Mom shared with me, were filled with wry accounts of people clinging to life rafts or the hulls of capsized boats, kicking at sharks that would have devoured them, had he not coptered down to pluck them out. No one in our family used such terms, but Johnny was proving to be a hero, his career a success story, while I seemed headed in a less noteworthy direction.

I'd hoped to complete my doctorate with a career-launching dissertation like Northrup Frye's legendary doctoral thesis on William Blake, *Fearful Symmetry*. A published dissertation would have given me a chance at a tenure-track teaching position at a liberal arts college hopefully similar to Scripps. From there I hoped to become a "public intellectual," writing about literature and ideas for thinking people. Once I'd become established in a college community, I dreamed of playing chamber music as a serious amateur pianist. Those plans were derailed by economic constraints. Not only had the Vietnam War cut federal support for the liberal arts, but growing numbers of liberal arts Ph.D.s were seeking a shrinking number of tenure track positions. Colleges and universities were hiring ever greater numbers of part-time faculty at much lower pay, with no job security.

My roommate, whose family could afford to keep her at Columbia, drew my attention to an ad in the *Times* for a secretarial job at Angel Records, a respected classical music label. She said it would at least put me near the music I loved. Though I had no desire for a career in the recording business, I was excited to be working for Angel's Director of Artist Relations, the elegant, silver-haired John Coveney. The office I shared with Mr. Coveney's assistant was lined with promotional samples of high quality classical albums, and I was allowed to keep any duplicates. The records I took home became my sole consolation for the tedium of typing letters and fielding phone calls for a volatile, imperious boss.

In a rare phone conversation with Johnny, I tried to put a positive spin on my job, offering to send him any albums he fancied from my bounty of classical freebies.

"Okay, thanks, but where do you go from there?"

It was the only time he'd asked about my plans for the future. I was tongue-tied, embarrassed to discover that he expected more of me than a secretarial job, after I'd poured everything I had into academe. I was at such a loss for words that I failed to tell Johnny about the one interaction at Angel Records that made my brief employment there worthwhile.

Mr. Coveney could morph instantly from the role of kindly confidant of Angel's roster of gifted artists, to a vicious critic behind their backs. He had me sit in front of his desk to place calls for him, so I could not help but observe the drastic contrast between his fine words and the expressions on his face. With an exasperated grimace he cajoled the aging opera star Victoria de los Angeles to record an album of less demanding Spanish folk songs rather than her favorite arias. When she reluctantly agreed, he dropped the receiver as if it were a moldy banana, and yelled to his assistant that de los Angeles was a has-been who should thank him for trying to salvage the remnants of her talent. In his next call, I listened as he pandered shamelessly to a young piano virtuoso.

The most heartrending call came from Maria Callas, one of opera's legendary divas. It bonded me to the great soprano for the rest of her too-short life.

Mr. Coveney's assistant had informed me that our boss was a longstanding confidant of Madame Callas, perhaps the only person she could still ask about her lost love, the Greek shipping tycoon Aristotle Onassis, who had discarded her to marry Jacqueline Kennedy. Mr. Coveney found it inexplicable that Callas could not get over this toad of a man. Onassis, he sniffed, had the gall to fall asleep and snore—"in his box seat, mind you, visible and audible to all"—during Callas's finest moments at La Scala. "Then," my boss fumed, "he had the nerve to marry Jackie Kennedy, who only wanted his money!" After that, Mr. Coveney opined, Callas demeaned herself by calling to ask if he knew where Onassis was and what he was doing.

By then I'd had a shorter but genuine taste of unrequited love for the charming, chronically depressed Steve Devere. Whether or not Callas had fallen for a toad, my heart went out to her. The day came when I answered line 1 and heard the great artist ask politely if she might speak with Mr. Coveney. She gave her name with no trace of self-importance. In her simple request was a world of pain borne with quiet dignity.

"Yes, of course," I replied, awestruck. "Please hold while I see if he's free." I hastily buzzed my boss on the intercom.

"Let her wait!" he barked. "I have better things to do with my time!" In fact he had no other calls or appointments. I couldn't bear for him to snub her. How to spare her the insult of being made to wait? Inspiration struck. I punched the button to line 1.

"You must excuse Mr. Coveney for a moment," I lied, *sotto voce*. "He's arguing with the phone company."

"Ohh, I *see*." The urgency in her voice melted into velvety tones of indulgence. I'd guessed correctly that Callas, who came from humble stock, would fully endorse his battle over a phone bill. In those days the Bell Telephone monopoly charged shockingly high rates and would occasionally bill customers for long distance calls they had not made. I trusted that the great diva would be too discreet to reveal her knowledge of Mr. Coveney's negotiations, and my falsehood would be safe.

After he'd spoken with her, my boss loomed in the doorway of the office I shared with his assistant, and crowed, "Onassis! It's always Onassis! How should I know where he is? Why should I care? Why should she? As I've reminded her more than once, it was *his choice* to marry Jackie Kennedy, for God's sake! Why can't she focus on singing and forget about that Greek ogre? *So undignified*."

Callas, I imagined, had no one else to turn to, and was too proud or ashamed to ask her friends for updates on Onassis. In the years to come I followed news of her sad decline, hoping she would find a more compassionate ally than Mr. Coveney.

Mr. Coveney and his assistant in his office at Angel Records,
December 1970. A Polaroid retrieved by me from the
company's Christmas tree, discarded after the holidays.

I left Angel Records for a slightly better paying job at a firm
that sold high purity chemicals, but was fired a few months later
for saying "yeah" rather than yes on the phone. I'd been closing
a sale to a jovial, casual-talking customer when the company's
owner—an elderly immigrant who considered "yeah" unacceptable for use by his employees, especially someone with a master's
degree—happened to pass by my desk. Feeling like I'd arrived in
a story by Franz Kafka, I threw the few personal items from my
desk into a paper bag and left the building. It was about three in
the afternoon. The lunch hour crowds were gone and the streets
seemed strangely empty, until I realized that the people who
hadn't just been fired were still at work.

The next day I was combing the *New York Times* classified
ads, and making the rounds of employment agencies that were, as
ever in those days, interested solely in how fast one could type and
take shorthand. Mercifully, one agent dispensed with the usual
grilling whether I sincerely wanted a secretarial career—a routine
charade for liberal arts grads whose prospective employers feared
they'd soon leave for a teaching or otherwise more interesting job.
"Here's a live one," she said. "It's an elite nonprofit, where some-

one with your education might not die of boredom. They won't accept anyone without a bachelor's degree."

The opening was in the Agricultural Sciences Division of The Rockefeller Foundation. Once hired, I could transfer, if there was an opening, into its Humanities program, where my background could be put to real use. I became a "Program Secretary" at the RF in September 1972.

That summer, before I started work at the Foundation, my mother invited me to join her for some sightseeing in Canada. The trip promised to assuage some of her loneliness as a recent widow, and perhaps to show me there was more to life than an elusive academic career. I took a train to Montreal, where Mom met me at the station and had me hail a cab to take us where she'd booked us in a cozy bed and breakfast. Montreal cabbies provided my first experience of the Francophone resentment of Canada's English-speaking majority. When Mom gave them the address of our B&B in her posh British accent, they pretended not to understand. But if I used my schoolgirl French they would nod indulgently, correct my pronunciation, and take us there.

The trip would also expose a more personal vein of negativity, in one terse phrase. I had no idea of its context, but the words communicated something longstanding, mutually understood, and disapproving. After we got settled at the B&B, we set forth to the city center on a cloudless day.

The cartilage in my mother's hips had worn down over the years. By mid afternoon she was in grinding pain. I found her a bench with back support in a picturesque public square. The weather was sunny and mild, and from there she could survey an array of artists and crafts people displaying their work amidst throngs of tourists. While she rested, I browsed around for about half an hour and returned with an inexpensive print. My mother examined it with a frown but no comment. All she could express was that she was ready to have an early dinner but wouldn't be able to walk far. I spotted an Old World French restaurant nearby.

The food was excellent, but by then she seemed displeased with my company.

In the B&B, as Mom's bedtime approached, I headed for the stairway down to the guests' lounge, where I hoped my bookish French would see me through a Paris *Vogue* I'd noticed on the coffee table. In the corridor I passed an alcove with a pay phone, and heard my mother's voice.

She did not see me until she'd summed up her side of the conversation with three sullen words: *Same old Becky.* Until that moment I had not heard this particular phrase, which my mother had uttered in a jaded tone that bespoke years of repetition, and a dark significance shared implicitly with her interlocutor. She looked up furtively, as if I'd caught her shoplifting, muttered something into the receiver, and hung up.

"Mom, what did you mean, *same old Becky?*" She stared back, expressionless. "What is *same old* about me? ...Were you talking to Johnny?" I waited for an answer. Her lips tightened. For one who had readily lectured me at exhaustive length, she did not care to explain herself.

Never mind. I'm exhausted. My hips ache and I'm going to soak in a hot bath.

In one dismissive command, my mother successfully stymied my pursuit of something she would never acknowledge, at least to me. That night I retraced everything we'd done on the trip, grasping for the root of this damning statement. Did she resent my mobility? Had she considered me selfish to indulge my love of art and explore what was on display in a town square for about half an hour while she rested on a well-positioned bench? All I knew was, by overhearing this snippet of conversation, I'd stumbled upon a nest of artillery where my brother and mother had evidently been taking shots at me for years.

Mom did not repeat *same old Becky* in my presence, but I was haunted by its tone and significance. What choice did I have, except to go on being the person with that nickname? I would not always be the same, nor old, but mostly clueless until after her death.

CHAPTER TWENTY-FIVE

It's Not What Happens to You...

My mother was lonely after we lost Uncle Wayne. I was bereaved in a less certain way. Steve Devere, my sometime boyfriend at Columbia, had followed his mentor to the newly formed philosophy department at the State University of New York at Stony Brook, where he'd been given a generous fellowship to complete his doctorate. Steve was the man I most wanted to care for me. No one made me laugh so hard or feel so alive. There was a strong attraction between us, but if I called during one of his dark spells he'd mutter, "Don't waste your time, Beck. I'm falling apart at the seams."

Steve's parents had been sent to a Nazi labor camp during World War II, entrusting their toddler son to a gentile family who took care of him until after the war. Eventually Steve's family settled in New Jersey, where his father made a living as a tailor. I was at Steve's apartment near Columbia when he received a package from his father—three beautifully made sports jackets, in tasteful colors and fabrics. Each one fitted him perfectly. When I admired how he looked in them, he snapped, "They're not my type. I'll never wear them." He never explained why he bore his father such ill will, though he told me that, speaking Yiddish, his dad was the funniest person he'd ever known.

Alas, this man I could not help loving was haunted by his parents' unspoken trauma. Were it not for his depressions we might have married, except that even in good times he tended to patronize me as a Pollyanna. When I mentioned this to my mother, she wrote,

> *So far as Steve is concerned I can imagine only too easily how being called a Shirley Temple/ Doris Day personality...must have hurt. But honey if you like to develop...the case for those who are trying to help themselves, as against those who are satisfied to sit back and feel bad, and ridicule the efforts of others who are "looking on the bright side"...well, all the sound arguments are on your side.*

Mom had met Steve at Columbia during a visit to Columbia, and without saying why, had not been favorably impressed. Until this letter I had not known that despite Uncle Wayne's devotion to her, he had also been disparaging.

> *Wayne when he was in the mood to belittle me used to be very nasty about "do-gooders". But I noticed that when he read* The Games People Play *he didn't comment on the chapter where this was listed as one of the few possibly beneficial "games"! — and stated that people who played it were much better off than the "do-badders"!*

I remembered Uncle Wayne's bitter account of how his father had promised to pay his way through college if he spent all his after-school hours working in his dad's print shop. It meant giving up his chance to play sports, spend time with friends, meet girls, and enjoy what was left of his childhood. But work there he did, trusting that his father would fulfill his end of the bargain. There was no describing the tone of humiliation in Uncle Wayne's voice—indeed, in his very sense of himself—that he'd been cheated out of his chance at a "pig skin" (old term for a college diploma), played for a fool by his own father. After such a betrayal, I thought, Uncle Wayne might have become a depressive type himself. That he lacked Steve's brilliance, charm and wit was perhaps why my mother chose not to marry him.

For years I compared all the men I dated to Steve, and found them lacking. It felt as though an invisible cord tied my mother's loss of Douglas to the impossibility of my partnership with Steve. Just as the Second World War had separated her from Douglas, the war's effects on Steve's parents had scarred him so that he could not fully love me.

A few months after Uncle Wayne's death, a colleague at the Welfare Department, where my mother was volunteering, recommended James Michener's novel, *Return to Paradise*, because the author described the war's effects on New Zealand. Mom wrote:

> *I had forgotten much of the almost pitiful lacks and deprivations which one grew to almost take for granted. So many women had to take any kind of man they could get, or else face a life of ignorance of what marriage was all about. The plain, the shy, those who lived in areas where there was hardly any male population—my heart aches for them. Your Aunt Gwenda and I were fortunate enough to have been of marriageable age between two World Wars, so we were luckier than most.*

In the same letter my mother confided that her marriage to my father was *the result of what one might describe as spiritual poverty and religious misconcept.* Marrying him, she said, had deprived her of *any further powers of selection.* I noted how carefully she chose her terms, writing about *the peculiar circumstances of life on the berry farm,* its financial problems having been *only a small part.* She mentioned having made desperate efforts to provide *some kind of normalcy for two small kids who had no one else to care for them.* These circumstances, she wrote, *made all of*

my bootstraps (including Ray, then Verne and my L.P.N. training)
part of the same picture. Yikes!

I'd grown up believing her story of the botched wartime cable
sent to Douglas, after which she'd never heard from him again.
What was all this about "spiritual poverty and religious misconcept"? Mom continued:

> *Douglas Elliott was the love of my life. And I*
> *belonged to a day in which the one man meant*
> *for one woman idea was the accepted thing.*
> *The agonizing I did when I lost him to a combi-*
> *nation of Christian Science and his mother not*
> *only shook my own confidence in my capacity*
> *to inspire love in others but drove me out of*
> *ignorance to a sort of "dedication." — "Giving*
> *my life to God" sounds too corny now for words.*
> *But I had been strongly motivated towards the*
> *idealistic since a child—still am for that mat-*
> *ter—and I honestly thought that was what I*
> *was doing.*

I tried to read between the lines. Had Papa sold her a
Theosophical bill of goods? She avoided illustrative details.

> *The idea of offering my services wherever they*
> *were needed most to my…approximation of*
> *"God" in return for some kind of real religious*
> *knowledge seemed…to make some kind of*
> *sense… (Roger talked of idealism in the religious*
> *field that I with my NZ background had had no*
> *access to. He claimed to have positive knowledge*
> *in many areas—including sex—that I lacked.*
> *And certainly in that terrible dust bowl of a berry*
> *farm—no blacktop on the road at that time—*
> *whatever capabilities I had were badly needed!)*

What kind of services had my father expected of her?

> *Everything else hinged on it.* [On what? Seeking religious knowledge? Being badly needed?] *"Do anything, go anywhere, stop at nothing and never complain," or words to that effect, was the motto I read somewhere of the British WAACS in World War I, so I adopted it for myself. Lord, Lord, how incredibly stupid. By the time Douglas and I were together again on paper at least, everything I did was with the reservation that "God" would show me what he wanted me to do.*

Not having direct verbal communication with God, she implied, led her to rely on *a number of yardsticks which were pretty devastating*, especially the one requiring her to *put every thought of self-interest out of the picture.* She summed it up in one disillusioned word: *Wow!*

I didn't think to ask why she hadn't written to Douglas when he failed to respond to her cable. Why put herself at the mercy of Western Union when the U.S. Postal Service might have proven more reliable? Why rush into marriage with my father when she could have waited a tad longer for the overseas mail?

Her letter was so freighted with marital mysteries that I hardly registered the substantive insights she offered regarding my brother's childhood:

> *Johnny had no bed of roses, growing up... If Annie Barley was a stinker to you, Ray Draine really was hateful to him. And the move to Camano Island from Getchell* [the elementary school closest to the berry farm] *nearly broke his heart. His love for Melody Kellogg was as real as any adult's.* [His letters to her] *were incredibly, touchingly beautiful. He'd write to ease the pain*

of missing her, and because I wanted to under-
stand him and help if I could, I'd read whatever
I saw. He used to keep Melody's letters in one
of those canvas bags banks used for carrying
change, and sleep with them under his pillow.

Mom wondered if Johnny had chosen me as the target for
the bad feelings he must have had, while showing more *helpful*
types of expression—humor, tact, sports and music—to others. She
mused whether the transference of negative feelings was probably not one's real enemy, as it may be an instinctive device inherited from more primitive times. The real enemy, she wrote, was
unconsciousness of what we're doing or why we're doing it. Looking
back on the extraordinary insight my mother expressed in this
passage, I had to wonder why she'd been unable to apply it to her
relationship with me.

Instead, she cited the psychologist Rollo May's observation that the experience of relating well to a sibling was valuable
preparation for a healthy marriage, and included—apparently for
my benefit—having a satisfactory relationship with any other person, even an animal for whom one feels responsibility and concern. This seemed to set things up for a verdict as devastating as
it was untrue:

You never formed the habit of consistently
expressing the pleasant side of your nature in
thoughtfulness and affection, which was a great
deprivation, in your own home. So it's no won-
der that lacking the chosen outlet for affection—
Johnny—and rejecting the alternatives of me or
Valla, you may give an impression of coldness
or indifference to others. Better times coming
though, if we make them.

In one fell swoop, her preceding insights about my brother,
even her seeming wisdom regarding negative transference of feel-

ings, vanished from my mind. The accusation that I hadn't been "consistently" pleasant, thoughtful and affectionate had to refer to the times I turned inward to recover from the trauma of her endless, singsong harangues. That she'd expected me to be *consistently* cheerful and affectionate, despite my need to recover from the stress of her monologues, seemed to reveal her own state of unconsciousness about the obsessive nature of and motivation behind the way she'd lectured me. Had she ever considered that continuing to accuse me of not loving her would amount to a great deprivation in my life?

It was stunning to hear that I'd "rejected" our beloved dog Valla, when I'd experienced nothing but trust, acceptance, and affection with that soulful animal. There were a few occasions when I needed to recover from Mom's lectures and did not feel able to play outdoors with Valla. The dog always seemed to understand and stayed nearby to comfort me. The compassion I felt from that gentle creature helped me survive emotional assaults that might have devastated a child without such an ally.

As a girl whose family had to relocate every couple of years, I was always the new kid, partially accepted in time, with the reservation routinely attached to those who hadn't grown up in that community. Kids had mocked me for being overweight, but no one had implied that my cautious reserve arose from coldness or indifference, except my mother. Many New Yorkers, I noticed, employed it as a survival tool.

In the early seventies it was virtually impossible to find a teaching job in a high school or community college in the New York area—unless you were a man avoiding the Vietnam draft. I'd taken a secretarial job at the Rockefeller Foundation for two reasons. It had a Humanities Division, to which I hoped to transfer; and its tuition reimbursement benefit—for courses taken toward an advanced degree, if passed with a C or above—was a viable alternative, albeit piecemeal and long-term, to having a fellowship to complete my doctorate.

My first two years as a program secretary at Rockefeller were spent in the Agricultural Sciences division, where I learned about its international efforts in crop development—the so-called Green Revolution—which won its director a Nobel Peace Prize. Then I transferred into the newly created Conflict Resolution Program, as program secretary to Elmore Jackson, a kind and gracious diplomat and former Assistant Secretary of State under Cyrus Vance. Elmore's knowledge of world affairs and low-key diplomatic manner were admirable, but there was little I could offer other than help polishing his letters to former and current State Department officials, foreign diplomats, and others involved with international peacemaking.

In my third year, the position of Administrative Assistant became vacant in the Humanities program. Though it was not considered a professional position I was glad for the promotion from program secretary. Unlike the administrative assistants in the other programs, I had a master's degree in the field, and had graduated from a top college with a humanities core curriculum. Thus I was given work normally done by professional staffers—screening and flagging promising grant proposals, advising inexperienced grant applicants how to construct effective proposals, and drafting the major grant descriptions—called docket items—for approval by the board of trustees.

It seemed ironic to be entrusted with the work of program officers scarcely older than me, who'd had the good fortune to complete their doctorates with fellowships that had been readily available before the Nixon administration's cutbacks. However, every division had one professional staff position that did not require a doctorate: that of Program Associate, whose duties were almost identical to what I'd already done as an administrative assistant. Earlier, I'd applied for that position in the Humanities Division, but it went to a woman who'd been hired a few weeks before me. Her master's degree, however, was not in the humanities, but I was told that her small advantage in seniority had won her the promotion.

I respected the foundation's regard for seniority, and focused on doing my best at the opportunities available to me. I kept alive the thrill I'd felt to take part in Scripps's three-year double course in the humanities—where professors of history, philosophy, literature, art and music would lecture in rotation, while their colleagues sat in the back row, lobbing serious questions along with the students. It was love of learning and the collegial spirit at its best. I was fortunate to have studied comparative literature under the eminent philosopher and polymath Philip Merlan, and dreamed of eventually contributing to that field. In my innocent idealism, a prestigious charitable institution like the RF would be a meritocracy, where someone starting on the support staff with a master's degree in the humanities could prove herself and rise up to become a program officer if she earned a doctorate.

Mom's early advice to Gwenda came to mind: *It's not what happens to you that matters, it's what you make of it.* It was difficult to imagine a future outside my ideal of being a scholar and educator, but I had to make the most out of a stalled career.

Mom with Gwenda, left, on her first trip back to New Zealand, each having done remarkably well with their lives.

CHAPTER TWENTY-SIX

A Gentleman Caller

When my mother began to work at the Bremerton Naval Hospital, she was assigned—destined?—to work on Ward M, tending the wives of Naval officers. She'd been on the job about a year when she wrote me that one of her patients, who'd recently died of cancer, had evidently expressed great appreciation for her care. Strangely, my mother had no memory of her, yet she'd received an ornate thank-you card from the patient's widowed husband, Captain E.J. Madden. A few days later a beribboned box appeared on her doorstep, with a freshly baked cake inside. Tucked under the ribbon was an embossed envelope with an invitation from Capt. Madden to accompany him as he drove his daughter Patricia back to college in Oregon. The forwardness of this invitation was disconcerting, since Mom recalled neither Mrs. Madden nor her family when they'd visited Ward M.

Curiosity made me ignore the price of weekday long-distance calls. I got straight to the point. "Well, Mummy, are you going to politely decline this invitation?"

Actually, Beck, I've already had dinner with Captain Madden. That was fast, I did not say. His manners were impeccable, she reported. He was a staunch Irish Catholic of comfortable means and, from all appearances, upstanding character. *He seems very*

169

nice. During dinner she'd agreed to accompany him the next weekend to his daughter's college near Portland.

Her next letter described their three-way conversation en route to Oregon as *innocuous chitchat*. She thought her presence might have spared the bereaved father and daughter the awkwardness of taking the trip by themselves. She was given her own room in a quality motel near the college, and taken to dinner at an upscale restaurant. She found it odd, though, when Patricia Madden introduced her to her dorm mates as "an old family friend," making no mention of her mother's death. The following day, Sunday, they attended Catholic Mass together, followed by an expensive lunch. Then the Captain bid his daughter good-bye and drove back to Bremerton with my mother, stopping in Tacoma for another pricey meal. Mom summed up the return trip as pleasant: *Reminiscences and so on, nothing too personal.*

What bothered me, and struck my mother as odd, was the strangely formal phone call she got the next day—"This is Captain Madden"— inquiring how she was feeling after the journey. Though touched by his courtesy, she wondered why he hadn't identified himself simply as Edwin Madden, since by then they were on cordial terms.

I was glad my twice widowed, once divorced mother in her early sixties had a respectable gentleman caller, but was his superior manner a bad omen?

Mom's letters thinned out in the following months. I found myself reading distressing lines about *living the old nightmare*. It didn't sound like the kind of nightmare she'd had in our family. *Will he call me? Will the doorbell ring and he be there? And if he doesn't call or come, how can I keep from wanting to know he is alright—and seal up the well of loneliness once again?* They'd been almost inseparable, she wrote, living a romance filled with tenderness and courtesy, *like something out of a fiction world.*

The reference to fiction was painfully apt. My mother's romantic idyll had morphed into a misery-making reality, with a well-mannered paramour whose alternate persona included being a heavy drinker with a nasty temper, and mistaken about Catholic doctrine. In Mom's quaint terms, Edwin had wooed her *ardently,* only to announce that *he could not consummate the marriage act physically.* His excuse was her divorce from Ray Draine, which he'd known about since the beginning of their relationship.

No point my asking whether the captain's self-restraint resembled impotence from overconsumption of booze rather than avoidance of sin with a divorced woman. Nor did I inquire how—before the era of computer searches—he'd ascertained that Ray was among the living, given the odds that he'd drunk himself to death. In Edwin's mishmash of Catholic canons, he'd convinced himself that the Church would consider my mother still married to Ray, overlooking the facts that she wasn't Catholic and hadn't married Ray in the Church.

A chill of foreboding moved through me as I read my mother's lament, the gist being that people had told her for many years that they loved her, while *doing nothing whatsoever* to ensure her happiness. My terror of her lectures had not faded. There still were times when she insisted that I did not love her, that any act of thoughtfulness on my part was a mere *gesture of duty.*

My eyes widened as I read that her *old paralysis* had come back, *the effort to not cry, to somehow face going to work...when one's throat is tight and one's solar plexus aches.* I was fairly sure she was describing the agony of romantic disappointments—beginning with Douglas Elliott, then Geoff Whisker, and perhaps more than one of three consecutive husbands. My heart was sad for her. At least when Steve Devere neglected to call me, he'd warned about his spells of depression. Far worse to be a widow facing yet another juggernaut of heartache. Edwin, in her view, was a man with serious cardiac problems who shouldn't be living alone. She finally called him out of *concern for his health.*

Eventually Capt. Madden confessed that he'd been overcome with shame to have stood at his dying wife's bedside, acting the role of a stricken husband while strongly attracted to her favorite nurse. He'd been unable to let a decent period of mourning pass before using his daughter's return to college as an excuse to see my mother again. Aha! I thought. He'd pressured his girl to bake that carrot cake!

When our birthdays arrived that December, my mother's card enclosed a check and an apology for not having had time to shop for a gift. Her liaison with the captain was troubled but serious; whereas, I had no social life to speak of, having lost touch with the friends I'd met at Columbia.

Mom's birthday message ended:

> *Becky honey, who <u>are</u> the successful people? Not necessarily those who win "fame and fortune." Many of them are personally a complete mess. The ones who can adjust to the ups and downs of ordinary living and still have something to offer others in need of comfort and encouragement get my vote. May be sour grapes. I think not.*

Funny, I didn't consider my mother capable of sour grapes. But why would she not be stung, when looked down upon by women with no need to work, like the officers' wives on Ward M?

When sober, Capt. Madden had squired her to dinner dances at the Bremerton Naval Officers' Club, with its stately white columns in Southern plantation style. One night she called to report an encounter she'd had in the club's marble-lined ladies room. She was freshening up at the mirror when a former patient, wife of an admiral, entered.

"Why, Mrs. McCormick," the woman asked, "what are *you* doing here?" in a tone implying readiness to alert the guards of an intruder.

Mom took a moment to compose herself, then replied: *Since you ask, I am the guest of Captain Edwin Madden, and I have as much right to be here as you do.* To punctuate the last words she snapped her purse shut, and returned to her table. *If you'd only seen how snooty she'd been to everyone but the doctors on Ward M—a woman with obviously little education!*

Edwin, Mom reflected, had probably not been such a heavy drinker when he was a step away from being promoted to admiral, the longed-for capstone to his career. There'd been another contender for the promotion, she'd learned, a man who'd obtained illicit access to Edwin's medical records. This unscrupulous rival had unearthed a minor cardiac event many years in Edwin's past, and spread rumors that Capt. Madden's health was shaky and an admiral's responsibilities might be too taxing for him. Ergo the slimebag was made admiral and Edwin was edged into retirement. By the time he met my mother, his resentment of this injustice had done actual damage to his heart, and self-medicating with alcohol had rendered him diabetic.

I was certain Edwin concealed his dark side from my mother until he knew she would never leave him. Swank evenings at the Naval Officers' Club hardly compensated her for what lay ahead.

In her letters Mom confessed that she fought not to be jealous of Edwin's daughter Pat, who visited him on some weekends from college. During such times Mom was left alone without so much as a phone call, feeling her home was *one big ache of emptiness, loneliness, and chores I don't feel energetic enough to do.* Her hips were so sore that the hospital assigned her to a less strenuous position in the nursery. She began to feel that her job was based on their doing favors for her: *I don't feel important or needed anymore.*

Her transfer to nursery duty, I responded, had likely been done out of consideration for her rather than lack of respect or need for her skills. After all, she'd saved lives in that nursery— proof of her value as a nurse outside Ward M.

As fate or Providence would have it, during my mother's stint on the maternity ward she came across a short article that would influence the rest of my life as a teacher, thinker and writer. It concerned another hospital, whose staff had been perplexed by the death of healthy babies in its nursery. All their newborns were kept clean, warm and well nourished. None had birth defects or diseases. But the ones who died differed in one way. They were called "boarder babies" because they'd been left there by birth-mothers who'd been unwilling or unable to take care of them, thus they were "boarded" until they could be claimed by relatives or adopted. It took awhile before anyone identified what these healthy infants lacked, compared to babies whose mothers were present and whose families came and fussed over them. The staff was too busy to provide the boarder babies with more than nour-ishment, cleanliness and shelter.

By process of elimination it was determined that these new-borns were *dying from lack of attention*. Once the staff realized this, the hospital invited volunteers to come and hold the boarder babies and talk to them. From that point forward none of them died, and they were eventually placed with families who wanted them. For me it was a profound revelation. That babies could die for lack of attention demonstrated in the starkest terms that attention is necessary to sustain human life. It is perhaps, over the long term, more necessary to our survival than food and shel-ter. Why, I wondered, is *attention itself* not given more consider-ation as a vital factor in many aspects of life?

Thanks to my mother's sharing of this article, a fertile seed took root in my mind. I began to ponder the presence or absence of attention as essential to our experience of wellbeing or happi-ness, goodness or evil. What if a person made it through infancy with enough attention to stay alive, but did not receive enough attention to feel loved and to thrive? Don't our pets and children compete for our attention, showing anger and resentment—even lashing out or being self-destructive if they feel neglected? By extension, wouldn't this factor be essential to the so-called prob-lem of evil? Because of the torments I'd experienced with my mother, how did it figure in my life?

The role of attention, its quality, power, and influence, became an integral focus in my teaching and writing. It proved essential to my study of women's perceptions of evil in works of fiction and nonfiction, philosophy, psychology and other fields of human experience.

I have no doubt that the quality of my mother's attention prolonged the lives of countless patients, as well as Capt. Madden's. Her ability to listen compassionately brought about a near-miraculous reconciliation with Edwin's estranged son. Mom had been involved with the captain for some time, knowing only that besides his daughter Patricia, he had a son studying for the priesthood. However, she was alone for a few hours in Edwin's home one weekend when a young man—who'd probably noticed the Captain's car missing—came in through the back door. He had long red hair, a scruffy beard and scruffier clothes. She was stunned when he identified himself as Bob Madden, Edwin's younger son, whom the Captain had never mentioned.

Putting him at ease, Mom learned that he had run away from home a few years earlier, when he'd called the police to stop his father from beating his mother in a drunken rage. When the cops arrived, Bob said, his father managed to clear up his speech, informed them of his rank, and lied, saying it was his son Robert who'd been violent! Hearing this, Bob fled out the back door, escaping arrest by knowing where to hide in the vast golf course behind their home. For awhile he crashed at friends' places and took odd jobs to survive. By the time he'd surprised my mother, he was living as a hippie in Port Townsend, a town known for countercultural types. He'd missed the chance to see his mother before she died because no one in his family communicated with him. News of her death had reached him slowly, on the grapevine.

Among the cognoscenti, Port Townsend was also known for yacht building. Bob had taken some art courses in college, but did not graduate because his father disapproved of such study and cut off his tuition. Bob had bluffed his way into the yacht-building industry by claiming he could understand architects' blueprints. With an artist's talent he quickly mastered that skill, and specialized in designing the ships' elegant, luxurious interiors.

Mom liked Bob instantly and stayed in touch with him. His father had offered to help renovate her downstairs guest room so she could rent it for additional income. He enjoyed showing off his carpentry and plumbing skills, but complained of needing an extra pair of hands. Mom arranged for Bob to drop by on the day Edwin planned to repaint her downstairs bathroom and upgrade the fixtures. With typical charm and whimsy, she brought forth the outcast son by announcing to Edwin that she'd found him another pair of hands. Thus she orchestrated a rapprochement between the Captain and the son he'd betrayed and cast off—a true display of angelic powers.

Ignoring their noxious past, Edwin jokingly complained to Bob that Rachel was bossing him around. Bob was moved because it was something his longsuffering mother would not have dared. During this magical occasion, Mom wrote, father and son had been hard at work on the plumbing when Edwin took a break and came upstairs. Giving her a sweaty hug, he said he'd been "finding something out."

Oh, what would that be?

"Familiarity breeds content!" he said with a silly grin. Later in the day he told his son: "Rachel has already made up her mind to marry me." News to Mom, but she didn't miss a beat.

Why not, if it suits me? It's leap year, you know!

After that, she said, they entered a *taking-it-for-granted-there-will-be-a-marriage state*, with no formal proposal from him. In happier moments, he'd ask if she'd decided which of their homes she wanted to live in. Those occasions alternated with communication blackouts that pushed her to the edge of despair.

By the end of her second year with Edwin, Mom was of two minds whether I should join her for Christmas and New Year's. I wasn't *any less her only daughter*, she reasoned in a letter. We'd become closer, in her view, than when we lived under the same roof. I was glad to hear this—until I realized she was suggesting that I not make the trip to see her. Someone once wrote that truth bites quick, but the pain of it lingers. As I spent the holidays alone, I wondered what kind of situation—or whose attention—she did not wish to share with me. Considering my historic lapses in tact, she might not have wanted me to speak my mind to her not-so-upstanding Naval officer boyfriend. In any case, I had to resign myself that, for the time being, my presence was less important to her.

My own love life had been a series of hope-filled disasters, and I prayed that my mother would finally escape that pattern. I tried to refocus my attention, away from loneliness and toward self-improvement. Stress itself could be the enemy. In New York I tried a relaxation technique called Silva Mind Control, which trained people to visualize positive outcomes for their goals and needs. The practice promised a payoff I'd always craved: the chance to have more energy with less sleep. I envied scant sleepers like Thomas Edison, who could thrive and be brilliant on three hours a night.

By then my mother was showing more signs of a heart condition. For years she'd struggled against an undertow of fatigue. We both tended to be insomniacs, she resorting to prescription sleeping pills. I did not, yet, and was almost always sleep-deprived. Here was our big chance, I thought. Silva Mind Control would relieve the stress on her heart, free her from sleeping pills, and help us get the rest we needed in fewer hours! I mailed her a check for the initiation fee. Wouldn't it be great if Silva Mind Control could zap Edwin's foul moods, and we could both turn our lives around?

She was willing to try, but found no Silva program anywhere. So she used my check for the initiation fee to learn Transcendental Meditation, and sent me a check to try TM myself. Shortly thereafter, in 1972, she reported that Edwin had become amazingly thoughtful, good-tempered, and sober. *The marrying bit seems almost inevitable.*

They took out a marriage license that he allowed to lapse, when Mom was recovering from hip replacement surgery and Edwin was cheerfully driving her to physiotherapy sessions. She was chagrined that he expected her to continue working after they were married—he with his comfortable officer's pension, and she with one prosthetic hip and the other disintegrating. When she returned to her job in the nursery, the Naval Hospital announced that all nurses had to be available for any shift, on any ward. Unable to comply, she retired early on a disability—heart disease.

Edwin then insisted that all he'd ever wanted was to marry and look after her, and to hell with the archaic customs of the Catholic Church. The same man who'd allowed one marriage license to lapse now accused her of foot-dragging. They began looking at wedding bands, and Edwin took out a second marriage license. He decided they would reside in his home, and Mom agreed. But when she mentioned that she'd like to bring her antique oak china cabinet and her plush new Lazy-Boy recliner that was comforting to her hips, Edwin refused, claiming those items would ruin his décor. License number two lapsed, along with his company and affection.

Alone again, she decided to fill her increasing spare time with charity work. She became a popular volunteer at the Office of Social and Health Services—a.k.a. the Welfare Department—delivering food to families whose public assistance checks had gone astray or run out, and they had nothing left to eat. She distributed donated clothes to women seeking jobs who could not afford suitable attire, drove people to doctors' and dentists' appointments, and other charitable tasks.

Sadly, she noted that after work we both had the problem of how, and with whom, to spend our leisure time. One of her letters stated: *I am proud of the way you have lived through your lonely New York life, Beck. Wish your choices had been easier.*

In a neighborhood paper I saw listed as For Sale a small grand piano by an unknown maker, price negotiable. The elderly couple selling it accepted my offer of several hundred dollars. My twenties seemed a mélange of hopeless romances, dateless dry spells, foundation work, part-time doctoral studies, and piano practice.

My mother filled her empty Sunday evenings by taking a course called Women in Society. She saw herself as less isolated than other women her age who, like her, were foreign born, widowed, and lacked close family ties. Because of the geographic distance, she explained, she was *not counting the close relationship between you and me. I am so glad of your letters, honey. They fill a very empty place. But I do wish you felt happier in your job.* In her term paper for Women in Society, my mother noted that Lesbian women had the same desire for continuity as other women, and shared—along with *"so-called gay men"* and heterosexuals—the capacity to be *"aggravated into violent states of possessiveness and jealousy."* She seemed oddly comforted by this discovery.

Without realizing, she'd become a textbook example of a woman perhaps better off without a particular man, but paying an extraordinary price in dignity and heartache to keep him. She loved a very troubled, arrogant man and was unable to give him up.

CHAPTER TWENTY-SEVEN

Mr. Lee's Beauty School

Her rocky romance with Capt. Madden seemed to put what Mom called my *teenage years* far into the distant past. Whereas, like it or not, I was in persistent contact with memories of helpless dread and futile efforts to bring clarity and closure to exhausting, nebulous rants about my *attitude*. I seemed to be the sole audience of a privately screened horror film, starring a mother who, when begged to bring one sleep-devouring session to an end, hissed that her death would be my fault.

Now, however, we lived on opposite sides of the country. She'd endorsed my move to New York, and since phone calls were costly we communicated mostly by mail. No longer hostage to her lectures, I began to question the platitudes she'd drilled into my teenage years. Living in New York awhile, I acquired some experience spreading sunshine, as it were—trying to please one feckless boyfriend after another. No amount of cheerfulness, I learned, could brighten Steve Devere's dark spells. And Jaime, the Cuban American I'd met when he attended Columbia Law School, spent so much time spreading his brand of sunshine at parties that he graduated near the bottom of his class. As a result he got only one job offer: translating articles in Spanish for an international law journal in Amsterdam.

I would have quit my secretarial job to cross the pond with him, but he didn't ask. The day before Jaime left, he leaned back jauntily on the back legs of a folding chair in the kitchen I shared with two roommates in Inwood, where I'd moved from the graduate dorm at Columbia. He smiled indulgently as I choked back tears, confessing that I'd miss him. Instead of anything reciprocal, he barked in a kindly tone: "Make sure you go out with other guys, you little shtunk!" At that point, for me, the thought of dating anyone else was literally nauseating. I counted the hours until Jaime's flight would arrive in Amsterdam, hoping he would call to say he'd arrived safely—as people close to each other used to do. When he did not call, I phoned my mother, devastated. Two weeks later a postcard arrived from Amsterdam's famous Rijksmuseum. "Rembrandts magnificent!" Jaime scrawled, adding that he'd met "an interesting woman" there.

About that time, in a letter, I took issue with my mother's lifelong advocacy of personal unselfishness as the best means to happiness. She decided to visit me in New York—perhaps to assuage my feelings of abandonment, perhaps to put off responding to my letter.

Mom and I were emerging from the subway near my apartment when a well-groomed Latino man offered to help her up the steps. She accepted appreciatively and, as we walked through the long exit tunnel to upper Broadway, he told us he was a physician trained in Brazil. Mom was impressed, and when he asked her if he could have our phone number, she gave him mine. After she returned to Bremerton I began dating him.

Raoul was suave, confident, and a good dancer. He took me to the city's best Latin dance halls, where Tito Puente, Eddie Palmieri and other salsa kings reigned. After a few months I wrote to Jaime that I was dating someone, keeping the details as vague as he'd been about the interesting woman he'd met. Surely, I thought, he'd be glad for his slow-moving little shtunk.

A week or so later, heading home from work, a lanky young man stood glowering at me across the intersection at 190th and Broadway. His features resembled Jaime's, with none of his characteristic warmth. Maybe there'd been a death in his family, I thought, and he'd come to tell me about it. Then a saner part of my mind noted that Jaime was unlikely to share any news of the family who'd threatened to consider him dead if he married me, a *shiksa*. Before I could ask what brought him back to New York, he announced, like a cop saying I was under arrest, that he'd come to take me with him to Amsterdam.

Right away he let slip a rankling detail—he'd spent all he'd saved from his new job on roundtrip airfare to New York, so I'd have to buy my own ticket one-way to Amsterdam. I'd just emptied my bank account to purchase a piano, and was no longer eager to drop everything to join him. Jaime surveyed my living room, saw the piano and, exuding business savvy, said I could easily afford the airfare if I sold it—"There's always a market for them." This I knew, having surveyed the market for pianos, luckily finding a sturdy grand at a modest price. His urgency was hard to fathom, even ironic. The moment had long passed when I'd have left for Amsterdam with him in a New York minute.

Raoul's case was quite different. He'd warned me not to call his work number because his hospital duties were all-consuming. But one weekend I ran out of cash and the banks were closed—no ATMs in those days—so I searched for the $20 bill stashed in the back of my dresser drawer for emergencies. Raoul was the only one who knew it was there. Furious, I called his work number and asked for him in a businesslike tone, referring to him as Dr. _____. The man who answered sounded surprised, and said the person I'd named worked there but was not a doctor and could not come to the phone.

Raoul apologized later, insisting that he'd meant to return the $20 before I'd notice it missing. This made matters worse. Wasn't he a doctor with a decent salary? He reluctantly explained that he'd been trained as a doctor, but got expelled in his last year of medical school due to "complications" with a woman on the school's staff. I surmised he'd gotten her pregnant, but did not press for details. It seemed he was working as a lab technician, hoping to finish his medical training in the States.

The evening after Jaime reappeared in New York, Raoul was waiting at the subway exit when I came home from work—a first for him. But Jaime had already installed himself in my building's lobby. The two sized each other up and appeared ready for a round of fisticuffs—each expecting to be chosen to spend the night with me. I told them to calm down and collect what was left of their senses. Jaime should return to Amsterdam and give me time to decide about moving there. Raoul should go back to wherever his place was, which I'd never seen. It didn't seem flattering to be fought over by a philanderer and a con artist, so I split with both.

In my farewell talk with Raoul, he confessed that it frightened him how easily he could make up stories about himself. Then the compulsive liar scolded me for trusting him in the first place. I never learned his actual background, nor even the country he was from. My mother, who'd been convinced Raoul was a better prospect than the faithless Jaime, was strangely silent about the outcome. We'd both been gulled by his deferential manner with her and his claim to be a physician.

Shortly after the farcical faceoff in my lobby, Mom ruminated in a letter penned under a hair dryer at Mr. Lee's Beauty School, near K-Mart on the outskirts of East Bremerton. There she enjoyed discounted prices, usually competent care, and the chance to encourage the apprentice beauticians—mostly single mothers struggling to get off welfare. For my sake, she wrote, she'd forego her chance to catch up on the besotted bickerings of Elizabeth Taylor and Richard Burton, and similarly edifying articles in Mr. Lee's assortment of high-tone periodicals.

In her view, *domestic proximity* tended to arouse feelings of love, especially when combined with sexual intimacy. But that did not mean that a genuine partnership was being forged. *I can honestly say, Beck, that I "loved" all of my husbands, but whether or not they were suitable partners for me is another question entirely.*

In a previous letter, I'd dared to suggest that she take her own advice about holding out for a better companion—rather than

Edwin, whom I'd tactfully described as "another booze hound"—and questioned the virtue of unselfishness that she'd drummed into me since childhood. Perhaps the environment in Mr. Lee's Beauty School inspired a more candid response.

She expressed regret that her religious training had led to the belief that any form of self-gratification was wrong, and was convinced that she'd *seen through that fallacy long before you kids started growing up.* Now, instead of noble self-sacrifice, she claimed to want only to learn more about life and how to live it, and to leave whatever conditions she encountered somewhat better off because of her presence. Then she took sharper aim:

> *If you had been a happy teenager enjoying life without any especially stressful condition, such as the combination of overweight and over-sensitivity with a brother like John, there would have been no need for me to be continually harping that the best first aid for one's own unhappiness is to try and make someone else happy. This is the best psychological device I know for the easement of personal pain.*

She now thought it better to substitute the idea of *thoughtfulness* for that bugaboo *unselfishness*, the scourge of my teenage years. How many times had I been reduced to tears and frozen silence at her accusations of selfishness? Had she ever been assuaged by my attempts at thoughtfulness? It seemed the goalposts had shifted slightly. Now she'd be judging whether I loved her by how well I met her standards of thoughtfulness.

As far as I could see, no efforts on my part could alter her claim that my relationship with her was my *Achilles heal.* It would not have helped me overcome my weight problem, which turned out to result from a sluggish thyroid. Nor would it have stopped my brother from calling me a pig and screaming that he hated me, or lessened my pain at his animosity. Nor would Mom's idea of thoughtfulness have protected either of us from being taken in by men who concealed traits that would undermine any healthy partnership. I had years ahead of me to hope for something better, but my mother felt she did not.

To have a seriously flawed lover in her sixties seemed better than solitude. Without Edwin, all Mom had for company was three afternoons a week running a volunteer food bank at the Welfare Department, and the occasional Scrabble game with another retired nurse. In my mother's volunteer work she really did bring sunshine into the lives of others, and couldn't keep it from herself, at least while she was there. She told me how the faces of the paid staffers would light up when she arrived, that she'd made a point of taking an interest in each of them. Her efforts so impressed the department's supervisor that they became close friends.

This administrator, Rosemary, was a member of an elite private club for women executives, whose officers she persuaded to create a new qualification for membership so that my mother could be invited to join. Mom was delighted to accept, as an outstanding volunteer who'd initiated an innovative charitable program. Her former career as a practical nurse was not mentioned. Vaulted into this rarified circle of female achievers, my mother proudly dressed up to attend club meetings, and entertained her new set of peers with a repertoire of amusing anecdotes.

Meanwhile, Mom and Capt. Madden alternated spells of harmonious companionship with nasty blowups followed by killer silences. In a moment of exhaustion, my mother passed out and fell, breaking a front tooth in her dentures. To get it fixed, Edwin revisited his old turf at the Naval dental clinic, where they greeted him warmly and did the job for free. He enjoyed taking care of her, she opined, *from a position of superiority.*

Having put Jaime and Raoul behind me, in the spring of 1973 I took an evening class at New York University to fulfill one of the language requirements for its doctoral program in comparative literature. There I met an earnest young man who'd recently graduated from Swarthmore. When I wrote to Mom that he and I were helping each other learn German, it struck a chord.

She'd been reading about the Swiss psychiatrist Paul Tournier, who'd written eloquently about how "beautiful, grand and liberating" it is when people learn to help each other. No one can develop freely or lead a full life, Tournier claimed, without feeling understood by at least one person. Tournier's idea rekindled her anxiety about what she called our *gap in understanding*. Since I was the one person who should understand her, there were a few points she wanted to clarify. From under the hair dryer at Mr. Lee's Beauty School, she confided: *My marriage to Roger was made under circumstances and for reasons so far removed from the conventional that there has to be some special importance attached to the potential of at least one of my children.*

It was rather mind-bending. As for special importance, my brother had received the National Air Medal for repeatedly risking his life to rescue others at sea. I being her child with no comparable distinction, why choose me to hear this justification for marrying our father? Why not confer this honor upon Johnny, with whom she had a special bond? Besides nearly confessing that she had not married our father for love, she also alluded to the possibility of reincarnation:

> *Years ago I read a book whose opening sentence began "When I chose my earthly parents" – and those words have remained in my conscious memory ever since.*
>
> *Wayne used to talk about "crossed conditions" and there being nothing accidental about accidents. I think he was right. …Our feelings or intentions often obscure our ability to make deliberate conscious choices for our own benefit.*

By the time she'd accepted Douglas's proposal via cable from London, according to her, she was operating on the premise that God would show her what to do. The problem, it seemed, was her difficulty receiving clear signals from God. She resorted to using what she called *devastating yardsticks,* the worst of which was *to leave aside every thought of self-interest in order to reach a "true" decision.* Another yardstick was willingness to be sent wherever she was most needed. What had protected her from *total disaster,* she confided, was her *sincerity of purpose.* In any case, she'd *learned a lot.*

What kind of "total disaster" had she meant? I gathered that the "peculiar circumstances" on the farm and the likelihood of total disaster to which she referred, was probably sexual in nature—given my father's moniker among Theosophists as the "Brother for Love." How badly had she been traumatized by what he'd ordered her to do—to the extent that she clung to the notion of sincerity of purpose, possibly to clear her conscience? She'd married my father for *ignorant idealistic reasons,* her letter concluded. She expressed hope, if not confidence, that I'd be more self-aware and have better luck.

In the summer of 1973 I experienced what appeared to be a supernatural confluence, while moving into the apartment I planned to share with my new boyfriend after he finished working at the summer camp he'd attended as a boy. The day I moved into this former hotel on the Upper West Side, an attractive young man stood near the entrance as if awaiting my arrival. "You must be Becky!" he called out cheerily without being told my name, and offered to carry my heavy boxes. He introduced himself as David, a fellow tenant in the building, and said he'd seen my face in dreams and felt he already knew me.

It got my attention. Wasn't seeing my Mom's face in dreams the reason Papa had persuaded her to marry him rather than her fiancé Douglas Elliott? Were David and I destined to be together? We seemed more than compatible. He was a Juilliard-trained pianist who'd learned ballet from his mother and shared my love of dance. He was smart, witty, with buoyant energy and catlike grace. My absent boyfriend, I decided, would have to find his own apartment.

During the next several weeks of rapturous romance, without my knowing, David spent some time outside my door listening to me practice the piano. When he invited me to meet his parents in Maryland, we took the train together, and after a cordial chat in his parents' living room, his mother invited me to play something on their fine Mason & Hamlin grand. I was shy, but managed to get through a favorite Bach prelude and fugue. David left the room, but his mother lingered. When I'd finished she murmured something to her son that I didn't quite catch, about degrees of talent. It made me uneasy, and everything else was lost to my memory.

After we returned to New York, David found excuses not to see me. When pressed, he said he was still attached to his ex-wife, who he claimed left him after a brief marriage. This was stunning. He'd shown no mixed feelings about having seen my face in his dreams, and in the weeks we'd spent together before I met his parents. I was heartsick in the months that followed, with David showing no interest in my company. One day I stepped into an elevator in our building and saw him standing beside a hugely overweight young woman, whom he introduced as his roommate. He seemed to glow with happiness, a state of being utterly at odds with the misery I fought to conceal behind a polite smile and greeting. Forcing myself to appear at ease until the elevator reached my floor, I stepped out, into my apartment, and called my mother, sobbing.

How, I cried, could David—so trim and agile, a trained dancer and gifted pianist—reject me in favor of someone so obese? I was so distraught that Mom's words did not register. But her follow-up letter mentioned that she'd recently experimented with another form of self-help besides meditation. She'd had a session with the "Inner Peace people," whose identity she did not clarify. It included a bit of automatic writing, presumably dictated by "knowledgeable sources" on the Other Side. Mom said she'd inquired about my problems with men. Perhaps moved by unseen forces, her hand wrote the following:

Tell your daughter not to worry. She will meet someone. Not now, but in the future. She has a great deal to work through but is doing a good job. Tell her she is being helped. There are those of us here who know what she really has to do. The music is good. She should stay where she is until she finds a suitable place. She will be given leads to follow.

The writing then touched upon my latest failed romance:

David is surrounded with entities but this is his problem not your daughter's. She has had enough trouble with hers and needs to be very careful with anything of a psychic nature. She should remember that she is a beautiful person and see to it that she reflects out this beauty in her presence, speech and bearing. She is fortunate to have you for a mother.

I wondered whether that last line had been written entirely on automatic. So I called, and our conversation went something like this:

"Hi, Mom. 'Just got your letter about the so-called automatic writing. You always say, 'self-praise is no recommendation.' But I guess it's okay if one's hand is being controlled by the Unseen!"

Very funny, young lady. It may be perfectly true that you're lucky to have me as a mother! I'm not sure if it was me or Higher Intelligence directing me to write those things, though I did not feel in control. But you can't argue with the warning about things psychic.

"Says she, who just dabbled in automatic writing! But Mummy, weren't you guided by psychic elements when you met Papa? He said he'd seen your eyes in his dreams! Didn't you feel the force of destiny when you met him? I felt it with David."

Sweetie pie, be careful using terms like destiny. Unseen forces can be devilish. Verne said that in order to be a responsible person he had to ignore a destructive inner voice he called Joe. It was Joe, he said, who told him to drive that park truck into the trees at Illahee.

"That was bad alright. But what's so terrible about someone who knew my name without being told, and seen my face in his dreams?"

That depends on whether there's mischief intended. You might recall that I began hearing voices when Ray left me.

"You told me that you'd asked the Unseen how to find him."

True. But I did not ask for guidance from God or even the good angels. That opened the door to any kind of entity, and the one that answered was up to no good. Looking back, it would have been better for all of us if I'd let Ray disappear.

"Ray was bad news, Mom. But David came into my life so wonderfully. We both love music and dance, and we seemed to share a beautiful feeling of being soul mates. Why would he suddenly drop me?"

God only knows.

"It hurt to see him with such a fat girl. He used to love how I looked."

Sweetie pie, I know how you've struggled to be slim. It's mystifying that a man would reject you for someone grossly overweight. Rather wicked, in my view.

"Do you think he was trying to hurt me?"

Possibly. Negative entities are cunning and have no conscience. The voice that called itself 'E' told me to drive to a real town and go into a real tavern where Ray would be in the back room behind a green door. Everything was exactly where 'E' said it would be, except that Ray was not in that room. Never had been.

"You think we've both been played for fools?"

In my case that's all I can conclude, but it was a great lesson. I was wrong to trust that voice, to pound on that door and scream for Ray to come out. They had to call the police to take me away. I was put in a jail cell, still screeching for Ray, so they decided I was crazy. I've never known such humiliation.

Memories flooded back of Johnny and me crouching in the back seat while Mom sped on dusty back roads away from the farm, muttering about enemies who wanted to take Johnny and me away from her. My memory blurred as to how we'd been placed in a foster home, and the brief, surreal visit to a clinic where someone who resembled my mother showed no warmth for me. I changed the subject.

"Oh well, Mummy, we got through it. Now I'm the one who's humiliated. Before he dumped me David even took me to meet his parents."

Normally, that would indicate a serious interest. Were his parents pleased that you also play the piano?

"His mother asked me to play something, which I think went fairly well. But after we returned to New York he stopped seeing me. How could David have dreamt about me and known my name if we were not meant for each other, like you and Papa?"

Becky dear, there are other fish in the sea. Don't compare your father's pursuit of me with this young man's brief attraction. My circumstances were circumscribed by the war, and by a sequence of events involving a strange New Zealand woman whose role I had no knowledge of until after Roger and I were married.

"What strange woman from New Zealand?"

I believe I've written to you about her, if you've saved my letters. Meanwhile, be thankful this fish has swum away!

CHAPTER TWENTY-EIGHT

"Brother IX"

Mom was right. She had written about this strange New Zealand woman. Among her letters was an account of how she'd been set up to meet the man who became my father before she left on her fateful cruise to Canada. The woman, Mary Fielding, was a very odd friend of her former patient, Mrs. Cole. Mary had met Roger Painter, a.k.a. Brother IX, in a commune of Theosophists in British Columbia. It was Mary who'd insisted on writing a formal letter introducing Rachel Williams to Brother Nine, which she brought with her across the Pacific and presented to him.

My mother prefaced all this by saying that Papa had been involved in *all kinds of offbeat religious activity—most of it Theosophist-oriented—in Florida.* He'd had a successful poultry business in Jacksonville, where he'd lived with his first family. *He had unconventional instincts to say the least. Orthodoxy was not for him.*

Though my father gave his first wife credit for raising my decades-older half-siblings, he'd found her to be, as Mom put it, *conventional and somewhat spinsterish, so they drifted apart.* Handing off the poultry business to his son George, Papa headed northwest to a colony of Theosophists on a small island near Vancouver, B.C. Mom pictured it as a higher-class prototype of the sixties and seventies' hippy communes. By the time Papa joined that group, he'd had several female companions, all drawn to him by a combination of spiritual and sexual charisma. The colony's leader was called Brother XII.

> *Roger became his second in command—known as Brother IX, or the "Brother for Love"—supposedly his specialty. This group collected funds and proselytes from all over the globe. Except for the fact that life was far from dull spiritually (?) and mentally, the ultimate end was disaster. The men had female counterparts (supposedly the "other half" of themselves) and in order to find out who was the half of whom there was some trading around.*

Brother XII took a fancy to Brother IX's then partner, chose her for himself, which gave her special status and the title Madame Zee, whatever that meant. After losing her, Bro. Nine began seeing a pair of eyes in his dreams. I was already familiar with the legend that my father had shouted "Those are the eyes!" the instant his future wife arrived at the berry farm. In Mom's telling, she'd been promised to him by the Unseen, in a recurring vision of her eyes which appeared at the foot of Roger's bed—consoling him for losing his "other half" to Brother XII. The dreams convinced him to give up his girlfriend gracefully, and his true mate—identified by her eyes—would come to him.

Soon the other Theosophists were in turmoil. *The colony (the Barleys had a considerable part in the project) fell into feuding, ran foul of British Columbia law, and ended up being disbanded by Roger—when Brother XII and Madame Zee fled to parts unknown to avoid facing charges for smuggling drugs.* My mother's letter went much further than the version given me as a child. The Theosophist colony that my father disbanded had called itself the Aquarian Foundation. *You see,* Mom wrote, *this Age of Aquarius stuff is in the family, as it were.*

Papa's plan was to find a piece of land somewhere, and make "the barren soil fruitful." He and a handful of followers traveled as far south as California searching for the right spot, and along the way the unusual woman from New Zealand joined the group. *Rather than visit a colony which no longer existed, Mary was invited to travel with Roger and his followers. She was a woman of plain appearance, a huge bosom, and a background of social impeccability plus Rosicruceanism.*

Rosicruceans, I would learn, are members of a centuries-old secret society of mystics, many coming from wealth and aristocracy, who practice various forms of benign or white magic, and are on cordial terms with Theosophists.

By the time Mary returned to New Zealand, Roger and the Barleys had purchased a farm in Washington—probably for back taxes, since the property had been abandoned during the Great Depression. My mother's letter continued:

> *Seems she had a very pathetic problem. Nobody discussed even going to the bathroom openly, let alone sex, in New Zealand at that time. So Roger, who was as devoid of sexual self-consciousness as anyone I've ever met, had her difficulty out in the open in nothing flat. (One of his "duties" as "leader" was to provide sexual as well as spiritual (??) experiences for his followers and show no favor or partiality!)*

The poor soul, as Papa had explained to my mother, had only a "vestigial vaginal orifice" but an "enlarged and very sensitive clitoris." She was tormented by guilt for "self abuse," though she was incapable of normal sexual intercourse. The natural and objective way my father responded to her situation, plus his complete acceptance of her as an individual, seemed just the therapy she needed. *He got her to think of herself as basically a non-physical spiritual being.* Her body, with its peculiarities, was merely *the physical vehicle allotted to her for this life.* Mary returned to New

Zealand *in a state of gratitude bordering on hero worship,* deter-mined to find *a suitable female companion for her hero—maybe even "the one" of his dreams!*

Mary was one of Mrs. Cole's Rosicrucean colleagues in Havelock North. In their circle, Miss Williams was considered a different type of person, unconventional in a religious sense, a highly competent nurse, and presentable personally. Could she be "the one"?

> *Mary, without my knowing she had any ulterior motive, or knowing a blessed thing about astrol-ogy, found out my birthdate etc. and sent the info. to this country for Alfred Barley to set up my horoscope and check it with Roger's. Seems there was some excitement at the berry farm (where they had located by this time). My "sun" was on his "moon" or vice versa. ...In the mean-while, all unsuspecting, I was offered the job of bringing Archdeacon Cole's widow to Vancouver Island. And seeing I was at that time engaged to Douglas Elliott, and they offered me my passage paid to England as part of my salary, I accepted.*

Whether any behind-the-scenes maneuvering on the part of Mary and Mrs. Cole had taken place, Mom did not explain. She did say that the institutionalization of her patient in Canada, the change from cold to hot war in England, Douglas's decision to return to New Zealand—and the sinking of the first passenger ship in the Pacific, which she said prevented her from joining him—all conspired to produce time on her hands.

> *Roger sent Annie Barley to check me out. And when this odd little character in her way-out clothes showed up in the fashionable Glenshiel Hotel lobby and told me about how her hus-band Alfred had just died, I thought how nice of*

her to make a special trip to Victoria to see me. Apparently she went back to the farm with the report that I was indeed probably "the one" Roger had been promised. 'Will continue the saga next time I write, if you're still interested.

Years before she wrote this letter, Mom had described her trip to British Columbia as a reward for the excellent care she'd given Mrs. Cole—not that it was part of a job, though the bonus could have been the cost of her passage to England. Among other facts she'd altered, I later ascertained that the hot war in Britain had not yet commenced, and that Douglas was en route to New Zealand to marry her while she was crossing the Pacific to Canada on a luxury liner. In any event, one had to share her conclusion that she'd led *a pretty fantastic existence one way or another.*

I never lost interest in the saga, but my mother never completed it. One thing it did seem to explain was a magical-seeming item that Mom bequeathed to me when I was in grade school. I'd come home after yet another round of ridicule for being fat and bookish, when she went into her bedroom and fetched a small suede pouch. *Here dear,* she said, *keep this safe among your things. Other people had best not see it, so do not wear it. It's called a Rosy Cross, and it's very special. It was given to me by a member of the Rosicruceans, and it's supposed to have powers of protection. I think you might need it now more than me.*

Handcarved from a single piece of ivory, the cross was embellished with carved wreaths of roses, yellowed and warped with age. Perhaps Mary had given it to my mother to fortify her for the challenges she might face as "the one" for Brother IX. I've not seen anything like it, either worn by anyone or in museum collections. Maybe Rosicruceans wear them only in their secret meetings.

Had my mother and I benefited from their powers of protection?

CHAPTER TWENTY-NINE

Rats in a Tank

When Captain Madden was sober, he and my mother shared a genuine bond of affection. Eventually he ignored his scruples about intimacy with a divorced woman, nevertheless finding flimsy reasons to postpone their marriage.

In harmonious times Mom accompanied Edwin to Mass at Our Lady Star of the Sea R.C. Church in Bremerton. There she got acquainted with Father Congor, the pastor, who'd known the Madden family for decades. One day, she wrote, Fr. Congor took her aside and told her he had no problem with Edwin's marrying a fine woman like her. But in his opinion, if they did marry, she'd be assuming the burdens of Job. "Between you and me," the elderly priest opined, "he's the kind of self-righteous old stick that gives Catholics a bad name." Fr. Congor thought it relevant to inform my mother that Edwin had purchased insurance policies for each of his children, separate from their college funds, and had held this money over their heads "as a sort of whip to keep them in line." The pastor was convinced that the Madden children's respect for their father was mixed with bitter resentment—so much so that, when it came to loving concern for Edwin's well-being, he said, "You're all he has."

Fr. Congor explained that, since her former husband had been divorced when they were married, and neither of them was

Catholic, in the eyes of the Church their marriage had never taken place. He offered to pass this on to Capt. Madden, but my mother replied *Absolutely not—until such time as Edwin has stopped drinking*. Fr. Congor nodded and left her with these words: "I believe that Edwin destroyed his wife's will to live. If he doesn't kill your spirit, you'll be my candidate for sainthood."

Mom suspected a sinister connection between the insurance policies Edwin had threatened to cancel if his children displeased him and the marriage licenses he'd allowed to lapse. They seemed to all be *some weird means of control*.

By then she'd been diagnosed with aortic stenosis, narrowing of the heart's main artery, and was prescribed nitroglycerin for when she felt too weak, and the tranquilizer Valium for when she felt overstressed. Since her cholesterol level was normal, the diagnosis actually came as a relief, for it enabled her to see her bouts of depression, weepiness, and inability to cope as physical in origin. She was touched by my offer to help if her disability benefits and Verne's small pension were not enough.

When I urged her to consider other options than seesawing with Edwin, she replied, *One has to play one's cards the way they fall*. Meanwhile, she planned to sell her house, rent a cozy apartment near the waterfront, and use some of the proceeds for a trip back to New Zealand. No more fretting about marriage. She would relax, meditate, and wait for something *easy and natural in the way of an opening* where Edwin was concerned.

After more than 25 years away from her homeland, a reunion with Gwenda and her New Zealand family seemed the perfect tonic.

During several years at the Rockefeller Foundation I'd seen no openings for college teaching positions for which I could qualify, so I remained. At least I'd been able to transfer into its Humanities program and win a modest promotion to Administrative Assistant. The term "glass ceiling" had yet to be coined in the mid seventies, but the women's liberation movement was surely growing. When word got around that the feminist writer and consciousness-raiser Gloria Steinem had been invited to speak to the professional staff in the boardroom, a lightning bolt seemed to strike the career-minded women on the foundation's support staff. We could hardly believe that Steinem had agreed to speak on condition that the [entirely female] support staff be allowed to attend, along with the [almost entirely male] professional staff, or officers. When the day came and a handful of us gingerly entered the boardroom, Steinem gestured for us to sit in the high-backed leather chairs that surrounded the magnificent elliptical teak table, whose central axis was discretely punctuated by a small, elegant built-in microphone. It felt almost rude to do so, but she insisted, and we were amazed to be in the same room with her. Beautiful, blond and serene, she peered confidently through her trademark aviator glasses.

If those in power at The Rockefeller Foundation were serious about their humanistic goals, Steinem advised in a calm, firm tone, they should create paths of advancement so that capable women could rise up in their ranks. The officers present sat expressionless, but among the rest of us a few fires of hope were lit. Sadly, after Steinem left, there was only one change in the rigid division between the clerical and professional staffs. The president announced in an all-staff memorandum that program secretaries were not obligated to fetch coffee for their bosses, though many continued to do so.

As more of my hopefully career-building years passed at Rockefeller striving for an elusive chance at a promotion to the professional staff, my mother felt moved to inform me of an article she'd read about a scientific experiment. I forgot its title, but the one I gave it was "Rats in a Tank." Mom summarized it as follows:

> *These rats were thrown into a tank full of water with a lighted platform charged with an electrical current and another platform unlighted but free from unpleasant repercussions. Naturally each rat took the lighted platform first and got*

shocked. The smartest rat stopped and looked around on his second immersion in case there was another and safer outlet someplace else. Others took a varying number of immersions before they too stopped and looked for an alternative. One rat kept shocking himself something like 400 times before he chose to (learned to?) do things differently.

She found this grim experiment uplifting, and managed not to hint that she had my stalled career in mind. It was heartening, she wrote, that even the stupidest rat finally learned that it didn't have to go on making the same wrong choices forever.

There was just one problem, she admitted. Anyone can learn to stop and look around for more satisfactory alternatives, but things get *more complicated when one appears to have no alternatives in sight.* In her case, she'd found no alternative to Edwin. But for all other cases of repeated mistakes and futile patterns, the message seemed clear. I pondered the implication that I was a dumb rat stuck in a dead end job, and wondered whether Mom considered my own lack of alternatives.

My old flame Steve Devere kept in touch, a bemused bystander to my series of romantic debacles. Supported by a generous doctoral fellowship in philosophy at the State University of New York at Stony Brook, he'd completed his coursework unburdened, as I had been, by a work-study job. While I was writing and typing up summaries of grant projects at the Foundation, Steve was heading down the home stretch—his dissertation topic enthusiastically approved by the Philosophy Department—when his mother died. Overcome by grief, he was unable to focus on thesis research. The rest of his fellowship was consumed in months of depression. I was doubly sad for him. He'd lost his mother, but also his motivation to complete the doctorate that would have made her proud and paved his way to a brilliant career.

Unlike Steve, I tried to resume my doctoral studies after an initial setback. In 1974 I reapplied to Columbia's doctoral program in comparative literature, and was accepted. The university could only offer me a tuition waiver, not a fellowship. If I had to cover my own rent and living expenses, there was no way I could return to Columbia, since it required its doctoral students to attend classes fulltime. My disappointment at being given an unworkable offer was mixed with anger at Steve for giving up when he was virtually guaranteed a renewed fellowship. Why couldn't he channel his grief at losing his mother into his studies? That's what I would eventually do, hoping to make my mother's spirit proud. However, to paraphrase the Bard, comparisons remain odious.

A few months later, Steve visited me in New York. As soon as we were together again all my dealings with other men seemed trivial. But Steve saw no cure for his depression. He hesitated to reveal the purpose of his visit, which was to tell me he would be moving even farther away than Stony Brook. Boston, he said, was a more manageable place for him to live, a "toy city" compared to New York. He had a few friends there, and felt he'd be able to find a job more easily.

There was something he was struggling to say, but couldn't, until we were in the subway and about to get off at different stations. We sat together in silence as the train approached his stop. Neither of us was demonstrative in public, but at the same instant an irresistible impulse surged through us. Ignoring the other passengers, we turned toward one another without looking and our lips met in an urgent kiss. Amidst the train's clatter Steve found it easier to tell me that he'd always cared, and was sorry he could no longer be there for me. "You understand, don't you, Beck?"

I looked at him with love and tears as the subway doors closed behind him.

Under the dryer at Mr. Lee's Beauty School, Mom wrote that she'd been praying that, if Steve was not right for me, my life would close one door and open a window. *So many things we want desperately at the time—so many seeming disasters, have in the long haul proved expressions of such Ultimate Intelligence, that their negative value is far outshone by the ultimate benefit.* My father's death, she decided, had led to a fuller existence for herself and her two children. Losing the berry farm caused us to move to *Camano Island and ultimately a decent series of school situations culminating in the college education which I doubt if Getchell* [the elementary school Johnny and I attended from the berry farm] *and Marysville High would have provided.*

She now viewed it as auspicious that Verne had died while he was head ranger at Scenic Beach State Park. She'd heard that the park was nearly closed, and the ranger who replaced Verne was working piecemeal at other parks with no personal authority or status.

Good news! her letter concluded. Her house on North Wycoff had sold, so she could afford roundtrip excursion airfare to New Zealand. With Edwin supposedly recovering from a stroke in the Seattle Veterans Hospital, my mother flew Down Under.

Not long after I'd become the Administrative Assistant for the RF's Humanities program, its Program Associate took two consecutive seven-month maternity leaves. During those 14 months I was given all her responsibilities, and not long after she returned to work she resigned in order to spend more time with her children. At any other time the Director would have given me the position she'd vacated, but the Foundation had a new president, who persuaded our boss to retire. A recently hired Program Officer in the Humanities Division, who'd previously chaired the philosophy department of a state university, was made Acting Director.

Unfortunately for me, before my boss was forced to retire, he'd found that this newly hired officer's writing style was unsuitable for the large grant project descriptions, or docket items, that had to be approved by the Board of Trustees. His work was given to me to rewrite. It didn't take the new officer long to discover that his efforts were not being presented to the board, and that I'd rewritten all of them. He must have resented me, though I'd only been following my boss's orders. As soon as he was made Acting Director, with authority to hire the next Humanities Program Associate, he gave the position to a less-experienced staff member, denying me the promotion I'd worked long and well to earn.

Ironically, the person who got the job was someone I'd encouraged to transfer into the Humanities program from a dead-end job in the foundation's library. She explained that she would not have applied for the program associate's position, had the acting director not persuaded her to do so. I could understand that it'd been almost impossible to pass up the chance at a career-making position at the foundation, despite knowing that I'd worked for it longer and had a master's degree in the humanities, which she did not. Several senior officers in other divisions told me they'd spoken to the acting director and strongly recommended me for the position, mentioning the foundation's traditional respect for seniority. But the man was impervious.

It was close to a knockout punch—losing what should have been ten career-building years at the whim of a philosopher whose specialty was supposedly ethics. In the years that followed, I sometimes wondered whether the person I'd invited to join the Humanities staff—whose bachelor's degree had been in religious studies—was ever troubled by her conscience. Crazily, I pondered whether Providence might have rewarded her if she'd refused to apply for the position out of fairness to one she knew had earned it. At such moments I imagined Steve Devere chortling that only a Pollyanna would imagine anyone acting against their own interests.

For too long, I looked upon philanthropic work in the humanities as the "career that got away." In any case, by my final year at Rockefeller I'd managed to complete all the course requirements for New York University's doctoral program in comparative literature. Unlike Columbia, NYU offered evening courses for people with day jobs, and did not require their doctoral candidates to take courses fulltime. NYU was lenient about leaves of absence, too. I took several when subsequent jobs were too time-consuming to combine with doctoral studies. That stopped when a professor warned me that, if I took another leave, even NYU might not readmit me.

By the time Mom called to say she was terminal, I'd passed the written exams for my doctorate, received an M.Phil. degree, and was submitting draft chapters to my dissertation advisor. For several months after my mother's death, I was able to work full-time on my dissertation. When I finally walked across the stage in Carnegie Hall to receive my doctorate in comparative literature on May 11, 1998, a few friends were in the audience. I hoped that Mummy and Johnny, Uncle Wayne and perhaps even Papa, were with me in spirit.

By then I was one of multitudes of individuals with advanced liberal arts degrees who worked as adjunct professors for meager wages, hoping against hope to win one of a vanishing few tenure-track positions. It went without saying—and took awhile for my Pollyanna heart to accept—that since I was older than most recent Ph.D. recipients, I would almost inevitably face age discrimination. In short, I would not be seriously considered for a fulltime position in academe no matter how capable and well qualified. In my estimation, the foundation work and other jobs I'd held, plus adjunct college teaching, fell short of anything one could call a career. It was no longer possible for me to fulfill my dream of teaching at a fine college like Scripps, a secure basis for becoming a "public intellectual." Whatever I could contribute to the world had to take a different approach.

I had to fight against what felt like the same force of doom that had deprived my mother of her true love, and caused her to set aside her own literary talents. Was it a factor in her unwillingness to accept that I loved her?

CHAPTER THIRTY

New Zealand Connections

I had no idea how my mother spoke about me during her first trip back to New Zealand, but my brother traveled there shortly after Mom returned to Bremerton. Johnny was a finalist for a life-changing position: Director of Flight Safety in New Zealand's Air Transport Department. He'd been stymied as Deputy Director of Flight Safety at the U.S. Coast Guard headquarters in Washington, D.C., and wanted to apply his experience and innovative ideas in a more responsive, less bureaucratic country where our family had roots. In NZ he met "rellies" who loved him instantly, and bonded with our cousin Grahame, Gwenda's surviving son, as though he'd found the brother he wished he could have grown up with. Johnny's heroic exploits and extensive training in flight safety were unmatched by any other applicants for the job.

Confident of his chances, he sent me a rare letter, overflowing with enthusiasm for the country. He sincerely liked the people he hoped to be working with, "instead of just being polite to 80 percent" of his colleagues in the States. New Zealanders had a great sense of humor, he reported, whereas "some household appliances had a better sense of humor than many Americans." If he got the job, he planned to move there within six months, and said I'd be crazy not to come, too. He was sure I could get on the faculty of most NZ universities. I was deeply touched by his optimism and confidence in my chances—feelings that stretched credulity, given our track record.

Shortly after Johnny's visit, Aunt Gwenda wrote the second of her three letters to me. She wanted to convey my brother's concern for me—something I'd never heard expressed by our mother. Gwenda did her best to capture his manner of speech: "I guess she's a pretty smart kid," he'd told her. "It's a mighty difficult job she has at times, and damned if I know how she figures everything out living in New York. *I* couldn't—the place frankly scares me, and I only wish I could get her away from it all and into a totally new environment—out here for instance." The trouble, she quoted, was, "We always seem to end up rubbing each other the wrong way."

Here was our only aunt, who'd never met me, taking upon herself a daunting task which I could not fully appreciate, not knowing what Mom had told her about me.

I would have rubbed my brother the wrong way again, had I the opportunity to ask whether his wife and children were as eager to uproot from the States as he was. Fortunately for me, not him, my concern was moot. Despite being unanimously chosen by the Air Transport Department to be their new flight safety director, the department's decision was subject to approval by New Zealand's immigration office. Then came a heartbreaking shock. A solitary immigration officer decided that the job should go to a New Zealander, even one substantially less qualified— overriding the Air Transport Department's choice for the job, notwithstanding that their chosen candidate had relatives in the country and intended to make NZ his home.

Decades later, Grahame confided that he could not forget the immigration officer's name, and lamented that the man had been granted unchecked authority. Grahame's lasting regret and sense of unfairness resonated with my difficulty forgiving the former acting director of the RF's humanities program for blocking my promotion to its professional staff. Though my brother remained in the Coast Guard and was promoted again in his foreshortened career, I felt closer to him realizing that we'd both known the pain of losing a

much hoped-for position for which we were preeminently qualified. We'd both been cut down by a lone individual using his power
to make an unjust decision. To borrow a phrase from Uncle Wayne,
"crossed conditions" propelled both of us onto different paths.

Aunt Gwenda's other son, Stuart, who'd been charming and
impishly funny like Johnny, had met a strangely similar fate. Mom
had the good fortune to meet him on her second trip back to New
Zealand, when she visited Stuart and his family on Rauponga,
the sheep station he'd bought next to the Williams' old home-
stead, Mangaotawhito, near the Maori village of Tikitiki, on the
East Cape of North Island. Stuart took his Auntie Rachel to meet
Mangaotawhito's current owners.

How odd it was, she wrote, to find herself *part of antiquity,*
saying, *I remember when there were no roads here, when it took
three days by stagecoach to get to Gisborne. The tennis court used
to be where your house is now.* Maori names sprang into her mind
*from regions long sealed away. There I was standing in the sheering
shed where I'd sorted wool as a girl.*

Mangaotawhito's sheering shed had not changed since my
mother saw it, when I took this photo in January 2007.

Before visiting Stuart, Mom received via Gwenda an impassioned letter from an old admirer named Mervyn, whom I'd never heard of. She enclosed it in her letter for my amusement. Mervyn had addressed her as his "Beloved Rachel," his "darling," and swore he'd loved her devotedly for 52 years! He'd evidently kept in touch with Gwenda since their tennis days at the Williams' station. When he heard about Rachel's homecoming he'd asked Gwenda if he could "borrow" her sister for a few days on the shores of beautiful Lake Tarawera. Left unsaid was that, once borrowed, his darling Rachel would be alone with a married man at his vacation home, wife not around. Mom asked Gwenda to inform him that her schedule did not permit.

Word of Mervyn's intentions somehow reached Stuart. On Mom's last day with him he announced that an old friend of hers would be dropping by. Within minutes, Mervyn pulled into the drive, effusing that his sweetheart of a half-century ago was "lovelier than ever." With devilish tact, Stuart disappeared to ensure his aunt and her admirer absolute privacy. Afterward, Mom said she tried to berate her nephew for leaving her stranded, but he made such wicked fun of the besotted Mervyn that she laughed till her sides ached.

Though I chuckled, I also searched for some clue as to why this married man had carried a torch for my mother for five+ decades, and marveled at the effect she could have on people. She mentioned vaguely that the idealism Mervyn claimed about her had helped him many times, *and may do so again in spite of the quaint figure he has deteriorated into now.*

What was in this idealism that had helped Mervyn so many times? How had she inspired him in their youth? Had she advised him this last time—as she had my half-brother Frank—to return to his wife and make the most of his marriage? The only clear thing was how confident my mother had been of her own wisdom, not just with Gwenda, their father, and Mervyn, but untold others.

Stuart had followed in his father Colin's footsteps and become a successful stock agent, but long hours away from home nearly ruined his marriage. Knowing next to nothing about sheep ranching, he'd bought Rauponga to keep his family together and change his way of life. Through sheer charm and effrontery he got expert instruction gratis from his neighbors at Mangaotawhito, plus the use of their costly heavy machinery. Family legend holds that one morning Stuart sauntered over to Mangaotawhito and announced, "Well, I'll be needing the backhoe today!" His chutzpah was impossible to refuse.

The Maoris loved Stuart for his camaraderie, rakish humor, and work ethic that made time for serious drinking. On one occasion, he'd hired a team of men for early morning sheep sheering, having agreed to celebrate a wedding the night before, hours away in Gisborne. The Maoris were awestruck when he showed up on time, in a tuxedo—having driven back in the wee hours—and after removing his jacket and tie, joined them for the long day's sheering.

Stuart was in his forties, apparently in excellent health, when he took the time to drive down to Gisborne and purchase life insurance for his wife and children. A few weeks later his eight-year-old daughter was getting ready for school and thought her dad was trying to be funny when he would not answer her, his face buried in the newspaper at the kitchen table. He'd had a fatal heart attack that shocked everyone but the Maoris.

Years later, when I traveled there, a tribal elder recalled that Stuart would sometimes stop and hold his side after he'd been working hard, joke about it, and resume working. They were sure he knew what he was doing when he bought that life insurance. Very few *pakehas* (Maori for white pigs, their term for European settlers) were offered places in Tikitiki's immaculately kept tribal cemetery. The Maoris honored Stuart with a traditional three days of mourning and full burial rites.

When Johnny died, Gwenda had already lost Stuart. In her quiet way she showed a strength of heart and grace of character that may have helped my mother pull through. Gwenda had maintained a rare lightness of being when threatened by her husband's drunken violence. Colin gradually succumbed to dementia, drinking uncontrollably until his early death. His grandsons told me about the time they were driving up to Colin and Gwenda's house and witnessed their petite grandmother diving out the kitchen window onto the lawn. Colin, they learned from Gwenda, had been smashing plates on the floor, but when he picked up a skillet and aimed it at her she chose the nearest exit, and defenestrated. One morning her son Grahame happened to drive by and saw her curled up asleep under a hedge near the house, where she'd hidden through the night. If Gwenda had shared any such matters with my mother, they were never relayed to me. Gwenda probably kept those trials to herself.

It occurred to me that Mom had been the first member of her New Zealand family to take on what they'd been raised to believe was the indignity of custodial work. Perhaps by the time Uncle Colin's drinking had cost him his career, Gwenda, who had not finished high school and had no other skills, considered herself lucky to find work as a hospital janitor. She supported her family and kept this job long after her three children had careers of their own.

My mother probably told no one else about Verne's shortcomings as a husband. If anyone asked Gwenda about her late husband, her daughter Heather recalled, she would say only that he was a most charming and amusing man when he wasn't drinking. She took to heart her sister's advice: *It's not what happens to you that matters, but how you respond.* She kept herself trim and fit by the daily practice of yoga. At 78 her photo appeared on the front page of the local paper, when a reporter observed her in a public park leading a group of practitioners in a backbend.

A month after my brother died, Gwenda wrote Mom a letter expressing admiration that her sister had schooled herself "to accept without railing, or bitterness, this tragic situation." She had continued to be "receptive to whatever may be garnered of profit from each day." Not many folk their age, she noted, "are able to live in the present and maintain a hospitality of mind." It was equally true of my aunt.

I was impressed that Gwenda, who'd dropped out of boarding school in her first year, was an avid reader whose letters were filled with wit and insight. Two years after my mother's difficult death, Gwenda passed away peacefully in her sleep at 87, nearly equaling the lifespan of her beloved sister.

After my mother's death, I came across a strip she'd clipped from a letter Gwenda had probably written shortly after Mom's last trip back to New Zealand. The context was a strong disagreement they'd had about the conduct of Gwenda's son Grahame, whose marriage was crumbling. In this passage Gwenda asked her sister to refrain from judging the manner in which she, Gwenda, spoke to her grown son. She buttressed her request by stating: *I cannot begin to understand, Rachel, the way you speak about Becky.* My mother had underlined these words, discarded the rest of the letter, and saved the clipping among the items left in the drawer next to her recliner.

Only then did I remember the first of my aunt's three letters to me, which she'd mailed after Mom's first trip back to NZ. She'd asked me to excuse her for writing out of the blue, but wanted me to know that she believed in her bones I was "a good person," and when she felt that way she was "always right." At first her letter struck me as a warm though unnecessary affirmation of the positive maternal comments I'd assumed Mom made about me during her visit. I did not know enough then to discern Gwenda's loving concern for the integrity and morale of her American niece—whom she would never meet, and who would come to realize the significance of her brave defense.

CHAPTER THIRTY-ONE

A Miraculous Extension

My mother returned from New Zealand to find her sometime lover in serious decline at the Veterans Hospital in Seattle. Taking an unauthorized peek at the chart at the foot of his bed, she noticed that Edwin was being given very high doses of insulin for a borderline diabetic. After she'd persuaded *his so-called rehabilitation team* to reduce the dosage, Capt. Madden regained some strength and was less groggy. Mom believed he would have soon died if kept at the previous level of insulin.

The same man who'd allowed their two marriage licenses to lapse, who'd brought a debilitating stroke upon himself during a drunken rage, was now partially paralyzed, incontinent, crankier than ever, and in dire need of fulltime care. He asked—more likely ordered—my mother to move in with him, with no mention of marriage. Sick as he was, I suspected his self-righteous gears were grinding away, directing him to preserve his good Catholic standing by looking like he'd hired a live-in nurse. Before I could think of a tactful way to put this, Mom wrote to say she'd told Edwin she'd *do nothing of the kind without benefit of matrimony.*

Meekly—or having no other choice—he agreed to a civil ceremony. I thought to myself: Right-o, Captain, no Church-sanctioned frosting on your wedding cake. But your pastor has made clear it's your problem, not your bride's.

I found it ironic, if not sad, that the previous year Mom had sold her house and moved into a snug new waterfront apartment in East Bremerton. She'd waxed effulgent about her independence—her own pension, her own car, no debts, and a ringside view of the Washington Narrows coursing into Puget Sound. I was worried that she'd signed up for another doomed relationship, and chilled to read her letter—a few photos enclosed—justifying what seemed like a forced marriage of convenience. *One day at a time is enough,* she concluded.

To me, one day at a time with an ill-tempered, arrogant, incontinent husband who expected 24/7 care, but who'd put off marrying her until his health went south, was hardly "enough." Had she lost all hope back in New Zealand, after that phone conversation with Douglas that she'd chosen not to tell me about?

Mom and the Captain were married in a judge's chambers, no priest present. Photo probably by Bob Madden.

Edwin was in a wheelchair during the ceremony, but his two sons helped him stand for one of the photographs. Beside him, my mother seemed a portrait of hope pushing away despair. *I seem to get slim only when I'm worrying a lot*, she noted.

I wondered whether the three smiling Madden children who appeared in other photos were relieved to have a stepmother to spare them the burden of hands-on care for their father. None of them had offered to help her. As Fr. Congor had suspected, she was all Edwin had.

Not abandoning Edwin in his hour of need might seem like self-imposed martyrdom, Mom wrote, *but one has to live with one's conscience.* Gwenda and other NZ relatives believed she was throwing herself away on a self-centered man who had treated her badly. The only way she could look after him properly, she'd told them, was with the respect and authority of legal status.

Respect and authority for what?—I refrained from asking. Enslaving herself to a demanding ingrate who couldn't commit when he was continent? It was obvious my mother loved Edwin unconditionally. Perhaps I would have appreciated her devotion more, had her love for me been less conditional.

For several years I'd been involved with a divorced man nearly twice my age, a scientist and officer in an international non-profit organization. Gerald was so similar in age and appearance to Frank Sinatra that women of a certain age would do double takes when they saw him on the street, with withering glances at me. He knew the philanthropic world, and considered it naïve to believe that I'd have a future at Rockefeller. The foundation's reluctance to promote people from the support staff to professional status was well known. Even someone with a master's degree from a top university, he said, who'd done well at officer-level work, would not be taken seriously. "The deck is stacked against you there, Beck. Finish your Ph.D. and to hell with them."

Gerald spent half his work life traveling abroad. The other half was spent commuting to New York from a large, comfortable home in Connecticut. Once he'd settled there for the weekend, he explained, he did not want to drag himself back into the city to see me. I had less need for his company on weekday evenings,

though, when he could see me, while my weekends echoed with
loneliness. Not so for Gerald, who filled his weekends with endless yardwork and visits from his handful of grown children. Of
course I could study and practice the piano, but in my late twenties I was embarrassed to go to movies alone, and longed to share
with him my love of theatre, museums, and concerts. Since he
was a man of culture and means, I wondered why our relationship did not warrant some kind of social life—dinners out, the
occasional play or symphony—even if I was much younger?

Though neither of us broached the topic, Gerald made it
known that, having endured a long, contentious marriage to the
alcoholic mother of his children, he did not wish to remarry. One
lonesome weekend my mother called and wasted no time asking,
*What do you have to offer this man that he cannot get elsewhere,
and might indeed be getting when he is away from you?* Though her
situation was less than wonderful in my eyes, she was certain—at
least after his stroke—of Edwin's need for her. How much did
Gerald really need me?

My mother gave up her independence and her cozy scenic
apartment in favor of a house that was wheelchair accessible.
Edwin's home on the golf course was not, and had to be sold. Not
long after she'd found a less upscale but spacious home on Almira
Drive in East Bremerton, and settled in with him, she realized
it was too difficult to care for him alone. Her letters became
brief and rushed. She put Edwin into a deluxe facility outside
of Bremerton for physiotherapy and overnight care. It required
almost all her strength, she wrote, to take him out in the afternoon and keep him mentally stimulated, with an occasional night
spent with her on Almira Drive. After one sleepover she wrote:

> *Any doctor expects to stretch out a hand and
> have some nurse or assistant slap something into
> it. They have no knowledge of how much they
> need to be waited on. Thank goodness most of
> the bed-changing incontinent care through the
> night is over. Tonight was the first in a long time.*

But I had an extra pair of pants on hand and all
was well. Except for cleanup work.

During my annual summer visit I stared in awe at her kitchen calendar. That August, and for months before, her graceful handwriting filled every day's box with reminders of doctors' appointments, specialists to call, prescriptions to fill. Every entry was devoted to Edwin's care, except for one hour on Friday for a wash and set at Mr. Lee's Beauty School. Mom was earning Father Congor's vote for sainthood.

To relieve some of the stress of caring for Edwin, she began attending group meditations. She befriended the young TM teachers who subsisted on poverty wages, living in dilapidated housing under the old Manette Bridge that connected East and West Bremerton. She hosted them and other meditators at buffet vegetarian suppers at her home. Daily meditation and the fellowship of young people created a supportive buffer zone around my mother for the first time since she'd left New Zealand. Mom said she was amazed to feel the weight of Edwin's demands falling away. Even he noticed her newfound equanimity and good cheer. When his condition worsened, he agreed to learn TM in his room at Harrison Hospital in Bremerton.

Late one night in May 1975 my phone rang.

Hello, Becky? I know it's past the time you should be in bed.

"That's okay, Mom. I'm not sleepy."

I wanted you to know that Edwin's vital signs are failing. If they continue at this pace he'll die in a week or two.

"Oh Mummy, I'm sorry. But this had to happen sooner or later."

It's not really his dying that I'm calling about. I've always felt that the death of the body is a natural process. When that's done the person's spirit is free to move on to its next assignment, so to speak.

I waited.

It's just that I know nothing about Navy regulations, death benefits, that sort of thing. I've been so preoccupied with Edwin's day-to-day care, I never thought of it.

"I presume as his widow you'll receive some kind of military pension."

One would think. But today a hospital administrator warned me that the Navy does not give pensions to surviving spouses who haven't been married at least a year.

"Probably some holdover from wartime. Too many young widows to support."

Well, I'm not young. Nor did I marry Edwin for a meal ticket. We've been married eleven months, and he probably won't make it to our first anniversary.

"I'll pray about it, Mummy."

Thank you, dear, but one has to roll with the punches. Sorry I kept you up.

Throughout my life my mother had cautioned: *Be careful what you pray for.* She considered it presumptuous to give Higher Intelligence too many specifics. As a young woman she'd stopped attending the Church of England because, in her experience, it had devolved into a stuffy social venue, where people muttered creeds and prayers they did not bother to enunciate. At Monaco Beach she'd accepted Muriel Ruff's invitation to take me to Methodist Sunday school with her daughter Suzanne, but only to learn something of the Bible. I was never encouraged to join any organized religion. Our family said no prayers before meals or otherwise. Prayer was considered entirely personal, so I was on my own—with just the warning not to pray amiss.

This was one occasion, however, when I believed a specific prayer was fully justified. With due respect to Higher Intelligence, I felt I knew almost as well as He/She that my mother had self-lessly made Captain Madden the center and purpose of her life. I had no qualms asking that Edwin's life be prolonged at least another month—preferably with no increase in his suffering—so that Mom could receive the pension she deserved as his widow.

From the back of a drawer I pulled out the utility candles I'd saved in case there was another New York City blackout, and set them on saucers to burn all night. Kneeling on my bedroom rug to pray, I felt surrounded by an assemblage of benevolent spirits in full support of my intentions before I could utter them. I appealed to God as Father and Mother, to Jesus, and to various saints and spiritual masters that entered my mind. Among them was Maharishi's deceased teacher whom he called Guru Dev. I'd heard from one of the meditators about a TMer who'd miraculously escaped a fatal car crash after crying out to Maharishi for help. Seconds before his vehicle was trapped in the pileup, a slow-motion corridor of time opened up for him, during which he safely maneuvered away from the collision. When this meditator finally got to meet Maharishi and thank him, the yogi replied: "Next time call on Guru Dev. He can come quicker." So I took his advice.

I also asked Papa, Verne, and Uncle Wayne to do whatever they could from wherever they were. This would be the third time my mother, then 66, would be widowed. It seemed right that their spirits would be concerned for her.

The next day, for no apparent reason, Edwin's vital signs leveled off. He lived two more months virtually pain-free, extending the length of his marriage to my mother to a year and one month. I thanked God and all the spirits who'd helped bring this about.

Mom called a few hours after Edwin died. She described how they'd spent a sweet, peaceful afternoon together. He was napping when she went to fetch his favorite lunch, a tunafish sandwich. When she returned he was sleeping just as she'd left him, only, in her words, *his spirit had left its prison.* She said it felt like he was waiting for her to return and meditate with him, as they made their first adjustments to life without each other's physical presence. *There was no need to notify the nursing staff until we had had that time together.*

Afterward, my mother reported, the loneliness and feeling of separation she had dreaded did not materialize. She had a sense of being eased through the mourning period, which she attributed to meditation.

I flew out to be with her for Captain Madden's funeral in August. It was a remarkably peaceful visit. My only record of it is a note I'd kept from Gerald, in which he assured me that he'd watered my plants, collected my mail, and missed me. Two months later, when I was back in New York, Mom got around to reading the names in the funeral's guest book, and noticed that I'd signed it. I'd figured she'd be the only one to read it, so I added, "I love you, Mummy." She wrote that it gave her a *warm feeling* to think of it. I could not help noticing that her comment about this warm feeling stopped short of acknowledging that she believed it was true that I loved her. Nor did she ever mention that my prayers might have contributed to Edwin's miraculous survival past their first wedding anniversary—securing her the captain's pension that would sustain her comfortably for the rest of her life.

When my mother returned to her volunteer job at the Welfare Department, she wrote about the unbelievable reception she got from everyone there—hugs, kisses, astonished looks of genuine delight. She went on about this for awhile, then advised me not to feel any less about myself for having never experienced such popularity. Funny, I hadn't thought less of myself in this way until she drew my attention to it. It would have felt better to be thanked for my prayers, less popular though I was.

At this point, Gerald had become the center of my emotional life. He loved to hear me practice the piano, respected my views on world events, and took an interest in whatever I was studying. He also used my apartment as an occasional dressing room to prepare for black tie events. After work he would change into his tuxedo at my place, downplaying the glamour of these evenings by complaining of boring speeches. He claimed to be doing me a favor not to make me sit through them.

I knew it wasn't the whole story. By not appearing with me he could avoid the gossip of his peers that he was dating a much younger woman of no professional or social status. When he returned to spend the rest of the night with me, he could not hide the glow of exhilaration for having mingled with—and no doubt impressed—another conclave of VIPs. I was proud of his achievements, and how elegant he looked. Still, a sad question arose. Would he have invited me to those events had I been able to complete my Ph.D.? Was I his backstreet woman?

For a few months I tried psychotherapy, which was covered by the RF's medical insurance. The analyst found my circumstances intriguing, but offered no advice. At first he let me choose whether I would sit across from him or lie on a couch staring at the ceiling as I talked. I much preferred to be seated and make eye contact, but after a few sessions he insisted that I use the couch. I found the treatment of no real help compared to meditating twice a day. In the many years that followed, I would remain convinced that meditation gives the mind an opportunity to heal at its own pace, besides releasing the daily stresses of life. Clinical research and my own observations indicate that people who meditate do not age as rapidly as non-meditators. The jury may still be out as to whether meditation is more helpful and curative than psychotherapy. But in my experience, it is.

My mother was relieved when I stopped the shrink sessions. She did not think I needed a therapist to tell me that I was the victim of *entrenched social attitudes*. She also believed that I had *a deep-seated resentment* of her, and that I tended to be *overwhelmed by events which, though painful, were not major tragedies*. She wondered if I was carrying over *some kind of trauma from a past life*. I lacked the self-knowledge then to suggest to her that I'd been traumatized in this life by her nightmarish lectures.

A year after Edwin died Mom visited me in New York and met Gerald. He called for us one evening in a chauffeured limousine and took us to a tony East Side restaurant for a candlelit dinner. When she and I visited the elegant ladies room, Mom murmured, *If I were fifteen years younger I'd go for Gerald myself.* Her tone seemed to imply that with her he'd have been more likely to make a commitment.

I was still in love with Gerald when I turned 30. Given his aversion to marriage and peripatetic career, I entered my spinsterish fourth decade very near despair. Though I was given professional level work at the Foundation, I had no apparent chance of joining its professional staff. I took evening courses to fulfill the requirements for a Ph.D. in comparative literature at NYU, but was a long way from obtaining it. All this contributed to a sense of not achieving much in either love or work.

I'd spoken ominously to Mom about my 30th birthday, to which she responded that this country's obsession with youth was absurd. Age was not something to feel sad about, she insisted, if it came with *increased maturity and expansion of consciousness. We need to say a strong "NO!" to things and conditions that are detrimental. Even if they seemingly overwhelm us, they're doing it without our consent.* Miracles could occur with a strong enough denial of what is bad, she wrote. She reminded me of the fierce *No!* she'd shouted when Johnny, as a toddler, capsized a pan of burning hot fat off the stove, and rather than being scarred for life, got just a bit pink and smiled at her. Her birthday card to me was inscribed: *I'm so grateful our better days are now and in front of us—instead of in the past.*

A year later Gerald was offered the chance to head an international research institute in South America. I was impressed, but wondered if I'd see much of him anymore. Ever so casually, he mentioned that I might accompany him and "possibly" we could be married there.

"And what would I do every day?" I asked, "Go out and pick daisies? What about my doctorate, my chance at a career?"

He looked down in silence, having expected a different response.

I was no longer an ingénue and, unlike Gerald, not fluent in Spanish. Although my doctoral course requirements were nearly finished, I had yet to prepare for the demanding written examinations. If I passed those, I'd have to research, write, and defend a book-length dissertation. What could I do in South America but be an alienated housewife? The man I loved was not asking me to marry him in New York, where our families, friends and colleagues could witness his respect and love for me. In my mind, a South American wedding bore an unpleasant resemblance to Capt. Madden's minimalist marriage to my mother, as though preserving his good Catholic credentials.

Since Gerald had sort of proposed, I dared to ask if he'd clarify one thing about our seven years together—something I would not have considered had my mother not been so blunt about it.

"On your weekends at home in Connecticut, when you were too tired to see me in the city, did you ever go out with other women?"

"Oh, occasionally." He looked weary and slightly annoyed.

"Did you sleep with them?"

"Well, Beck," he said, as though seeking sympathy, "they were much older than you, and it's very difficult to get out of doing what older women expect of a man." He made being unfaithful to me sound like gentlemanly duty!

Mom was right. At least he hadn't asked any of the others to join him in South America. Or had he? Blood rushed to my face. Hard to say which stung the most—rage at his infidelity, or shame at my being so clueless.

"You may not believe this," I said, "but all the time we've been together it never occurred to me that we were not exclusive. I assumed that if you were too tired to come into the city on weekends to be with me, you'd be too tired to go out with someone else." I'd taken him seriously when he'd expressed regret that his past infidelities had contributed to his wife's drinking problem, and heard this as the basis of a decision I'd assumed he had made, not to inflict that kind of pain on anyone else.

His eyes widened, either in surprise or pity. No comment.

"This might be old hat for you, but it changes everything for me."

He did not apologize, nor did he offer to marry me in New York, where I could finish my doctorate. So I broke it off.

Gerald turned down the South American offer and accepted a different position in Washington, D.C. There, I would learn, he dated a woman two years younger than me, who had a Ph.D., a professional position, and a drinking problem.

To compound my dismal romantic situation, I was devastated to lose the professional position at Rockefeller that I'd

worked toward for ten years. I gradually realized that I was joining the ranks of countless others with similar or worse cases of
thwarted careers.

My mother sent me a bottle of Vitamin E, and a bag of des-
sicated liver tablets for their richness in B vitamins, vital to the
nervous system. She enclosed this note in the package:

> *Not that anything ingested will cover the psycho-
> logical impact of poison released by feelings of
> being unfairly treated, lonely, and in general the
> victim of circumstances. The Indian/Buddhist
> doctrine of Karma makes a lot of sense and is
> probably inescapable. In other words we are con-
> tinually for good or ill setting up the conditions
> we find ourselves in, and it is up to us to look for
> the means with which to change them if they're
> something less than we want.*

Blaming oneself, she added, was an erroneous waste of time,
and so was defending one's actions and feelings. This seemed
contradictory. She seemed to say that I'd brought upon myself the
injustice of losing a position I'd spent years working and hoping
for, and by every reasonable criterion had earned. Yet I mustn't
make the mistake of defending my actions and feelings, which
seemed justifiable.

I tried not to cast blame, though the outcome was bitter
proof that the world was hardly a meritocracy. John F. Kennedy
had famously remarked, "Life is unfair." I was one of multitudes
not blessed with outward recognition and career status. Mom's
idea that I'd set myself up for disappointment at the Foundation
was troubling and unjust. An interior voice seemed to whisper
a more positive message: Maybe I was not destined for a career
processing grants supporting other people's research and creativ-
ity. I could do grant-quality work of my own, with or without "professional status."

After Captain Madden's death, his elder son and daughter accused my mother of marrying their father for financial gain. They resented that the fine house they'd grown up in had been sold and the proceeds used to purchase the home now occupied by their stepmother. It meant they could not receive the inheritance he'd promised them. The probate process became so distressing that, seven months after Edwin's death, Mom took another trip Down Under, turning to her New Zealand family for consolation.

Bremerton had a lumberyard and an auto parts shop whose signs had adjustable lettering similar to old-time movie marquees. Rather than announcing sales or new merchandise, they posted pithy maxims that my mother would occasionally inscribe on the backs of envelopes to me. During my end-time at the Foundation, the lumberyard advised: "Forgive your enemies. It bugs them." Across town, the auto parts shop proclaimed: "A bird in the hand can be messy." Both seemed apropos.

CHAPTER THIRTY-TWO

New Home, Old Homeland

Though Mom patiently repeated her mantra and did everything else we'd been taught in the TM program, she admitted that she'd never felt what other meditators called moments of "transcendence." No matter. When it came to acquiring her dream home, she'd surely tapped into what Maharishi Mahesh called Creative Intelligence. From the terrace of the second floor rental unit where she lived before marrying Edwin, she used to gaze down longingly at the boldly designed home with a wraparound deck that projected out over the Washington Narrows' shore. She told a fellow tenant in her building that she'd love to own the place, but it was not for sale. Shortly after Edwin's death, her former neighbor called to report a For Rent sign on the property she'd coveted. Mom grabbed her checkbook, drove over and offered to buy rather than rent it. Reluctant to sell, the owner quoted a rip-off price, which my mother accepted.

Soon I received a rapturous letter, illustrated with an artfully drawn—who knew she had this talent?—ink sketch of my mother's new home. She described the thrill of stepping onto her deck at high tide and looking straight down at the crashing waves. From there she could toss out scraps of bread or leftovers and watch as gulls swooped in from nowhere, shrieking, diving, and catching bits in midair. Through the floor-to-ceiling windows of her living room she could see the Seattle-Bremerton ferries dock and depart, and spot a kingfisher perched on her deck's corner rail. The bird shot out so fast toward its prey, she wrote, that a blink would cause her to miss its takeoff. At other times, a pensive old blue heron chose the same promontory. Its ponderously slow launch left one unsuspecting of the bird's amazing ability to swivel in midair, its wide wings swirling sideways while lowering its long bony legs to brake.

It made her happy, she wrote, to hear the sound of people enjoying themselves as they sailed down the Narrows in fine weather. Sounds of laughter and chatter rose up from the water, crystal clear and filled with "good clean fun." At sunset, she quoted Milton: *The sinking sun is taking leave, and lightly guilds the edge of eve.* From her deck, the sun was gilding the rim of the Olympic Mountains. *The water between this new home of ours and the Warren Avenue Bridge is just rippling with light.*

I was touched that she referred to the place as ours.

On my first visit, I dropped my luggage and stepped out on the deck to immerse myself in the sight and sound of waves pulsing under the boards beneath my feet. Mom handed me a bag of scraps for the gulls. She smiled at my amazement as they swirled, shrieking, and catching most of the bits before they hit the water.

When low tide came, Mom made a wry face and pointed toward the shore, where a gaggle of plump adolescent gulls—as large as their mother—were nipping and screeching at her to be fed. As my mother chuckled knowingly, I wondered whether this amusing scene had a subtext for her. Perhaps a daughter in her thirties, with no marriage prospects and no one else to visit but her mother?

Mom on her deck at mid tide, the Warren Avenue Bridge behind her.

The Christmas after Edwin died, my mother visited me in New York, where I tried my best to overcome her aversion to the city that she shared with my brother. I was proud to watch her lean over the mezzanine's balustrade at City Center—where I'd splurged on first row seats—enthralled to see the Alvin Ailey dancers perform their famous "Revelations" to live Gospel music.

That day, we'd walked arm in arm, staring up at the enormous Christmas tree in Rockefeller Center, and down at skaters in its sunken ice rink. Johnny and his children were with his wife's family in Connecticut, for years Flavia had celebrated the holiday with friends at Lake Stevens, and Uncle Wayne had ferried into his next realm of existence. Mom and I tried to make the most of being alone together in this teeming metropolis, remnants of the small family who'd spent their first Christmases on the berry farm, then at Monaco Beach and at Verne's succession of state parks. I was sad that Mom had been widowed three times, whereas I'd never had a serious reciprocal relationship. As we clung to each other keeping loneliness at bay, there was no further mention of her dislike for New York City.

Back in Bremerton, Mom was inspired by Julie Harris's portrayal of Emily Dickinson in "The Belle of Amherst," a public television special. *What an incredible gift your Emily had!* During the performance she jotted down two verses: "Nature must be too young to feel, Or many years too old," and "Parting is all we know of Heaven, And all we need of Hell." At first, she admitted, she found no sense in the line "Parting is all we know of Heaven…" It had seemed to her *a case of the magic of words losing track of meaning.* Later she wondered whether the poet meant that *in our human state we can't hang on to any blissful experience forever, so parting is inevitable.*

I could not comprehend the sadness of my mother's long history of partings—from Douglas Elliott, Geoff Whisker, her father, my father, Ray Draine, Verne McCormick, and Edwin Madden. Six years earlier, when I had no choice but to leave Columbia's doctoral program, Mom had not wanted to read my master's essay on Dickinson, perhaps assuming that no American poet could equal her beloved Keats and Wordsworth. Now she was determined to read all of Emily's poems at the library. *And how about sending that paper of yours?* She asked me to remind her of a poem I loved—*something about a little bird, and hope.*

I pulled down my volume of Dickinson's collected works and wrote it out for her:

> Hope is the thing with feathers—
> That perches in the soul—
> And sings the tune without the words—
> And never stops—at all—
>
> And sweetest—in the Gale—is heard—
> And sore must be the storm—
> That could abash the little Bird
> That kept so many warm—

I've heard it in the chillest land—
And on the strangest Sea—
Yet, never, in Extremity,
It asked a crumb—of Me.

The thought of that poem sustained me at times. Someday, I promised myself, I would memorize "The Chambered Nautilus" by Oliver Wendell Holmes, a favorite of hers that might have pulled her through some dark times.

Recently she'd met a woman who was studying calligraphy, and said she would commission her to write out a beautiful passage from Keats that she quoted from memory:

A thing of beauty is a joy forever:
Its loveliness increaseth—
It can never fade into nothingness,
But still will keep a bower quiet for us
And a sleep full of sweet dreams, and peace,
And quiet breathing.

She told me to hang the framed poem in my bathroom, of all places, but it never arrived. Instead, for the Valentine's Day after her visit, she shipped me a compact Hoover vacuum cleaner. It was still working 35 years later, perhaps due to infrequent use, when I donated it to the Goodwill.

In 1977, when my mother was ready to branch out from her state of widowhood after Edwin's death, two women she did not know very well invited her to join them for a road trip around England, Scotland and Wales. At first it seemed a great way to share expenses and have company on a journey to her ancestral homeland, and auspicious that Roberta, who'd invited her and offered to do all the driving, was a retired English teacher. Roberta was tall, stout, never married, and bossy. Maureen, equally rotund but placid, was a housewife whose husband seemed to disappear in Roberta's presence. For the entire trip the two large women occupied the front seat of a compact rental car, leaving my mother and Maureen's short husband to sit in the back with obstructed views.

At the time Mom gave no hint of the alienation she'd suffered on this trip. She'd mailed me a series of upbeat, awe-filled postcards from Westminster Abbey, the Tower of London, Stonehenge, the field where the Battle of Hastings was fought. She penned her first letter from England sitting across from Cleopatra's Needle—*How incredible!*—on the Thames Embankment, not far from a monument to Arthur Sullivan—*of Gilbert and Sullivan fame!*—and a statue of Robert Burns, whose immortal lines she'd recited throughout my childhood (à propos of my behavior): "*O would some Power the gift He gie us, To see ourselves as others see us.*"

Despite having to pinch herself that she was *really in England, really in England,* she noted that their first hotel in London was so shabby and uncomfortable that they decamped in search of tolerable lodgings. On their way out Mom noticed a small plaque: "Benjamin Franklin lived here in 1703." The furnishings may not have changed.

Not mentioning to her companions that a former fiancé had once trained there, my mother persuaded them to visit the famous Kew Gardens. None of them, she reported, had reckoned on the Gardens' vastness. *The others gave out, but I just stayed for hours.* After her death I would better understand why.

When they drove on toward Wales, Mom said tears flowed from her eyes when she first set foot on Welsh soil, as though her genes resonated with the land of her ancestors. She sought out the old village church where her grandmother, Mary Davies Williams, had been baptized and married. Mom's grandmother was legendary in the family for having realized that the Williams' morale was caving in as badly as their land, which had been undermined—literally—by the coal industry. The Williams men were demoralized, drinking heavily, with no chance of compensation for their losses. As the story went, this little country woman who'd never set foot outside her village, sold the generations-old collection of pewter she'd received in her dowry and used the proceeds to buy passage from the port of Cardiff for her eight children, her husband and his brothers—on a ship bound for the colony of New Zealand. There the Williams men could acquire land and return to their gentlemen's occupation of sheep farming.

As a child I'd heard the story of Mary Williams' tragic death. Despite her heroic efforts, her husband and his brothers continued drinking in their new land. They were hung over one morning when she asked them to harness a horse to the buggy she would take to market. When she climbed into the seat and signaled for the horse to depart, the animal's forward jolt flipped the unhitched rig back like a catapult. Her body was thrown up and back in an arc, coming down headfirst, which broke her skull, killing her instantly. It took her death to sober the Williams men and motivate them to apply themselves to the opportunities she'd made possible for them in New Zealand.

My grandfather, Morgan Williams, was one of Mary's sons, who would eventually need another strong Williams woman to convince him to stop drinking.

Mom was proud of her courageous grandmother, but made it clear that her own mother, Alice, née Evans, was only half Welsh, the other half being English, a Manning. Mannings, she said grimly, were known for their stubborn, humorless nature. She would occasionally accuse me of having too much Manning blood—though she had twice as much. I once asked Mom why she never spoke of her mother. She responded reluctantly—in a tone of let's not talk about this ever again—that she was ashamed of her mother for allowing herself to get fat, lying in bed reading books most of the day, and leaving her, Rachel, to manage the household at Mangaotawhito. She confided that she'd wanted to look up to her mother and respect her, and vowed that her own children would never have to feel ashamed of her.

From Wales, Mom wrote that her grandfather's birthplace, the village Gabalifa, was now engulfed by the city of Cardiff. There she managed to find her grandparents' church, St. Hilary's,

...a little gem of a church with a stone baptismal font and arch over the altar dating back to Norman days. Like all these old churches its yard was full of gravestones so old one could not read the names. I had a delightful talk with the vicar who brought out his old old parish books and found the actual records of not only my grandparents' marriage but my grandmother's baptism. He gave me duly certified copies of both events as a memento!

Alas, I never located these documents among my mother's papers. Why were they not among her other precious mementos? Had she given them to my brother? I would never know. When I got to Wales and found the same little old church, there was no vicar on duty. How I wished I could have shared my mother's experience. All I managed to do was tell my companion what I'd learned from my mother—that the stone baptismal font and arch over the altar had been there since the Norman Conquest.

CHAPTER THIRTY-THREE

A Dark Stretch of Path

After Captain Madden's death, my mother and I set out more or less together on the Transcendental Meditation movement's path to enlightenment. Belonging to it gave us a new bond, and fellowship with a wide range of spiritual seekers. On our opposite coasts, we faithfully meditated twice a day and took occasional "rounding courses" to deepen our knowledge of the teachings of Maharishi Mahesh Yogi. Regular meditation promised to clear away layers of stress, make us more calm and alert, and increase our chances of spiritual awakening.

TM retreats took place in secluded facilities rented from private country schools vacant during academic breaks, monasteries serving as venues for contemplative getaways, off-season resorts and the like. Participants did "rounds" of traditional yoga positions and stretches, breathing exercises, and meditation in their rooms. Interspersed with rounds were gatherings of all attendees to view grainy videotapes of the movement's founder as he responded to wide-ranging questions on meditation, the nature of enlightenment, and impediments to achieving it. Each video screening was followed by a discussion led by young, personable TM instructors, with varying degrees of skill handling an unpredictable array of questions and comments about normal and strange personal experiences.

Rounding courses could evoke bizarre and ineffable sensations—the result of what TMers called "unstressing." Sites of old injuries could reactivate vestiges of physical and emotional pain that would make themselves felt before fading away, as if to complete an unfinished healing process. Some participants' skin would break out in rashes, then clear up, leaving them with glowing complexions. Buried trauma, rage, humiliations and frustrations could resurface—some tied to specific memories, others passing in a blur of sensations that the mind was sloughing off. It was my experience—shared by many—that meditation provides the mind a safe space to clean its own house.

On a rounding course in Oregon, my mother wrote that she'd felt a terrible piercing pain in her side, as though she'd been shot with an arrow. She witnessed it, however, through a sort of protective observational scrim, and as she continued meditating the pain disappeared without a trace. *It must have come from a previous life,* she surmised. At the time I did not think to ask whether that searing pain might have come from a great wound in her present life—possibly when Douglas Elliott's mother screamed, "Get that woman out of my house!" and her spineless sweetheart had obeyed.

We were instructed not to dwell on thoughts or feelings that came up in meditation. We were told that the origin of, or our emotional or physical reaction to these marks of stress, was irrelevant. What mattered was cleansing our consciousness of the residue of suffering and harmful actions or thoughts, as we gradually cleared the path toward what Maharishi called Cosmic Consciousness, a sort of entry stage to enlightenment.

After a few years Mom and I were eligible to receive TM's "advanced techniques" to enhance our mantras. These seemed to be extensions of our mantra's initial syllables, meant to deepen our meditation and bring us closer to Cosmic Consciousness. The most advanced TM program at the time was training for the *siddhis,* a Sanskrit word meaning "perfections". The program's content was carefully selected by Maharishi Mahesh Yogi from the yoga sutras of Patanjali, an ancient yogi master—*sutra* being Sanskrit for thread or stitch, root of the word *suture*.

So-called "flying" was one of the *siddhis* taught in the TM Siddhi program. After we'd established a comfort level meditating with our mantras, *siddhi* trainees were supposed to insert, or stitch, specific ideas or commands into their consciousness, such as the refinement or improvement of the five senses. Of all the sutras that constituted the TM Siddhi program, the one for levitation or weightlessness was most subject to sensationalism. Maharishi insisted that under no circumstances were TMers to show their "flying" abilities to the non-meditating public. Still, news articles emerged, with fuzzy photos. Meditators who took to it more readily found themselves—though sitting cross-legged on the floor—able to briefly pop up an inch or so and zip through the air to land a few feet from where they'd taken off. At TM centers and retreats, "flying" rooms were equipped with foam rubber mats to cushion such landings. Those trained in the Siddhis were called Siddhas, and could "fly" at home on individual foam pads attached by straps that crossed their legs. I suspect that plenty TM- trained Siddhas did not achieve lift-off, and got better results from the sutras that focused on refining the five senses.

The goal was to enter a level of consciousness that permitted one to transcend gravity and fly about unimpeded. To my knowledge this was never achieved in the West, though I heard that some meditators, in lotus or half-lotus position, could lift off and traverse up to ten feet. When asked why so few TMers managed to fly, Maharishi reportedly answered, "Too much gravity." Perhaps a sly insinuation that Western consciousness in general was leaden. Hermit yogis in the Himalayas were reputed to levitate and fly around easily, but outsiders were forbidden to observe them.

In the late seventies word got around that the first Westerner, a Canadian TM teacher, had achieved enlightenment while on an advanced training course in Switzerland. This man, whom I'll call Reggie Cantwell, had been addressed by Maharishi Mahesh Yogi in a group discussion as "the enlightened man from Canada," in response to some especially discerning comments Cantwell had made during the course. News of his unprecedented recognition by Maharishi preceded Cantwell's return home to British Columbia. But rather than a congratulatory welcome or homecoming celebration, most of his fellow TM teachers greeted him with poorly veiled envy and resentment. They were stunned when their former colleague accused them of being "demonic" for this reaction. If they'd been true seekers of enlightenment, Cantwell asserted, they would have been eager to learn from his experience. This won him instant *persona non grata* status among TM authorities.

Unsurprisingly, reports of Cantwell's reception aroused sympathy and interest among more independent-minded meditators. He developed a renegade following of loyal friends and fellow TMers in Canada and meditators in the States who wanted a perspective on what being enlightened would feel like in today's Western world. By the time my circle of New York meditators heard about him, his informal gatherings in British Columbia had evolved into seminars that charged attendance fees to cover their expenses. One or two had already taken place in Fairfield, Iowa, a short distance from Maharishi International University, the North American hub of the TM organization. A New York meditator I respected attended one of those seminars, and recommended Cantwell's lively, more interactive approach to enlightenment. I was intrigued, and traveled to Fairfield for Cantwell's next seminar, where we were amazed to see grim-looking people with video cameras filming us as we entered the place Cantwell's team had rented for the occasion. It seemed they were there to intimidate or identify us as subversives within the TM movement. Their subterfuge made us all the more determined to give "the enlightened man from Canada" a fair hearing.

For several years, most people who attended Cantwell's seminars found Reggie to be consistently challenging, charming, and convincing. I encouraged my mother to try a seminar in Seattle or Victoria, B.C., and we found it exciting to have an inside track on something spiritually bold and promising. We were both repelled by what sounded like TM's provincial rivalry. Separately and occasionally together, we attended about two Cantwell seminars a year, for six years. Steady practice of TM and the Siddhis had not bridged the emotional gap between us, and I secretly hoped that the first Western enlightened man would identify the source of our difficulty.

Reggie was handsome and agile, with the mobile face of a thespian. His mild, resonant voice could bolster as easily as cut someone down. Before teaching TM, he'd earned a college degree in theatre arts and was licensed to teach in the Canadian public schools. Widely read, he seemed knowledgeable about ethics and psychological theories, attuned to world events, and conversant with Western and Eastern religious teachings. He never spoke of his father, but said his mother was a psychotherapist who did not meditate.

Seminar participants brought some of their deepest problems to him. They approached the microphone with some trepidation, but trusted Reggie's judgment as he probed their feelings and circumstances with laser precision. Eventually, individual trips to the microphone evolved from occasional personal explorations—either self-initiated or arising from group discussions—to the seminars' most climactic moments. They grew to be called "confrontations." When someone was "confronted" at the mic, Cantwell would expose the qualities he perceived as "demonic" in that person's thoughts, feelings, and relationships. He distinguished these from thoughts and emotions arising from "pure feeling." The latter were always by nature truthful, non-hostile, and not limited to self-interest.

Unfortunately, as the only supposedly enlightened person at these gatherings, Reggie became the final arbitrator of what stemmed from goodness or malevolence.

If people had misgivings about his insights, they either deferred to his judgment or stopped attending the seminars. Two friends of mine left after a few hours; others stayed, withholding judgment in order to learn more about enlightenment.

For over five years I did not go to the microphone, nor did I avoid doing so. I was not afraid that Reggie would expose something ghastly in my psyche. My deepest conundrum was the impasse between my mother and me, the often concealed but ever present weapon she held against me: that I did not love her, despite all evidence. That kind of problem never seemed to come up in Cantwell's seminars. Still, I was an active contributor to the group discussions, and Reggie seemed to respect my working toward a doctorate in comparative literature.

Neither did my mother approach the microphone. Reggie was impressed with her reservoir of wisdom and extensive knowledge of English poetry. Since she was apparently his oldest seminar participant, he was deferential and pleased to be taken seriously by her.

Cantwell looked surprised when I began attending the seminars with a slightly younger man, a gifted musician in the doctoral program in composition at the Juilliard School. Half Asian and half European, Anton Lee had been a popular rock musician in his country, but wanted to prove himself as a serious musician. He was well on his way, studying under two renowned composers, Elliott Carter and Vincent Persichetti. Reggie, however, acted as though he had Anton's number in a different field of expertise.

One day, while he was elaborating on how people conceal various forms of demonic motivation, he looked over at Anton and asked the rest of us, "On a scale of one to ten, how much do you think Anton knows about evil?" Some guessed five. A few wagered up to seven. I thought maybe three.

Cantwell turned to Anton, who was sitting Sphinx-like in the last row. "So," he asked with a half smile, "how extensive is your knowledge of the demonic, Anton?"

My new boyfriend kept silent, perhaps mildly amused. Reggie answered for him: "Ten, eh?" Surveying the audience, he glanced back at Anton, whose ineffable expression suggested a faint glint of pride.

Then Reggie shot me a look that said: Watch out with this guy. I thought it was odd for him to be so blunt about an elegant young man of few words who expressed himself mostly through music. But I was infatuated and not yet acquainted with his dark side.

Anton and I stayed at my mother's house for a couple days after we'd all attended a seminar in Victoria, B.C. Treating my mother with what could be taken for traditional Asian respect for elders, Anton, by some sinister intuition, sensed that my mother would not defend me if he were to falsely accuse me of deceitful intentions—the details of which I do not remember, as they were far too convoluted in their imagined malevolence for someone of my slap-the-truth-in-someone's-face-like-a-wet-dishrag nature. I was horrified to have to defend myself, but my mother clearly enjoyed watching him reduce me to spluttering in shock before I could put together a coherent response.

He and my mother seemed to relish a devilish alliance of sorts—she admiring his performance as master accuser, cool and calculating in the unreal enormity of his attacks. I got hoarse trying to disprove him, and was dismayed by my mother's gloating silence. Why had she not, in fairness, mentioned to Anton that in her experience I was an honest person whose acts and intentions deserved a measure of trust and willingness to reserve judgment?

Till then, the only person who'd ever come to my defense, I would realize later, had been my mother's sister Gwenda, who'd never met me. She'd been concerned enough about how my mother spoke about me to write me a letter insisting that she knew in her bones I was a good person.

A decade or so after Anton and I had split up, we crossed paths in my neighborhood, and ended up having a frank conversation. Looking back on our relationship, he made a telling remark that sounded weirdly disappointed. No matter how much I'd argued with him, he recalled, my anger never became "dark." The term gave me pause. It moved me to ask if his motives had been dark when he'd falsely accused me at my mother's place, forcing me to defend my motives and integrity in front of her? No answer. Reggie might have been right about Anton's knowledge of the demonic.

I mention this better-left-forgotten episode because my mother referred to it a few weeks before her death.

CHAPTER THIRTY-FOUR

Changing the Acoustics

Those not involved with the Cantwell seminars might have suspected that Reggie's followers had been drawn into a personality cult. Several of those closest to him did eventually share the costs of living in a picturesque old three-story mansion in Victoria, though it was not run as a commune. Those who lived farther afield, like my mother and the group of New York meditators to which I belonged, considered ourselves independent of mind and disinclined toward hero worship. Most of us still took TM rounding courses, fitting in an occasional Cantwell seminar if we had time, and remained open to learning about enlightenment from a range of sources. Reggie even joked about religious cults whose members were duped by egomaniacs.

Still, there was something dicey about Reggie's perceived authority over others. Though he'd been called "the enlightened man from Canada" once by Maharishi, when word got back to Mahesh that Cantwell was running seminars of his own, the TM founder-guru rescinded his appellation and made clear his disapproval. Some took the news of Maharishi's reversal with a grain of salt, as perhaps suggesting internecine rivalries and an overblown threat to the global revenues of the TM organization, whose initiation fees, meditation retreats, teacher training courses, and charges for so-called advanced meditation techniques generated considerable income. Cantwell's market share, so to speak, was minuscule, so why the fuss?

Most of Reggie's followers did not question his methods or motives. They were glad he was willing to share his insights as a Western enlightened thinker and observer, and felt he had a right to charge reasonable fees for the rental of facilities for his seminars, travel costs and living expenses. They may have also assumed that an enlightened person would avoid the bad karma of taking advantage of others.

Of course, any kind of spiritual or intellectual trust is empowering. Without the armaments of humility and constant self-questioning, it is catnip to negative forces. Legend has it that Francis of Assisi, besides being able to converse with birds and other animals, could actually see devils. The saint observed that hardly any devils wasted their time at the local marketplace—already a cauldron of greed and corruption—and instead prowled in droves around the walls of the monastery, constantly targeting the virtues of his brother monks.

With few sensing anything amiss, the most powerful moments in Cantwell's seminars began to change in character. In his early gatherings, participants would bring up a difficulty in their personal lives, and Reggie would invite them to step up to the microphone for a more in-depth dialogue with him. He would then probe for any lingering resentment, anger, envy or other destructive feelings he perceived as demonic—which he defined as untrue to the individual's goodness, honesty, and respect for others. Over time, ominously, these times at the mic became known as "confrontations" rather than dialogues. As Cantwell ever more boldly accused people of being demonic, their trips to the mic began to resemble—for lack of a less fraught term—exorcisms.

I was at a seminar in Canada when Reggie responded to a rather inept question from a young American with an abrupt declaration that the guy's spaced-out passivity was demonic. Within seconds his naturally pale, boyish face flushed dark red as his features engorged into brutish contortions. His body seemed to inflate as though occupied from within by a large, hostile beast. Shocked by the transformation, the seminar audience was pulled into a grueling spiritual battle. As a community of spiritual seekers, we were determined to help this man— by means of our combined will and intense prayer—to drive out this grotesque, malevolent entity that was clearly alien to his nature. At the moment when our shared energies felt most keenly focused on opposing this hostile spirit, it was gone. At once, the atmosphere around us seemed filled with fresh air and sunlight. The exhausted young man's face and body resumed their natural form—bathed with relief, gratitude, and a new chance at innocence.

It would have made a believer out of almost anyone. But a believer in what? God's power over evil, or Cantwell's ability to invoke demonic forces in order to play with his own power? This hindsight did not occur to me for some time.

I was at a two-week seminar in Victoria, B.C., when Reggie, for no apparent reason, ordered me to step up to the microphone. I was surprised, because nothing sinister was at work in my psyche at the time. For me the seminars were another form of higher education, a chance to learn how to transcend the bounds of my less than fulfilling life—all the more enjoyable because I didn't have to write term papers or worry about grades. Though helpful in relieving stress, the practice of TM and Reggie's seminars did not resolve the tensions between my mother and me, but at least we could share these activities occasionally. Mom was not at this seminar, however.

Being called upon for no obvious reason aroused some of that feeling of entrapment from the days of my mother's lectures. I had no illusions that what she'd claimed was my *Achilles heal*— my relationship with her—was a thing of the past. Reggie, however, knew little of our history. If he were really enlightened he might have more carefully exposed that vein of terror.

Any hesitation on my part would signal reluctance to let Reggie identify whatever was demonic in me, so I stepped right up to the mic.

242

Perhaps I had a look of dismay that betrayed me, for Reggie skipped his usual search and discovery phase. Offering no specifics, he said my frame of mind was demonic, and spoke in a manner I had not seen him employ with others. If I did not change, he threatened rather like a Mob Godfather, I'd have to leave the seminar.

"What'll it be, Rebecca? Stay here with your friends, or take the next plane back to New York, alone?"

I was perplexed. Why didn't Reggie identify my problem first, as he'd done with everyone else I'd seen at the mic? Where was the revelatory insight that demonstrated his ability as an enlightened man to see the inmost intentions of other intelligent people? Instead, he took a cheap shot, using his power to expel me from the seminar—and threw in some fear-mongering, in my potential shame and embarrassment if I had to leave my friends and return alone to New York.

Not focusing on the shabbiness of his threat, I tried to get by on his terms.

What could I say to convince everyone I'd had an insight into my personal evil? Sure, I had my own rap sheet of sins— envy of naturally thin girls, disgust at my own pudgy-from-birth body, risking ill health by depriving myself of needed sleep, taking chances with men who had no serious interest in me. Not exactly criminal, but hardly free of inequity. Then there was the problem of loving my mother but having to protect myself from her lectures by withdrawing into stoic silence. And though the era of her endless rants was over, I strongly suspected that her recurrent accusations that I did not love her did not arise from honest motherly love. When Reggie called me to the microphone none of my personal sins felt bad enough to justify my being there. So I decided to try something vague enough to be indisputable.

"It's not what I've done that's the problem," I said flatly. "It's what I've thought." It was general enough to cover a lot of bases. I hoped it would work.

It did all too easily. The audience gasped. I had an immediate visceral sensation that friends as well as relative strangers were recalibrating—downward—their estimation of my character. Reggie sat back, evidently satisfied.

Then came pangs of conscience. My statement shocked the other participants, but I knew it had been less than honest. Did I have thoughts bad enough to qualify as demonic? Wasn't it Reggie's job to help identify them? I'd dug a deep hole for myself, not wanting to disappoint Reggie and lose my credibility in the seminars.

At the mic, part of me hoped that Reggie could provide some extraordinary insight into my psyche that I was meant to gain from him. Another part of me knew that I'd thrown him a fuzz ball and was curious how the supposedly enlightened Western man would catch it.

"Okay, Rebecca. We'll take a break now and see how you are when we return."

What? He wasn't going to shed any light on my allegedly demonic state of mind? I could return to my seat with no group effort to drive out an evil spirit? Reggie could have confronted me—which I deserved—for not being truer to my own standard of honesty.

Fortunately, I'd always trusted in a Higher Source of enlightenment than Reggie's, so I stayed behind and prayed that the Holy Spirit would release me from whatever was evil in my thoughts. And if that wasn't possible, please not let me be victimized by it.

After the break Reggie did not ask me back to the mic. "How goes it, Rebecca? Had a breakthrough?" Smiling omnisciently, he said, "You look fine to me."

I'll admit to some relief that I hadn't been forced to reveal the nature of my therapy during the break. My prayer had not been a breakthrough but an act, done countless times before, of total reliance on God's mercy. My conscience, however, did not let me off the hook. It took years to realize that I'd failed to respect myself enough to challenge Reggie in this encounter. I'd sold myself short by making something up to sound acceptable, rather than asking Reggie to identify what was demonic about my state of mind that would justify his ordering me up to the mic.

It might have deterred him from doing more damage to others.

Unlike all my previous experiences at Cantwell's seminars, this encounter planted a seed of suspicion. Till then there'd flourished a genuine atmosphere of fellowship, honesty and discernment among the participants, whether or not a seminar was in session. They produced a high quality of what Reggie called "acoustics." At their best, his gatherings fostered the kind of honesty that, perhaps, my mother and the contemporaries of her youth had sought in their New Zealand branch of the Oxford Group. Whether in a seminar or during our free time, an insincere statement resounded with bell-like clarity. As did the truth.

My clearest experience of these acoustics occurred when Mom and I were attending an earlier, one-week seminar in Victoria. We shared a suite in a bed-and-breakfast place where several other New York meditators were staying. One morning Mom went to breakfast ahead of me, and sat at a table with my friends Karen and Brian. As Karen told me later, the three were chatting casually when, apropos of nothing, my mother announced: *Becky does not love me.* The conversation stopped, as she and Brian both registered the statement as untrue, if not dishonest. "Rachel," Karen replied, "it's obvious to anyone who knows Becky that she loves you very much." Brian concurred. My mother, it seemed to them, was neither pleased nor reassured to hear this. She sat there silent, pokerfaced, and soon left.

Other friends at this seminar mentioned that, when I was not around, my mother had made similar comments to them. They were disturbed and felt there was something disloyal in the way she spoke about me, going so far as to say they could not imagine their own mothers speaking like that about them. One was so concerned that he asked my mother if she actually loved me.

Strangely enough, at that time there were no discernable hostilities going on between Mom and me. What she would later describe as her *nightmare monologues* had ended by the time I'd finished college. When I was in graduate school she'd rescinded the F she'd given me as a daughter when I was in high school. But here I was in my mid thirties, and behind my back she seemed to be trying to betray my integrity as her daughter in the eyes of my friends, and perhaps others who didn't know me. I didn't try to name it, but I sensed ill will in my mother's statements about me. Meditation had not disarmed it, nor had it been exposed by Reggie's perceptions of the demonic.

The end of my involvement with the Cantwell seminars came during Reggie's last appearance in New York, September 1986, at the Essex House on Central Park South. My friend Brian had invited his new girlfriend, Margie, a devout Christian unfamiliar with TM or Eastern spiritual traditions. When Margie asked Reggie how the pursuit of enlightenment related to Christian values, he lost all propriety. Not bothering to explain the seminar's custom of having people step up to the microphone to be "confronted" in order to explore personal problems and expose whatever might be evil in them, Reggie peered at the newcomer and said, "Your question, Margaret, happens to be demonic."

Margie blanched. Brian sat speechless beside her. He should have come to her defense, I thought, but since he did not and was my friend, I tried to help out.

"She asked a valid question, Reggie," I interjected. "Why don't you answer it instead of calling her demonic?"

Annoyed with the lack of deference in my tone, he sneered, "Rebecca, you do realize that you're doing the equivalent of shooting yourself in the face with a squirt gun?" Glancing across the room, he declared, "I'm a fighter, you know."

"So am I," I muttered, "if need be."

Reggie stared at me with an expression of surprise, suspicion and disdain.

By coincidence, Reggie had been exploring in the seminar his newfound appreciation of the teachings of Jesus. A question flashed across my mind, which I put to him: "Do you think Jesus would have spoken to me the way you just did?"

In seconds the acoustics of the seminar changed. Reggie found himself on defense, at an uncharacteristic loss for words.

"If you don't like the way I handle things, Rebecca," he snapped, "you know where the door is."

Reggie glowered as I stood up amidst the rows of blank, stunned faces. Their silence engulfed me as I reached for my coat and left the room. I could hear my own pulse as I padded down the plush carpeted corridor toward the elevator. Exiting the Essex House onto Central Park South, I felt comforted to join the flux of unenlightened pedestrians. Redfaced but unnoticed, I strode toward Columbus Circle, observing the fringe of pigeon droppings atop the gilded monument to those who'd drowned on a long forgotten ship, the Maine. It wasn't Cosmic Consciousness, but nonetheless reassuring, to be on familiar pavement, heading home. My pulse was back to normal as I passed Lincoln Center, turned left on my street, entered my building and exchanged nods with the desk attendant.

Within an hour the silence in my apartment was broken by someone calling from an early model car phone. It was Gary, one of Reggie's most devoted American followers, who'd been with him since the first Cantwell seminar in Fairfield, Iowa. He was driving back to Pennsylvania with his wife Marilyn. They'd sat near me in the Essex House.

"Becky, Marilyn and I want you to know that we are with you." Gary's voice wavered in and out on the car phone. "When you spoke up we were afraid to say anything. But after you left we started hearing Reggie differently. He was the one playing the fool, not you. The whole seminar fell apart." He told me not to be upset. "We're sorry you left before we could back you up."

All I could say was thanks, it meant a lot to me. They'd never called me before. I was touched they'd taken the trouble to ask Information for my number.

A few months later, in early 1987, a British Columbia newspaper printed a muckraker-style exposé of Cantwell's seminars. He was cast as a cult leader who'd offended the TM movement by calling himself enlightened. The article may have mentioned some improper overtures I'd heard that Reggie had made to a few female seminar participants, and it probably interviewed some disgruntled former seminar attendees who'd been accused of being demonic. I did not see the article, but word traveled from Reggie's former Canadian friends that after it was published he'd sold the house given to him and his wife by her parents. They said he'd kept all the proceeds and moved to eastern Canada, leaving his wife penniless.

I later read that some Eastern spiritual masters do not believe even the most disciplined devotees can achieve a steady state of enlightenment. In their view, one can always descend from elevated levels of awareness and insight to imperfect states, especially when swayed by selfish desires. Reggie might have experienced a flash of enlightenment while training in Switzerland with Mahesh. But he did not remain close to this master teacher, to make sure he could sustain that level of consciousness. Back in Canada, surrounded by admiring friends, then in the seminars they helped him to organize, he was tempted to enjoy having power over others, judging them as good or evil with impunity. Toward the end of his popularity, he'd tried to destroy the engagement of a long-term seminar participant and his fiancée, and abandoned his own beautiful, devoted wife. He'd accused relatively innocent people of serious evil, myself perhaps included.

How strange, I would ponder, that my mother and I had witnessed a phenomenon not unlike my father's break with the Theosophists in British Columbia, under the perfidious leadership of Brother XII.

After the collapse of the Cantwell seminars, my mother and I came upon the teachings of Dom John Main, a Benedictine monk who espoused a form of meditation closely linked with the Judeo-Christian tradition. There were no fees for secret initiation ceremonies or advanced techniques, just a basic mantra available to all, and an emphasis on the healing capacity of mindfulness as a form of prayer. Like TM, this organization was international in scope and held meditation retreats, but my mother and I did not attend one together. For us, meditation and prayer returned to the private sphere.

CHAPTER THIRTY-FIVE

Closing a Deal

In June of 1978 my brother was awarded the United States Air Medal for the rescue of seven Greek seamen from an oil tanker, the Argo Merchant, that ruptured in a violent Atlantic storm the night of December 16, 1976. Amidst 20-foot waves and 40-knot oil-splattering winds, facing certain death if a fragment of the wreck were to fly up and damage his propeller, Johnny switched gears deftly back and forth, swinging his helicopter down pendulum-style to hover near enough to the pitching deck to evacuate three men, and repeated the perilous maneuver on a second trip to save four more. Depositing them all on the Coast Guard cutter that had called for his help was no mean feat, as that vessel's deck was tossing dangerously. He'd made these forays leaning barefaced out the side of his cockpit in order to see, as his windshield was coated with oil. The medal's citation acknowledged "Lieutenant Commander Painter's innovative actions, expert aeronautical skill and valor throughout this mission…in keeping with the highest traditions of the United States Coast Guard."

Johnny put the medal in a drawer. I didn't hear about it until Mom sent me a copy of a book about the disaster that described his role in the crew's rescue.

Decades later I would learn that my brother's heroism had fulfilled a fortuneteller's prophecy before he was born.

The award won him a promotion to Commander and elevation to Deputy Director of Flight Safety for the Coast Guard, a desk job in Washington, D.C. By then his marriage was shaky, his wife refused to make the move from Cape Cod to join him, and they decided to divorce. The luster of his new position faded quickly. Though he did not confide in me, I suspected he'd been boxed in by the Director of Flight Safety, who stole or brushed off the new second-in-command's ideas, or feared being outperformed by him, or all of the above. Johnny had so little to do that he enrolled in a master's degree program in management relations, sponsored by the Guard.

It took him awhile to convince his new sweetheart, Nancy—a divorced nurse and skilled amateur sailor who'd been content to share indefinite living arrangements—to marry him. Though I hadn't been invited to the wedding, any feelings that I'd missed the wonder of this occasion evaporated when I saw the photo Mom had framed on her dressing table. There was Johnny in his officer's uniform, bursting with joy and pride in the woman he'd chosen—freely, this time—to share the rest of his life. The photo's color faded over the years, but the radiance of my brother's joy did not.

They were newlyweds when Johnny invited me to visit them in a leafy Maryland suburb of D.C. When the couple picked me up at Union Station, the first thing I noticed was how tender and vulnerable he was with her. From the back seat I overheard the conclusion of their tête-à-tête over an auto repair bill.

"Those guys are all crooks!" he yelped. "What do they care?"

"John darling, you have a right, like any customer, to question the charges. Maybe they made a mistake. No big deal." Serenely confident, Nancy murmured, "I'm sure you'll settle the matter easily." My brother's disposition morphed from futile pessimism into the mindset of a seeker of justice. I had to smile. Nancy had his number, having sensed that beneath the officer's garb lurked the occasional timidity of a once scrawny little boy. She'd deftly restored him to the stalwart persona he'd earned by risking his life to save others.

There was one problem in their marriage that he never divulged. The damage had been done when we learned about Nancy's bouts of depression, when nothing could cheer her up, including his irresistible—to others—sense of humor. Perhaps he'd been too bewildered to tell anyone, or ashamed that the woman he loved so helplessly was capable of shutting him out, commanding him to stay away from her. I'd seen for myself that Johnny's childlike tender heart was at her mercy. My deepest intuition was that the cold abyss of rejection he'd been thrown into at the hellish extreme of her mood swings—and endured without seeking help—dealt a mortal blow.

In 1983 they'd been married two years, when Johnny sent me a postcard on one of their sailing trips. That he would bother to write to me was unusually communicative, but the real shocker was his spastic penmanship. The card reached me shortly before his first full-body seizure, when he was diagnosed with one of the fastest-growing inoperable brain tumors in the annals of oncology. From the first symptom—a trembling in one hand that he'd joked about in the postcard—to his death in Walter Reed Military Medical Center, took six months, including two months of remission.

Afraid he might die at any moment, Mom made arrangements to stay near Walter Reed for several weeks. She believed in rigorous bedside care—backrubs with rubbing alcohol to prevent bedsores, bed baths and other ministrations seldom performed in modern hospitals. She was as skilled as any nurse, but had only an LPN's license. Nancy, an RN, might have pulled rank.

Three days after she'd flown to Bethesda, Mom called. Her soft, resonant voice quavered in a strange high pitch: *Becky, you won't believe this. John told me to leave! He said my presence was upsetting to Nancy, and it would be easier on him if I just went home.* In a unique state of panic and humiliation, she could barely admit that she was already back in Bremerton, too mortified to contact her friends, who'd expected her to be long gone. How could she bear to be perceived as unwanted by her dying son?

Johnny's dismissal of our mother might have struck me as impossible, had I not witnessed his vulnerability to Nancy. Still, her predicament was stunning. Unlike Mom and me, she and Johnny had always been simpatico—sharing that secret, damning phrase she'd refused to explain: *same old Becky.*

I'll never see him again, Mom vowed bitterly. *That's what he wants. He can die in Nancy's arms.* She would not attend his funeral, she decided, if there was one.

"Maybe it's better to wait, Mummy. Sooner or later they'll regret how they treated you." This did not console her, but she listened. It felt unreal—knowing how I'd been disparaged in their private communication—to be reassuring our mother that she would be reconciled with Johnny before his death.

Photo taken by Nancy of Johnny on their sailboat prior to his seizures.

Two months later he was released from Walter Reed, cancer in remission. The tumor remained dormant long enough for the

50-50 possibility that he might recover. How difficult it must be, I wrote to him, to hover between equal chances of living or dying. His situation, my letter wagered, required more heroism than his rescue missions at sea, and I assured him that he was up to the challenge.

He'd begun to take seriously his chances of survival, when a worst-ever seizure landed him back in the hospital. This time Nancy called me, rather than the mother-in-law she'd claimed to love—in effusive letters Mom had occasionally read aloud to me—more than her own mother. But that was before Nancy had pressured her dying husband to send his mother home.

I was touched to learn, afterwards, that it was Johnny who'd made Nancy's mother feel appreciated when she visited him in the hospital. He'd made a point of asking her to bring him her homemade rice pudding, insisting it was his favorite dessert—which was actually ice cream—when chemotherapy had nauseated him so thoroughly that he could hold down nothing but ice chips.

On the phone Nancy said he was failing quickly, and I could have a few hours the next day to see him. I booked a roundtrip flight on the short-lived Trump Shuttle to Washington, D.C., praying that somehow we could settle our troubled accounts.

The trip seemed to float through time and space. I boarded the plane amidst a flock of pinstriped executives, and skimmed complimentary copies of the *New York Times* and the *Wall Street Journal*. Unencumbered by luggage I disembarked, breezing past the baggage claim onto the street and into a waiting cab, whose driver proved correct saying he knew the quickest route to Walter Reade Hospital. My purse quickly produced the right amount for his fare plus a generous tip, and within seconds I was walking through the famous hospital's entrance, stepping into an elevator that glided to my brother's floor. Its doors opened onto a ward suffused with an aura of gentleness, kindliness, even holiness.

When I asked for my brother's room number at the nurses' station, their curious once-over suggested that he was a patient they considered special. Counting the numbers approaching his room, I felt drawn by a childlike instinct of his need for me. My heart reached into the stillness as I entered. It was a gift to find him alone.

"Hi, Johnny." I was the only person who still called him that. His face was turned away toward a wall. I could tell he was awake, so I went to the foot of his bed and squeezed his toes through the blanket. "It's not going to kill you to look at me." As his head turned to meet my gaze, his eyes conveyed volumes of fear, sorrow and shame, as direct as when we were kids on the berry farm, before he started school.

A recently botched biopsy of brain tissue had left him unable to speak. The corners of his mouth turned down in a deliberately failed smile—a peculiar expression of his that used to convey all-purpose cynicism. Now it telegraphed a terrible hopelessness that he might have revealed only to me.

I defied it, saying, "Johnny, you have nothing to fear." The set of his mouth returned to neutral. He'd never been drawn to anything spiritual, so I chose my words carefully. "I just know that wherever you're going next, it'll be the *best*, because you've earned it." I said this matter-of-factly, looking at him as though it was obvious.

His gaze narrowed slightly, as if to say, Go on, then I'll decide if you're crazy.

"Whatever else you've done that you don't think is so great, you've risked your life to save others. That is very special, and you will surely be rewarded."

His eyebrows lifted, as if thinking aloud, Well, if there *is* such a thing as a next life, with so-called rewards.

I hadn't seen this kind of openness from him since childhood, when he took for it granted that I loved him and understood his fear. So I took a chance on something deeper. "I feel in my bones that life is a continuum, and this world is just one stop." He stared back, more pondering than dismissive.

Nancy arrived and asked if I'd like some tea. Never had I craved a cup more. When she returned, I took the chair next to Johnny's bed, facing Nancy, who sat with her tea at the foot. The chemo made him too nauseous to swallow liquids, so I got a cup of ice chips and reached over to feed him some from time to time so he'd feel included. He crunched them sociably, which made me feel more accepted.

Not much of a raconteur until that moment, I took on a once-in-a-lifetime role, and began describing for Nancy some of my brother's childhood exploits. Johnny had never heard me speak about our past. Neither had I. I hope it wasn't because he couldn't talk, but he was uniquely attentive, gazing tenderly across his feet at Nancy, absorbing her every response. It gave him a chance to witness her loving interest in things he had not shared about himself.

Nancy heard how, as children, Johnny was taught the clarinet and I the piano by Flavia Van Dyke, a very proper lady who was our surrogate aunt, and lived in Lake Stevens, Washington. I explained that we had a much stranger de facto family member, Wayne Trubshaw, whom we called Uncle Wayne, who'd been a friend—more like a follower, but I didn't go there—of our father. He would faithfully visit us on weekends and holidays, when he wasn't driving a school bus in Marysville. Flavia and Uncle Wayne had been our family, who spent Christmas and Thanksgiving with us. We had no blood relatives to interact with—our mother's people being in New Zealand and our father's other children much older and residing mostly in Florida.

On holidays and other occasions, I explained, Uncle Wayne would pontificate about supernatural and paranormal phenomena, displaying a vast vocabulary of quasi-scientific esoteric terms. He and our stepfather Verne would converse for hours about concepts such as "meridian etheric polarity action." I dropped this phrase casually, savoring Nancy's blank look. Johnny looked ready to wince at whatever Wayne's verbiage signified.

He was not going to hear it from me. Instead, I recalled being shocked to discover that our mother, whose vocabulary was enormous, had no idea what meridian etheric polarity action meant. Once, while Verne and Uncle Wayne were debating sundry occult topics, I asked Mom in the kitchen the meaning of that four-word phrase. She'd rolled her eyes and said, *I haven't the slightest, nor do I care to ask!*

One of Uncle Wayne's many strange ideas was that liquid dish detergent was toxic, so he refused to use it. The few times we visited him in Marysville, after Johnny's clarinet lessons from Flavia in nearby Lake Stevens, Johnny would stash a knife and fork in his clarinet case because he didn't want to use any implements that Uncle Wayne had washed without benefit of soap. The rest of us tolerated our host's dubious eating utensils to avoid offending him, but Wayne never noticed that my brother brought his own. Nancy tilted her head, staring at him. He looked toward the ceiling.

Flavia, on the other hand, was proper and fastidious. Nevertheless, she had to deal with an entrenched medical establishment that considered her profession a form of quackery. For many years the State of Washington made it difficult for chiropractors to obtain licenses to practice, so the shingle Flavia put up on the office she'd transformed from a private home in Everett simply stated her name, followed by "D.C." and "Health Services." I'd been told that Flavia had probably saved my brother's life before I was born by straightening out a dangerous kink in his spine. When I looked at Johnny, he shrugged to signal no memory of it.

Word of mouth brought Flavia a sizeable clientele for chiropractics, but she kept a parallel career teaching music that continued into her nineties. She taught my brother clarinet and me the piano at no charge, on condition that we take our lessons punctually and prepare as rigorously as her paying students— who eventually spanned three generations. After Flavia got him started, Johnny virtually taught himself, acquiring considerable skill. Johnny hadn't told Nancy about the music competitions he'd won in high school. These were Northwest national competitions—Washington, Oregon, Idaho and Alaska—where student musicians, ensembles and concert bands performed before professional adjudicators. I described how Johnny won a competition, still playing the dented metal clarinet he'd learned on, that was attended by the president of Selmer Instruments, perhaps the finest maker of clarinets in the country. The man was so impressed that he gave Johnny a Selmer clarinet and offered him a scholarship to attend the Juilliard School of Music in New York. Nancy's eyes widened, staring at Johnny as if to ask, How could you not tell me this? He looked again at the ceiling. By the time he met Nancy he'd stopped playing and sold the Selmer. Maybe he lost the heart for it after being barred as a cadet from playing in the Coast Guard Band. When I mentioned that he'd turned down the scholarship to Juilliard, quoting him as saying that if he had to play music for a living it might take the fun out of it, she gave him a melting look. Better left unsaid whether he might have been happier on the road not taken.

All this reminiscence filled the hospital room with a homey air. I'd been inspired to share parts of my brother's life story that he hadn't got around to telling the woman he loved. I hoped he'd allow himself to appreciate more of what he'd given to the world.

Nancy learned that, though Johnny's tin clarinet could not produce a rich tone, what the president of Selmer heard him play flawlessly was Mozart's Clarinet Concerto, a virtuoso piece for any high school musician. Johnny's boyish exuberance was similar to Mozart's. When he got older he read several biographies of the composer, and was delighted to learn that young Wolfgang also had an impish sense of humor and relished caustic put-downs of the pompous. I did not say that they were kindred souls in vulnerability as well, and in having to face an untimely death while young and happily married.

My brother's favorite living musician was Bob Dylan. Long before Dylan's songs were acclaimed for poetic genius, Johnny wrote down all his lyrics and kept them in a three-ring binder. Once, while stationed in Corpus Christi, Texas, he called me to report his amazement that he'd been able to attend a live concert of Dylan on tour. None of the songs sounded like the recordings, he said, bursting with admiration. Dylan kept reinventing his songs. "He's a real improviser," Johnny declared, "like Mozart." This was not entirely new to Nancy, I gathered, as she looked at her watch. She said it was time for him to venture out of his room a bit, and left to fetch a wheelchair.

I fed Johnny—who seemed a bit happier—more ice chips. As Nancy rolled the wheelchair in and helped him out of bed, I noticed that he would have to sit on its cold vinyl seat with his bare bottom, because his hospital gown tended to open in the back and would not cover him when sitting. So I grabbed a spare towel and slipped it onto the seat before he sat down. A look of unexpected comfort brightened his face, and he gave me a quick nod of gratitude. Nancy let me push him, and the three of us cruised slowly down the corridors, until she suggested that I might want to speak to him alone, and left us in a vacant lounge.

As I stepped around to face him, Johnny seemed to tense up. Deprived of speech, his mouth tightened as though he wanted to say something, but I was the only one who could talk. Searching for something reassuring, I said tentatively, "Johnny, you've always been straight with me." It had been true sometimes, in our childhood.

He looked sideways and turned his head away, as if to say that he could not agree and did not feel good about it. I could see how honest he'd become, and how badly he wanted to be reconciled. As his head sagged downward, my heart groped for a solution.

"Okay, let's do a deal." He looked up. "If you'll forgive me for all the things I've done that bothered you, I'll do the same for you, and we'll call it even."

A wave of relief seemed to wash over him, followed by the feeling, if not the normal shape, of a smile. His right side being paralyzed, he held out his left hand. I took it, and he squeezed my hand with remarkable power. His eyes blazed into me, when until that moment he hadn't made more than fleeting eye contact in all his life. It was the most vehemently caring gaze I'd ever received. As he held his grip and did not look away, it felt as though he was trying to fill a pit in my heart. Maybe he wanted to compensate for all the years when he didn't—or acted like he didn't—care about me. He seemed to be willing me the strength to carry on without the brotherly support I would have so wanted and needed.

Nancy reappeared. I gave Johnny's hand a last squeeze, said goodbye, and waved a grateful farewell to Nancy. As I walked down the long corridor to the elevators, I glanced back at him several times. Each time I found him watching me steadily, smiling, still there in his wheelchair, not returning to his room. Each time I looked back, he smiled and waved, as if confirming that he'd always be there for me. The last time I turned, I noticed how amazed Nancy appeared, perhaps wondering what had transpired.

He could not tell her, and neither could I. It was something only we could share, because we knew the whole story.

CHAPTER THIRTY-SIX

Flowers

Things were finally right between Johnny and me. But what about the mess he'd made with Mom? He was much closer to death than when he'd asked her to leave. He could no longer speak, let alone apologize in writing. Nancy remained the dominant presence in his life, but gave no indication that she'd stand in the way of Mom's return. Nor had she voiced any intention to invite her back. By default, the ball landed in my court.

My mother barely managed a positive response when I called to describe my farewell visit with Johnny. Her words—*I'm glad for you, dear*—had a hard edge. Not the same as being glad for us as brother and sister. It felt as though she still wanted him to suffer for turning her away. As in our childhood before he started school, I found myself trying to protect him.

"Mummy, I think you should go back and see Johnny again."

Well, that's another matter. It's good you settled accounts with him after all these years.

"Mummy, he needs to see you before he dies."

He didn't want me around. At least he's reconciled with you.

"But you're his mother. I can't fill that role."

Never mind. You're his sister. That should do.

"I don't think he had the strength to cope with whatever was happening between you and Nancy. You have to forgive him for caving in. He was helpless and dependent on a moody wife."

I don't see what use I'd be, if he cares for her to the exclusion of his mother.

"He's got very little time left. I'm sure he regrets hurting you and wishes he could have another chance. How's he going to get that if you stay on your high horse? ...Besides, I took a look around that hospital room. Can you believe, no one's brought him any flowers?!"

Silence. She of all people could feel for a dying patient with no flowers.

But I wouldn't know how to get there on short notice.

"Not much to it. You pack a bag, go to the airport, pick an airline, hand over your plastic, pay full price, and head for the gate. [This was an era before security checks.] Then you call Nancy and tell her when you're arriving." I assumed Nancy had come to regret her prima donna performance, and at this stage she wouldn't dare tell Mom to stay away. "When your plane lands, you take a cab to the hospital, catch an elevator to the 9th floor, and ask for Johnny's room number at the nurses' station. I guarantee he'll be so grateful you returned."

Well, I'm not sure I can do it.

"Of course you can, Mummy. If you don't, Johnny won't be able to die at peace with himself."

Well, I'll think about it. Goodbye, dear.

"Don't think about it, do it! Then call me. Bye, Mom."

I'd gotten pretty bossy, defending my brother from his last attack of a killer bee. Though I'd never shared their special bond, I knew he'd be devastated to miss his chance to repair it. For Johnny, it would have been a fate worse than death.

Mom called two days later. It was wonderful to hear her soft plummy voice free of bitterness. She said the first thing she did, when she got to Johnny's room, was walk over to his bedside and put her hand on his shoulder. Whereupon—still unable to speak—he leaned his head on her arm and looked up at her tenderly.

To my mind, this childlike gesture expressed sorrow for what had happened before, total love for her, relief and gratitude that she'd returned. He would have known instantly that she'd forgiven him, and been reassured of her love, which he'd needed more than mine. I shared his relief.

Some of Nancy and Johnny's friends insisted on reimbursing Mom for her airfare, and offered her a place to stay. I didn't need to ask whether she'd brought any flowers. There were bouquets aplenty in the hospital's shop.

Johnny died a few days afterward, at 4:20 in the morning. If Nancy or Mom had been in the room, he could have died in their arms. My guess is he took leave alone, at peace, knowing he was loved—and perhaps avoiding a scene between Mom and Nancy.

Years later, on my flight back to Bremerton, when it was our mother's turn to take leave, I recalled the moments I'd shared near the end of my brother's life. Now that his spirit was free and our earthbound unease with one another was over, it felt possible he'd arranged for the seat to be empty next to me, to remind me of his presence. I hoped he'd take good care of Mom in the next life—and help me out, if he could, while I stayed in this one.

CHAPTER THIRTY-SEVEN

The Chambered Nautilus

Less than two weeks after Johnny's death in 1983, Mom spent Christmas with me in New York. It was consoling and special that our friend Mary-Jo Kaiser was able to join us for dinner at my apartment on Christmas Eve. Mary-Jo had been teaching Transcendental Meditation in Bremerton when she met my mother. She became like a second daughter, privy to many of Mom's thoughts and feelings that I knew nothing about unless Mary-Jo shared them with me. We became close friends when, after studying awhile in Switzerland with Maharishi, she stopped in New York before returning to Bremerton, and ended up living and working in the City for the next nine years. I cherished her memories and insights about my mother, especially the ones that resulted from spending this evening with us.

Our family's tradition was to open our gifts after dinner on Christmas Eve. As the holiday approached, I spent hours trying to memorize "The Chambered Nautilus" by Oliver Wendell Holmes. My plan was to recite the poem before my mother opened her special gift from me—which I would preface by telling her how all my life I'd been in awe of the vast repertoire of poetry she knew by heart. I wanted to honor her by learning this one that had meant so much to her. Mary-Jo knew about my plan, and was eager to see it carried through. Though I could not match Mom's plush timbre and diction that made this poem numinous for me as a child, I got through it without stumbling.

As my mother had been before I was born, I'd been inspired by Holmes' image of a broken seashell, a ruined ship of pearl no longer occupied by its frail tenant, whose life had been crushed by the ocean's powerful forces. The creature's "irised ceiling" was broken open, exposing its years of "silent toil," the way it had left each "past year's dwelling for the new," and "stole with soft step its shining archway through." The imagery had moved me and untold others to think of our uncharted, unfolding lives—how once-immediate experiences get sealed off by time and changes in circumstance. I lost some of my voice at the end, when the poet thanks the broken shell for its message sung through "deep caves of thought":

> Build thee more stately mansions, O my soul,
> As the swift seasons roll!
> Leave thy low-vaulted past!
> Let each new temple, nobler than the last,
> Shut thee from Heaven with a dome more vast,
> Till thou at length art free,
> Leaving thine outgrown shell by life's unresting sea!

Mary-Jo knew how much I'd hoped my mother would feel my love and admiration for her as I recited this poem from memory, as she opened my gift to her. We were riveted as she opened the little jewel box that held it—a beautiful pendant of ammonite, an extinct ancestor of the chambered nautilus, cut and polished with gold highlights that revealed its delicate spirals, the fossilized artistry of the creature's ancient toil.

Very thoughtful, dear. Very tasteful. Thank you.

Such brevity and reserve was unlike her, especially when someone—not necessarily her daughter—had put such effort into honoring her. Neither Mary-Jo nor I could figure whether my mother had been truly pleased, by poem or pendant.

Years later, Mary-Jo confided that on one occasion, after listening to my mother's litany of complaints about me and her insistence that I did not love her, she reminded her friend Rachel of the Christmas Eve when she'd personally witnessed my love for her, giving her that pendant and memorizing the poem it signified. Mary-Jo recalled that instead of being reassured, my mother responded in silence—sullen, as though annoyed to be offered a perception of me that differed from her own.

But my friend had left something important unsaid. Mary-Jo did not reveal it until several years after my mother's death, when I was struggling with an early draft of this memoir. She said she'd kept it from me for fear of how much it would hurt me, but finally decided that knowing about it might give me a fuller perspective of what I was dealing with in writing about my mother.

"Becky, in the twenty years I knew Rachel," she said with grave reluctance, "she did not have one good word to say about you." That was devastating enough. Mary-Jo also wanted me to know that she and her mother, Lucille, had independently developed the same technique to avoid having to listen to their friend's rants against me. It took awhile before Mary-Jo admitted to Lucille that it was hard for her to stomach Rachel's litany of complaints about me. The only way she could escape them, she told her mother, was to wait for Rachel to take a breath. Then she would quickly change the topic. To Mary-Jo's surprise, her mother—who had not yet met me—replied that she too had found Rachel's complaints about me obsessive, and had developed the same technique. They'd both observed that, unlike most mothers, Rachel never balanced her negative remarks about me with anything positive.

It took years for me to ponder the significance of this revelation. What spurred Mary-Jo to reveal it, she explained, was seeing me struggle to understand why my otherwise kind, gracious, inspiring mother had continued to accuse me of not loving her. It seemed she'd left no room for what other mothers might have found worthy of pride in a daughter who'd earned a master's degree, was gainfully employed, and had a small number of good friends in a city where she had no connections but still had a future.

It was painful to hear about Mom's persistently negative judgments—which she'd probably shared with other friends. Nevertheless, I knew Mary-Jo had divulged this out of compassion, and respect for my quest for understanding. I was grateful she'd presented me with an essential piece of the puzzle, which helped me identify a pattern that had been largely hidden from me.

CHAPTER THIRTY-EIGHT

Hummingbird Time

Old age is not for sissies. Mom loved this chestnut that she attributed to Bette Davis. She refused to waste her golden years alone, reading whodunits and the National Enquirer, watching the *boob tube,* waiting for the phone to ring, or calling a diminishing handful of old friends. Duplicate bridge was reputed to be both mentally challenging and sociable. She took a class, and within two years became a popular player at the Bremerton Bridge Club, attending tournaments and accumulating points in a national ranking system. On the club's off days she hosted games at her home. Among her partners was Oscar Cooper, a wealthy retired banker.

Mrs. Cooper was several years older and unable to play bridge, having lost much of her eyesight. One afternoon at the club, the players briefly noticed the wail of a passing ambulance. Oscar later concluded, showing no emotion, that it had been the one taking his dying wife to the hospital. A few months after her death, Oscar began to offer to drive some of the club's widows to local bridge tournaments in his Lincoln Continental. He emerged from these trips with a short list of ladies whom he invited in pairs on brief sightseeing excursions. My mother mentioned this to me as though she were simply a bemused observer.

I had no idea she'd participated in Cooper's screening program until one of her Sunday evening phone calls resounded with a tone of triumph. *By the way, Beck, Oscar has invited me for the first time to drive with him to Eastern Washington—alone.* It sounded like she'd won an Olympic gold medal. No longer would she have to compete with Florence Mortensen and Gertrude Lingstad!

"Why do you think he chose you, Mummy?" I asked, when my real question was what took him so long.

My sense of humor, of course. I was the only one who teased him.

By then the two had known each other for ten years and, though he prodded, Oscar never got a straight answer about her age. He got the same line she'd given other club members: she was pushing 100. If pressed for her secret of youth she would whisper conspiringly, *Glands. I get them freeze-dried at Helen's Health Food.*

They'd been dating a few years when Oscar fished her driver's license out of her purse when she wasn't looking. By then he cared nothing that she was eight years his senior. He'd sold his house in West Bremerton and rented a waterfront apartment about 50 yards down the road from her home in East Bremerton.

My mother was proud to be seen with a younger escort, a man of means, dining at fine restaurants, and traveling with deluxe accommodations. She enjoyed being chauffered to her doctors' appointments in his Lincoln. *It saves me the effort,* she told me, *and does wonders for my gasoline bill.*

After I met Oscar, and commented on his personality as indirectly as possible, Mom admitted that his company was not scintillating. In fact, she'd labored to elicit any response from him on topics that interested her. He brushed aside anything to do with nutrition, of which she had extensive knowledge, world affairs did not concern him and, unsurprising for a banker, he was a die-hard conservative. When he asked me where I stood politically, I answered, to get a rise: "Bleeding heart liberal with vegetarian proclivities." No comment, but the ghost of a smirk.

For most of their relationship his manners were impeccable, but there was something suspect about other aspects.

Dr. Bright, Oscar's longtime physician, was another right-winger. Mom referred to him as Dr. Notsobright, because he'd failed to ask about his patient's consumption of alcohol, though Oscar had causally related ailments. With a flick of one hand, she informed me that Oscar had not functioned sexually for years—an upshot of the heavy drinking that never came up with Dr. Notsobright. No point their sharing a bed, she commented breezily. *Besides, we each want our own space.*

Her casual air stirred me to ponder how fully she'd dealt with Verne's absence of affection for her. Now she felt no need to avoid the subject.

Otherwise they were as good as married. Each day Oscar joined her for lunch, then returned to his place to sort through his mail, run the occasional errand, and take a nap. Every evening he had dinner with her, either at a fine restaurant or enjoying her home cooking while they watched his choice of TV shows. At ten p.m. he would rise from the easy chair formerly occupied by Capt. Madden, and announce "I'm leaving," without so much as a goodnight peck on her cheek. Mom would remain in her Lazy-boy recliner as he let himself out the door. He would then cruise downhill in his Lincoln the few yards to his apartment, though it would have been an easy, healthy walk.

One summer I accompanied Mom and Oscar on a road tour of the Olympic Peninsula, exactly scheduled so we'd arrive at restaurants known to serve drinks at lunch as well as dinner. I was perplexed at the sight of my heretofore health-conscious mother smiling approvingly as her elderly boyfriend ordered martinis for two. Then refills! Before taking up with Oscar she might have imbibed, at most, a bit of Sherry once or twice a year.

Despite old age not being for sissies, I could hardly believe that my mother—who knew she had a heart condition—was knocking back martinis with this guy. The sight gave me a chill of foreboding. Couldn't she see, where booze was concerned, it was a lot smarter to be a sissie?

"Mummy," I pleaded, when we got home and were free of Oscar for a few hours, "I'm really worried about your matching drinks with Oscar. He's used to hard liquor and you're not. You've told me his health has suffered from so much alcohol. Why are you jeopardizing yours by trying to keep up with him?"

Lips clamped, hands trembling, she glared in defiance. I forged ahead.

"Why not let him drink while you enjoy a nice hot tea? Or nurse along some light wine or beer? At least beer has a few B vitamins."

She brooded for some time, composing the following retort: *Did it ever occur to you that your mother might actually* like *martinis? If I were to choose tea or beer or wine, it could be perceived as indirect criticism. And, as you may recall, I prefer to avoid discord.*

I shook my head in defeat. She'd convinced herself she was taking the moral high ground, leaving her *little sister in the body* to suffer the consequences.

In the next two years my mother had three heart attacks. Oscar's gentlemanly demeanor eroded the more she came to depend on him. Two or three times, she reported, he'd threatened to stop seeing her, though she managed to charm him out of those taunts, which I considered demeaning and intolerable. I reminded her that she had several interesting female friends with whom she could socialize. Maybe Oscar should stew in his own juice awhile, with her not around to intimidate?

In a tone implying I was rather thick, Mom said she'd already weighed the pros and cons, and decided that Oscar's company was preferable to that of her women friends. Though she did not say so directly, I gathered that she enjoyed being envied by her widowed friends who lacked male company. In her view, I suspected, they did not need to know about Oscar's dark side.

Perhaps my mother had not wanted to upset me, or did not wish to acknowledge that my warnings about drinking with him had been justified. She'd chosen not to tell me about her first two cardiac episodes. After the third, she asked me to come to Bremerton to help her transition from the hospital to a local rehabilitation facility. That summer, 1993, was the first of my visits when she did not greet me at the door with a welcoming smile. By then she was a frail and somber 84, and I was there not as her guest but as the daughter who would look after her home, visit her in the hospital, and manage things if she did not recover.

Soon after I entered her hospital room I asked when she'd be allowed to come home. It was a shock to hear my constitutionally upbeat mother's leaden response: *Frankly, I'm not eager to come home.*

"Why, Mummy?" I was afraid it had something to do with me.

She muttered grimly: *I don't want to watch Oscar drink anymore.* Quite a turn from her fierce rebuke two years before—that swill about avoiding discord and not drinking safer stuff while he guzzled martinis because it might, God forbid, imply criticism. I agreed completely with her current sentiment, but felt she'd have been more honest not to gloss over two facts. One, she was no longer capable of drinking with him. And two, the shock to her previously alcohol-free system for having done so—despite my pleas—had precipitated her decline.

For several years Mom had been buying fresh eggs and vegetables from a charming retired Marine originally from the hills of Tennessee. I'd met him on a previous visit, when he explained that he was leasing farmland near Bremerton to stay far away from his family, who were prone to feuding and drinking. He'd mentioned being a member of Alcoholics Anonymous, so I gave him a call.

When he heard my mother's reason for not wanting to come home from the hospital, he promised to do anything he could to help. Helen Scales, a retired public health nurse and one of Mom's best friends, was an AA member who'd stopped drinking decades before. From both of them I learned that people did not always join AA voluntarily. Some did only after "interventions" orchestrated by experienced AA members.

Sitting up in her bed at the hospital, Mom asked why I hadn't been spending as much time with her lately.

"Well, if you must know, I've been plotting and scheming."

Do you mind telling your mother what about?

"Not sure I should tell you. If it doesn't work, you'll be even less inclined to leave this place."

Becky dear, I feel worse being left out of things.

Trapped, I tried a jaunty response. "Okay, how about if I tell you, then you tell me if I shouldn't have told you?"

A faint smile. *Fine. Out with it.*

Helen, the Tennessee Marine and I were planning to corner Oscar and ask if he'd stop drinking for her sake—fortified by invitations to attend AA meetings with them—so she'd be willing to come home. He could easily refuse.

"Well, Mummy, should I have told you?

Certainly. Even if he doesn't stop, I'll know that you cared enough to try.

The next day Oscar seemed amused by the hillbilly Marine's gung-ho AA pitch and agreed to attend a meeting with him. Afterward, Oscar complained about how much the AA members smoked, and said the hardest thing he'd ever done was stop smoking. He resented being surrounded by people puffing like chimneys to compensate for not drinking, and refused to attend another meeting.

Nevertheless—to borrow a Reggie Cantwell phrase—the acoustics had changed. Oscar insisted he was not an alcoholic, but promised to stop drinking "for Rachel's sake." Mom agreed to be transferred to a rehab facility. She asked her housekeeper, whose services she shared with Oscar, to make a tiny mark on the label of the bottle of Jameson's whiskey he kept on his kitchen counter. As time passed, the bottle of Jameson's remained on the counter, but its contents, their housekeeper reported, did not decrease.

Alone in my mother's home, the passing days offered me an eerie foretaste of when she'd really be gone. One evening I felt so cut off from close friends that I broke a silence of many years and dialed my old flame Steve Devere in Boston.

"Beck...?" he recognized my voice immediately. In an instant the feeling of separation vanished, and we exchanged the essentials of two decades spent apart.

Steve made understanding sounds as I recounted my failed romances since we'd parted. Still single, he seemed both sorry and relieved that I was also unattached. Having long since lost interest in finishing his Ph.D., he chuckled that I'd taken so long to complete my doctoral course requirements and pass the written exams—the stage at which he'd left off. Instead, he'd become fascinated with computers, mastering a complex software program that determined employee benefits for large companies. He'd become the director of human resources at a technology firm on Route 128, and was positioned to retire early with a comfortable pension. A few years back he'd won the trifecta at a racetrack and banked all his winnings. Quite a nest egg, he boasted. He could afford to travel wherever he wanted and could easily visit me.

"Really, Steve?" So eager to see him, I gushed inappropriately how beautiful my mother's place was, that I had the use of her car, and we'd have such fun tooling around Puget Sound together—as if I hadn't already told him why I was out there. He promised to call back with his flight information so I could pick him up at the airport.

The next few days I breathed in anticipation of Steve's call, but something told me not to call him again. It was the last time we spoke.

Meanwhile my mother's roses were in glorious bloom, and she was not there to enjoy them. Each day I took her a fresh assortment of the most magnificent blossoms, set off by sprigs of greenery clipped from her shrubs. One of my happiest moments was when she told me, as if it was quite a surprise, that I had a talent for floral arrangements, since her eyes never tired of looking at them. I was reminded of that Keats poem she'd intended to have written out and framed for my bathroom—a thing of beauty being a joy forever. Flowers wither and die, I thought, only fresh ones are beautiful. Probably not what Keats had in mind.

One night in the rehab facility, while telling me a joke, her voice became hoarse and shallow. Some persons who'd just died, she said, were waiting at the Pearly Gates in a long line of souls being processed by St. Peter. While they were waiting, a man in a white coat and stethoscope emerged from inside the Gates, descended to Earth, and was allowed back through the Gates ahead of everyone else. Hey, the souls in the queue asked, How come that guy gets to go back down to Earth, come up here again, and cut in front of us? *Well, St. Peter explained, even God likes to play doctor now and then.*

My laughter echoed uneasily down the empty halls. "Mom, you're not breathing very well."

No dear, I'm not. You'd better call the charge nurse.

Annoyed to be summoned so late at night, the nurse came to my mother's doorway and accused her of hyperventilating. "Just take your sleep meds and call it a night," she snipped. Not bothering to examine the patient, she strode off before I could protest that my mother had been doing nothing of the sort.

"Mom, I'm afraid if you take a sleeping pill you might not survive the night."

She agreed, and told me to go back to the nurses' station and ask them to call the hospital for an ambulance. *If they say I'm hyperventilating, tell them I'll take responsibility for my own treatment.* I was fiercely glad to obey.

Despite their reluctance to make the call, the ambulance arrived quickly. In seconds, the medics assessed my mother's condition and rushed her to the hospital. I followed them closely up the hill in her car, tapping the horn to let her know I was right behind. Her lungs had filled up with fluid, they said afterward. She'd diagnosed herself correctly, and sending for them had saved her life. The problem—unidentified till then—was congestive heart failure.

At dawn I drove home, and stood in her kitchen. Her refrigerator door was studded with decorative magnets posting pithy quotations, jokes and cartoons. Taped firmly in the center was a large, signed announcement—DO NOT RESUSCITATE—

identifying my mother as a dues-paying member of the Hemlock Society. For years she'd claimed the right to end her own life if it became unbearable, telling everyone close to her *Under no circumstances do I wish to be kept alive as a vegetable!*

I washed a few items in the sink, wondering if by some miracle my mother could live a few years longer. I was not ready to lose her, and hoped that time would resolve the tensions between us. Miraculous things had happened to her in response to prayer, but I had not experienced anything vaguely miraculous directed toward me. Couldn't I have a sign that it was not the end yet, that I'd have a chance to be reconciled with her?

By then winter had arrived. Two large round wooden planters, once resplendent with flowering plants, flanked either side of the sliding glass door to my mother's kitchen, their contents shriveled at the foot of tall bamboo stakes Mom had once inserted to support them. Shortly after submitting my above question to the Unseen, I looked through the glass door and noticed a hummingbird darting back and forth from atop one planter's bamboo stake to its counterpart in the opposite planter. As though trying to summon my attention, it whirred in a zigzag pattern and hovered before me at eye level between the two planters, tapping firmly on the glass with its beak.

I'd never seen a hummingbird on my mother's waterfront property, nor anywhere else in Bremerton. When she was still gardening, Mom had expressed sorrow that hummingbirds were disappearing in Washington, and lamented not having seen one in years. I stared at the tiny rare bird, doubting my eyes.

It rapped again on the glass door as if to assure me it was real, and stayed there, as if determined to communicate with me. So I directed two thoughts toward it: I accept that you're real. Are you here in response to my request?

The bird tapped again, its tiny dark eyes locked onto my gaze as if to convey a clear affirmative. Then it shot up a foot or so and hovered with its beak next to the glass, without breaking eye contact, as though waiting for me to acknowledge that I understood its answer.

I nodded, sending it another thought: Since you seem determined to verify this exchange, I accept that we have reached an understanding.

At this point the hummingbird zipped down to its previous position, rapped again on the glass door, as if to say Roger and out, and was gone.

At the hospital that evening I described this uncanny episode to my mother. For her ears, I modified my question to the Unseen (by which I meant some form or messenger of God, which I am sure was understood at the time)—as being simply whether she would get better.

Mom reflected a moment. *Maybe it was a miracle. Hummingbirds are rare and precious in these parts, and do not appear in winter. 'Wish I'd seen it.*

CHAPTER THIRTY-NINE

Open Heart Surgeries

Three heart attacks had left my mother with minor valve damage, detectable in a faint, nonthreatening heart murmur. Otherwise, at 85 she'd rebounded quickly in rehab, coming home to resume her gardening, bridge playing, and road trips with Oscar Cooper. I was happy for her, and glad to return to my life in New York. All seemed well, until Mom called with unwelcome news. Oscar was planning to "celebrate her recovery" with a drive down to California's Napa Valley, where he looked forward to sampling its fine wines. When I asked if she would participate in the wine-tasting, she did not answer.

What followed, perhaps, was her way of avoiding the trip, where she may have lacked the will to protect her own health. Unfortunately, my mother chose an even more perilous route, which she did not discuss with me beforehand. Eventually Mom told me that, after her successful rehab program, her cardio-pulmonary specialist began posing questions with a fiendish sense of which buttons to push. Was she "venturesome?" Did she want to "avoid the possibility of a stroke"? Somehow he'd realized that, more than death, she feared losing her wits. If she'd been so unwise as to try downing double martinis with a heavy drinker, how could she not think of herself as venturesome? The cardio was, in fact, pitching an unnecessary and extremely risky surgery for someone her age. Claiming it would reduce her—remote, he forgot to say—chances of a stroke, he got her to agree to elective surgery to repair the slight valve damage. He referred her to a colleague in Seattle, who he claimed was one of the best heart surgeons in the Northwest. She was unaware—and I might have found out for her, had I known of this subterfuge—that elective heart surgery for any woman over 65 was considered highly inadvisable, if not openly forbidden, by most physicians and hospitals nationwide.

The first I heard from my mother about this was her call to say she was scheduled for surgery the next day. It would take about five hours and finish about eight p.m. New York time. She tried to make it sound like no big deal, simply FYI. No need for me to come out there, she said.

That evening I had to go to a friend's apartment to print out chapters of my dissertation because my printer was broken, so I called the hospital and left my friend's number. Eight o'clock passed, then nine, ten, and eleven. By midnight I was petrified, unwilling to risk leaving my friend's place for fear of missing the hospital's call during the time it took to walk home. (No cell phones back then.) I sat frozen by the phone, praying.

Five hours and several calls to the hospital later, a nurse—not the surgeon—told me my mother was still bleeding, so they had to sew her up and reopen the incision the next morning. This meant her 85-year-old ribs would again be pried apart and held in a vice while they tried to locate and fix the "bleeders" and install a pacemaker. This they did, only to notice afterward that they'd installed two pacemakers, not one. So they reopened the incision and repeated the whole ghastly process to remove the extra pacemaker—then reopened it *twice again* to stem the stubborn bleeders.

Within three days my mother endured an unbelievable *five open-heart surgeries.* That she survived them testified to a lifetime of effort to remain fit via moderate exercise and the study of nutrition. This elective surgery, while eliminating her heart murmur, took an unconscionable toll.

Though she'd barely escaped death on the operating table, she told me by phone that I should stay in New York. That changed when I got a call from the surgeon himself, on a Saturday afternoon. Sounding both urgent and exasperated—as though my mother was misbehaving, rather than he with his five unnecessary surgeries—he informed me that she was refusing her liquid meals, and without sufficient protein her body would not heal. The next day I caught the first available flight to SeaTac, and took a cab straight to the hospital. That Sunday my mother's ward seemed devoid of staff. I found her slumped in a large armchair next to her bed, her short legs dangling inches from the floor, ankles swollen the size of cantaloupes. She greeted me with a look of surprise, relief and despair. I stood there, appalled, not knowing what to say or do.

Oh Beck, I've been stranded here for two hours and can't reach the call button. I was supposed to sit up for twenty minutes, but I've been forgotten. I'm very weak. Might not make it.

I lunged for the call button and ran out to find help getting her back in bed. No one was available, and I couldn't lift her alone. Waiting for someone to come, I found a cardboard box to serve as a footrest, and gently massaged Mom's feet and ankles. Her surgeon, I mentioned, had called me to say she was refusing her liquid meals. She couldn't swallow much of anything, she said, because she had *trench mouth.*

"What? Wasn't that something people got in the First World War?"

Mom explained it was a type of fungus infection that would normally have been stopped by her body's healthy bacteria, but they'd all been destroyed by the antibiotics she was taking. *My mouth feels like it's clogged with fur.* The liquid meals she was supposed to drink made her gag. Mom made them sound ghastly, but they turned out to be an old standby, Ensure, whose familiar cartons I'd seen in her own fridge. She must have consumed so many in lieu of fixing meals for herself that she'd sickened of the flavors. There had to be something else nourishing she could drink. I explored the ward's coffee station, whose small refrigerator held half-pint cartons of skim milk.

"It sounds crazy, Mummy, but you could try this blue milk." Her eyebrows rose warily. "It may not be your favorite, but it has protein, which the surgeon says you must have in order to heal. And it tastes nothing like Ensure."

Mom had raised my brother and me on whole milk, fresh from local farms, whose top layer of cream she'd save for tea. She used to grimace at the mention of nonfat milk, calling it an unnatural product consumed only by people *too clever by half,* who for the sake of a few calories deprived themselves of vitamin-rich butterfat. Circumstances having changed drastically, she acquiesced to sipping the odious skim through a straw. I wondered whether her cooperation spoke of a will to live or simply conflict avoidance, given my determination to keep her alive.

I had not forgot, but found it too painful to mention, the terrible weeks that followed her hospitalization for a fourth heart attack a year before. She had not asked me to return to Bremerton to stay at her place and visit her in the nursing home. In fact, she'd refused to have a phone put in her room, and spoke only to Oscar. The only way I could obtain news of her progress was to call him at night after he'd returned from visiting her. He wouldn't say why she would not let me call her, only that she wasn't doing very well. It hurt me terribly to be shut out. But I had to focus on the present.

The Seattle hospital where my mother remained after the heart surgeries—I would discover in a meeting with their doctor-patient liaison—had no statement of patients' rights. Since administrators like her could influence the standard of my mother's treatment, I tried to suppress my rage, asking why my mother—a patient who happened to be a nurse—was the only one who'd noticed she had trench mouth? How could she have been left for two hours sitting in a chair that cut off the circulation to her feet? Calmly meeting the administrator's gaze, I explained that I was not litigious by nature, but if the hospital did not improve her level of care, I could become so. She stared back—affectless, as the shrinks say.

The next day Mom's surgeon stopped by her room while I was present. I told him I reported that she was now drinking skim milk for protein. Nodding warily, he asked who I was. His face reddened as I identified myself. Rather than shake my hand, he picked up an unused, toy-like breathing gauge from a cart near my mother's bedside, and demonstrated how she should inhale deeply and exhale into it with enough force to make a red ball rise in a notched plastic column that would estimate her lung capacity. She should do this ten or more times per waking hour, he instructed, when any idiot could tell that his patient was too weak to even reach for the device. Could it be he'd heard that I'd mentioned the possibility of litigation? Otherwise why grace us so promptly with his presence?

He and I were operating in very different theatres of rage. Mine required that I look past his near fatal professional arrogance and focus on the discrepancy between his professed concern for my mother's recovery and the hospital's inattention to her post-surgical needs. After his demonstration of the breathing gauge, I asked if he would please examine her for trench mouth, and leave instructions that she not be left sitting in her bedside chair for two hours at a stretch. He gave me a withering glance and left. So much for one of the best heart surgeons in the Northwest.

Each day until my mother was released from the hospital, Oscar picked me up in his Lincoln and we took the Seattle ferry to visit her. He'd been making daily trips before I arrived, and she'd asked him to bring her copies of the *Reader's Digest*. So he wouldn't get bored sitting with her, she had him read to her his choice of articles and amusing anecdotes, and test her vocabulary in the magazine's legendary—at least in our family—Word Power feature. I reminisced that my brother and I had been raised on Word Power. Mom would bet us 25 cents on fairly challenging words, but 50 cents for the most difficult ones—like *Areopagite, monopsony,* or *surd.* "Hmmph," Oscar grunted. "That's Rachel for you."

In our family the term 50-center got applied to any obscure word we'd never heard before. Teaching college, I found myself referring to the occasional arcane term as "a real 50-center." Everyone seemed to understand, though it didn't look as though their mothers had grilled them much on that feature of the *Digest*.

Mom was painfully weak, but her nurse insisted she get up and walk 40 feet daily. When Mom said the exertion was too much for her and she might do better after a few more days of rest, the nurse sighed, "Honey, I've been through this many times. The ones who don't get up and move are the ones who don't make it." Mom gave Oscar and me a look of helpless misery. But I suggested we each take one of her arms to help hold her up, and as a team we completed the required steps.

Her surgeon wanted to wash his hands of us. After Mom had been there a week he dropped by again and offered to send her home with me. Or, he added perkily, he'd be glad to refer her to a Seattle nursing home that would surely have an available bed. His cheerily acidic tone suggested that we deserved each other.

My mother had already heard of this third-rate facility. *My daughter is not a trained nurse,* she rasped, *and I will need round-the-clock post-surgical care.* She mentioned a well-regarded new rehab center in Bremerton.

"Fine. Whatever," sniffed the illustrious surgeon.

After a devastating five surgeries, my mother's heart was too weak to prevent fluid from pooling in her lungs and elsewhere in her body. After she'd finished the rehab program in Bremerton she needed extra oxygen, delivered through cannula placed in her nostrils, and was prescribed diuretics to help reduce the buildup of fluid. She could not return to the bridge club because the restroom was down hallway too long to accommodate her sudden urges to urinate. For a few months she hosted bridge games at her home. When bridge became too taxing, she and Oscar played gin rummy.

He learned how to fill her portable oxygen canister from the large tank that was replaced each week by truck. He found her a wheelchair he could fold up and store on the back seat of his Lincoln. For a year or so they resumed dining out at fine restaurants. In between, she relied upon Meals on Wheels, whose generous lunches she shared with Oscar.

By the time my mother called to say she was terminal, her body had developed an unbearably itchy rash, in reaction to the diuretics that were keeping her alive. The itching caused her such unrelenting misery that she refused any form of diuretic. All of them made her itch. This decision moved her primary care physician—a conscientious young woman who'd grown fond of her—to throw up her arms in dismay. My mother quoted Dr. Bartlett as saying, "Rachel, you know what this means. There's nothing more I can do for you." But the good doctor did one more excellent thing. She prescribed Hospice care.

The morning after I arrived in Bremerton, the Hospice team, who'd already visited Mom, was waiting to meet me. They explained that my mother's end would not come quickly. With congestive heart failure, her lungs would gradually fill with liquid and she would need ever stronger amounts of oxygen. They would provide whatever drugs she required for pain relief and comfort, including morphine.

The first few weeks Mom was able to get around with a walker, relieved to be free of the horrid itching. A Hospice aide came each morning to bathe and dress her. Every other day a Hospice nurse checked her vital signs and said she could be reached whenever needed. Hospice volunteers were available, if requested—one to keep my mother company while another gave me breaks from the stress of care-giving. A clergyman was sent to speak privately with her. As he left, he told me in all sincerity that it was he who'd been inspired and uplifted.

My mother viewed her body's disintegration with a nurse's clinical candor. I looked up *edematous* to make sure I understood what she meant about her swollen legs and arms. What pained her most, however, was not her physical decline. It was Oscar's absence and the irreversible rift he'd caused. Mom recalled how he'd been filling out her checks to pay her bills, so all she had to do was sign them. When he saw the amount she had to pay for fire insurance, he insisted she was being overcharged. He was certain an insurance broker he knew could find her a cheaper policy, but she had ascertained years before that only an expensive customized policy would insure her residence, because it had been built out over the water. She lacked the strength, though, to argue with Oscar about this. When she asked him to fill out the check to renew her existing policy, he threatened to leave her if she signed it. Too depleted to charm him out of this ultimatum, she signed the check and asked him to mail it. As he left, Mom said, *he shut the door with a sickening thud.*

The next day she heard the familiar sound of Oscar's Lincoln pulling into her carport. She listened as the car doors opened and closed, but there was no ring of her doorbell. Oscar drove off, leaving behind the folding wheelchair he'd kept in his back seat.

All that cruelty for a fire insurance bill he did not have to pay? It was bizarre.

However—aside from the callousness of Oscar's desertion—I couldn't help seeing a providential aspect. I no longer had to plan every meal to suit his taste, as Mom had insisted during my previous visits. He would no longer control the television programs we watched, changing channels regardless of whether we were enjoying a show not to his liking. I was sorry he'd subjected my mother to an ugly betrayal in her last weeks of life, but part of me was relieved that he would not impede my chances to be reconciled with her.

One evening, after I'd served a tasty vegetarian meal that Oscar would not have appreciated, Mom remarked, *If Oscar were here he would only get in the way. And there would be tension between you.*

"What would you do, Mummy, if he apologized?"

I suppose I'd have to forgive him, but it could not be the same with us. I've reached a point where I cannot pretend.

We did not discuss it further. By walking out on her when she was terminal, Oscar betrayed the dignity they'd shared as a couple, and belied his persona as a gentleman. She saw no reason to defer to him anymore. I'd never seen one. I hadn't forgotten the previous times she'd mentioned that Oscar had threatened to leave her, when she was in better health. After each of those occasions, she said he'd called or dropped by the next day, as if nothing had happened. She'd gone along with it, I suppose, *to avoid discord*, and hoped for the best. This left me wondering about the odds that someday he'd follow through on one of them.

After he dumped her, Oscar tried to call my mother three times. Twice I answered the phone, and was told to say she was unavailable. The third time she took the call—before phones had caller ID—and as soon as she heard his voice her tone darkened. *Excuse me, I am occupied at present,* she announced, as though to a complete stranger, and handed me the receiver. As I took it from her, his voice filled the air between us as he called out "Rachel, I love you." She gestured for me to hang up. After that he stopped calling.

As the days passed with no further word from him, I regretted that my mother did not receive the apology she deserved, and hoped Oscar loved her enough to regret this the rest of his life.

One day Ada Mae, my mother's old friend and Scrabble partner, paid a visit. When I was in the kitchen I overheard Mom in the living room saying, *Becky is doing her best, but I miss Oscar.* Part of me was surprised that it didn't hurt my feelings. Though my presence was inadequate, at least she had someone who'd never abandon her.

Nevertheless, a strange bond existed between Oscar and me, after our trips together on the ferry to Seattle, visiting Mom after her heart surgeries. In the weeks before her death I called to let him know how she was doing, and he thanked me.

For years I'd asked the Powers That Be for the chance to spend a meaningful length of time with my mother before she died, a time for us to be reconciled. A hummingbird had signaled that this would indeed happen. I would have seven weeks.

CHAPTER FORTY

Hospice to the Brink

Shawn, my mother's Hospice nurse, introduced herself the Monday after I arrived in Bremerton in late October, 1996. She was a young single mother, warm and confident though new to the program. Lucy, Mom's Hospice home attendant, already had a key to the place, having established her protocol. A husky, no-nonsense middle-aged woman of breezy gallows humor, Lucy let herself in at nine each morning, shouting "Arise, sunshine!" She wore tasteful pantsuits with colorful blouses and accessories, a deft touch of makeup, and was proud of her reputation as a human angel. Out of Mom's earshot, Lucy told me she'd had at least twenty patients die in her presence, several having waited for her to arrive before doing so. She expressed sympathy for Nurse Shawn, so young and unfamiliar with death. "The first one is always difficult, but after that"—she palmed an arc in the air as though defogging a windshield—"all in a day's work!"

Within a week tensions erupted where least expected.

It was assumed I would fix our meals, but the kitchen cabinets—previously stocked with a useful array of pots and pans—were bare. One small saucepan remained, possibly for the oatmeal Mom, until recently, still cooked for herself. When I asked where everything else had gone, she said she'd donated them *to Welfare families who could make greater use of them*. I didn't ask whether she'd expected me to borrow such things from the neighbors. It looked as though she'd anticipated a quicker exit.

Repelled by the nuked aroma of microwaved popcorn, in New York I'd become used to making my favorite snack fresh from a hand-cranked popper. Mom dismissed my plan to buy one in Bremerton, along with a mid-size cooking pot and frying pan. She emphasized the need to avoid clutter. Clutter where? I thought. On her empty kitchen shelves? I also suggested, since autumn on Puget Sound was often too cold and rainy to go for a daily walk, that I could get an exercise machine to use while we watched TV in the evening. It would cost less than joining a health club. Mom warned, *I am acquainted with people who've purchased such machines, only to feel guilty for not using them.*

Up from buried depths sprang the memory of that rosy pink scale Mom had brought home while I was packing for my freshman year at college. How delighted I'd been at what I'd taken to be her thoughtfulness, and relieved that the rich girls at Scripps would not see me using our rusty old scale. How my thanks had been cut short by her icy reply, *What makes you think it was meant for you? You seem to want the best only for yourself.* This time, however, there would be no tearful self-defense on my part. Since I'd readily dropped everything to take care of her, she had no grounds to insinuate selfishness on my part. Still, I could not muster a response. We could afford such things now. Why didn't she want me to have them in our last weeks together?

Calmly, the next morning, I reminded my mother that I had given up—gladly and without regret—my teaching job, most of my consulting work and income, my social life and other activities in New York in order to be with her. If she didn't want me to have cooking utensils, a popcorn popper or an exercise machine, she might allow me to purchase them with my own funds.

I'm sorry you feel that way, she replied dismissively. *But since you've made up your mind, I have no choice but to accept your decision.*

In the box for November 2 on her kitchen wall calendar, she wrote in block letters: *BECKY WANTS TO GO BACK TO NEW YORK*. Underneath that she noted: *Legs retaining more fluid. Weight gain from 110 to 118 lbs.* Ever the watchful nurse, she'd begun recording the symptoms of her final days. What was false and, as I saw it, deliberately unfair to me, was that attention-grabbing statement in allcaps—put there defiantly for the Hospice team to notice, perhaps to arouse their suspicions about me.

It felt like the kind of insidious betrayal she'd attempted by going around telling my friends in the Cantwell seminars that I didn't love her. I scratched it out, trying to reassure myself that, in any case, being a live-in caregiver was bound to be stressful. Besides basic cooking implements, I needed to maintain my fitness and to enjoy simple pleasures like popcorn.

Part of me still felt like the little girl who'd waddled twenty feet behind my brother and Annie Barley, as logging trucks roared by on the road past the berry farm. A more circumspect aspect of my psyche was aware that the years when I'd been judged an F daughter were behind me. I'd saved my mother's letter in which she'd lifted that particular curse—which also revealed her long memory of having burdened me with it.

After Shawn finished checking on Mom, I walked her out to her car.

"Are you stressed out?" she asked.

"No, just upset about what Mom wrote on the calendar. Why doesn't she appreciate my being here enough to let me have a few essentials and comforts?"

"My mom and I also had a difficult relationship," Shawn answered. "I think some kinds of maternal opposition and lack of encouragement actually come from envy."

It seemed implausible in my case. Truly enviable things, in my view, were a successful career and a viable romantic partnership, neither of which I had. I imagined that my mother felt the same, but in fact I never knew what she held against me. Something prompted me to ask Shawn if she was close to her father, since I'd grown up without mine, who evidently hadn't wanted me in the first place.

"My mom wouldn't let me get close," Shawn said. "I was adopted, and she was always jealous of my dad bonding with me."

With that, Shawn and I struck a solid rapport. "Guess what!" she confided, "I just came from a patient who'd died and fallen out of bed, and his wife didn't even know!"

My eyes widened in sympathy. "Gosh, you get one shock, then you have to tell the guy's wife and deal with hers!" Since Lucy had already told me that Shawn would be off the following week, I added, "You deserve a vacation!"

"Yeah," she smiled, "I'll get one all next week." She climbed into her car, revved the engine and winked. "Y'all have a fine weekend."

Next week the Hospice social worker, Dee, called to ask if she could spend some time with me after she'd chatted with my mother. She took me to lunch at the Boatshed, a popular restaurant built on a dock near the picturesque old Manette Bridge, and asked about my work. She seemed interested in my two jobs, teaching college in the Bronx and finding grant support for the United Negro College Fund. Our conversation shifted to my mother's difficult life in this country, far away from her New Zealand family, and her sequence of mismatched husbands. Dee drew out of me that I'd been my mother's confidante since childhood, functioning as a little adult and hearing perhaps too much about her troubles.

As Dee probed further, I admitted to feeling betrayed by my mother at various times throughout my life. The most recent, other than the calendar block letters, was earlier that year, when my dissertation advisor encouraged me to submit one of my chapters as a paper to be read at an international conference on literature and ethics in Wales. I was thrilled when my paper was accepted and the invitation came for me to attend. Not only would my doctoral research and ideas be presented to scholars from around the world, but attending the conference in Wales gave me a chance to visit my mother's ancestral homeland. I couldn't wait to phone

Mom with the news. Finally I had something happy to report, something she could feel proud of. But as soon as I'd delivered this joyful news she snapped, *Well! Don't expect me to help you get there!*

It was impossible to convey how stunned and hurt I'd been by those angry words. All I could offer Dee was my memory of the rest of that phone conversation.

"But Mummy, I'm not asking you to help pay for the trip. I'm earning enough now to cover the cost. All I wanted was for you to be happy for me."

Why do you have to go? Can't you just be glad your paper was accepted?

"Why on earth would she not want me to go?" I asked Dee. It defied logic. Of course I went to Wales, presented my paper, and felt honored to be chosen to moderate a panel discussion. On the last day of the conference a good friend flew in from New York to travel with me around Wales. We had a delightful, fascinating time. I'd have gladly told my mother about it, but did not offer to, for fear her lack of interest or animosity would cast a shadow over my radiant memories. Now, half a year later, when we had many hours to talk, it was sad that she never asked about my experiences in Wales.

Dee offered to serve as a facilitator if I ever wanted to express my feelings to my mother in the presence of a third party. I thanked her, but said I had no interest in forcing my mother to deal with unpleasant truths. Dee said she felt no such impulse in me, but I wasn't sure. Part of me did wish someone like Dee could get my mother to explain, in my presence, why she'd never accepted—since my adolescence—that I loved her. Now that I was her fulltime caregiver, she seemed to ignore rather than retract this longstanding judgment. It was confusing and hurtful, but there was still time.

I told Dee that I'd been blessed to be reconciled with my brother before he died, and had to trust that during Mom's final days there'd be some kind of resolution, so we could each part with a clear conscience. Dee nodded somberly. When we

returned, her manner toward my mother was warm and solici-
tous, as if assuring her that nothing we'd discussed had lowered
her in Dee's esteem.

The next evening Mom seemed strangely conciliatory. She
asked if I'd found any suitable exercise equipment. I had not.
She expressed disappointment that my new popcorn popper did
not work well. Putting her to bed that night I asked if Oscar had
called again. She shook her head.

"People are weird," I said, to comfort her.

We're all weird. I'm weird!

Lucy was giving my mother a bed bath one morning, and
asked what her life was like growing up in New Zealand. I was in
the room when Mom responded with a wealth of facts I'd never
heard from her, such as: On her father's sheep station there were
ten people to feed, usually by killing one sheep a week. Besides
her family, there was a "cow boy" who tended the cows, a shepherd
who helped her father with the sheep, a fence man who repaired
the fences on their 1100 acres, an untrained Maori girl who served
as a maid, and an older Maori cook. Though one was old and
the other young, the two women were referred to as "the girls,"
and ate their meals separately in the kitchen. When shearing time
came, her father hired extra hands, so two sheep were killed each
week to feed them. They raised chickens for eggs, kept cows for
milk and butter, and grew their own potatoes and other vegetables. Every six months they would *set in stores* from as far away as
Gisborne: medicine, dry goods, sewing fabric, spices, tools.

She'd never gone into such detail before, but did so to entertain Lucy. There were no cars in those parts, Mom recalled, so
almost everyone rode horseback. The Gisborne East Cape was
twenty years behind the rest of New Zealand in getting electricity, so they had no refrigeration. Most homes still used kerosene
lamps. *My family was isolated from people of congenial background
and education.* She'd been educated at home by her mother, then
won a scholarship to attend boarding school. There was no free

high school education back then. That part I knew, but appreciated far more as an older woman.

By coincidence, the night before, Lucy, Mom and I had seen on TV the movie "My Darling Clementine," directed by John Ford, which featured a stagecoach chased by bandits. "Rachel," Lucy asked, "did you ever ride in a stagecoach?"

Why certainly. Mom was happy to expound. Her boarding school in Gisborne was a hundred miles from the Williams sheep station, so she had to ride for three days in a stagecoach not nearly as fancy as the one in the movie. Along the way she spent two nights at small pubs—combination guesthouses and taverns where respectable people would stay. *I don't think the Wild West was ever as wild as they portray it in movies. And women were not allowed at the bar.*

"Were you afraid to travel alone?" Lucy asked.

Oh no, there was no danger in those places. People were civilized.

"Maybe in New Zealand," I muttered. Lucy shot me a look that said, Don't go there—your mother's on a roll!

That movie was frightfully misleading. People never rode their horses at such a hard gallop in real life. The horses couldn't take such abuse. It would have killed them!

Along with Lucy I learned that when my mother attended Gisborne High School, she boarded in a residence called Miss Sheldon's School. This was the first time I'd heard the name of the place where the legendary headmistress had humiliated her for not knowing how to wash her corset, where she'd been embarrassed to wear her aunt's hand-me-downs, decades out of fashion.

Mom explained to Lucy, as she had long ago to me, that leaving her family's sheep station to attend boarding school made her realize that her home life had not been normal. It fell upon her to make their house presentable to guests for some kind of social life. I enjoyed overhearing her entertain Lucy, describing how she'd taught herself to hang wallpaper, planting the wobbly legs of the farm's pole ladder in her father's rubber boots to steady them. How many mothers, I asked myself proudly, had leveled a hilltop in New Zealand with her father and some Maori farmhands, then measured out and seeded the grass for a proper tennis court?

Lucy and I were fascinated to hear my mother explain that she'd cultivated an upper-class accent so that the society people who attended her tennis parties would feel comfortable with their hostess. Her main concern in adopting this accent was *to avoid the stagey, pretentious demeanor of many upper class British. It's so easy to role-play*, she observed drily. I was struck by the insight.

Mom was pensive after Lucy left. She wondered aloud how much of Oscar's gentlemanly manners had been simply playing a part. His father had worked in Washington's logging camps, she'd gathered, as did Oscar before his rise in the banking system. That was not to say that people could not become gracious by cultivating good manners. *I've never forgot what Cary Grant once said about himself—that he'd pretended to be someone as charming and gracious as his movie personality, until he eventually became Cary Grant!*

I'd brought some consulting work to do for the College Fund when my mother did not need tending. Late one afternoon I was at my computer when Mom pointed out that it was a glorious sunny day, and urged me to take a bracing walk before evening. From a hilltop in Manette I gazed in awe at Mount Rainier's snowy slopes, glistening pink as the sun set on Puget Sound. The phone was ringing when I returned. Whoever it was hung up when I answered. I wondered if it was Oscar.

Mom didn't feel able to speak by phone, even to our old family friend Flavia, my beloved first piano teacher. She felt it was time to say goodbye to her, and asked me to call and do the talking.

Near my mother's age, Flavia had chosen not to marry, giving up the one man she might have shared her life with—a man she told me about but would not name. A year before she died, seven years after my mother, she said she'd had no difficulty, and no regrets, choosing to pursue her two careers—music and chiropractic. With the exception of attending the Palmer College of

Chiropractic in Iowa, she had not left her family home in Lake Stevens. Like her father, who'd served as Lake Stevens' first postmaster, she'd become a local institution, honored as grand marshal of the town's Memorial Day parade. The street that ended across from their house was named Van Dyke Road.

Flavia a few years after Mom died. She lived to 95.

When I called, Flavia addressed me as though I was still her young piano student. "Oh, how nice to hear your voice, Becky dear. How is your angel mother?" Before I could answer, Flavia anxiously informed me that she'd written twice to the nursing home where my mother had stayed earlier in the year. Receiving no reply, she'd written to Oscar, asking him to please drop her a line about Rachel's condition. She'd enclosed a stamped self-addressed envelope with a blank piece of paper inside, to make it easy for him to respond, but he didn't.

In better days, Oscar had driven north with my mother to Lake Stevens, where Flavia guided them around the area's scenic attractions, and he took the two ladies to dinner at the best local restaurant. Mom whispered for me to tell Flavia what had recently transpired with Oscar. I did, and Flavia responded simply, "You must remember he was good to her for quite some time."

As I described the aftermath of their breakup, Flavia seemed to understand why her friend had turned away Oscar's calls: "Your mother has entered a new phase of her life, perhaps the last, and matters like uncertain love ties are no longer important."

Flavia asked if I thought my mother was approaching the end, or was there a chance she'd make another amazing comeback. In the three years since the open heart surgeries, she remarked, "Your dear mother has risen like a phoenix bird several times. I almost fell over a few months ago when she called to say she was back to driving her car!" Sitting at Mom's bedside, with her listening to my side of the conversation, I tried to answer as tactfully as possible.

"She is getting shorter of breath and is slowly retaining more fluid."

Flavia's cheerful tone vanished. "That's not good. It means the heart is failing." She apologized for being unable to drive down to visit us. The trip from Lake Stevens had become too long for her. "It's been several years since I could trust myself to drive at night, Becky. I am so glad you are with her, though."

After a pause, she added, "You must know that you are the person closest to her heart." Why had Flavia felt it necessary to tell me this? I fought back tears, hoping it was true, but not sure I could believe it. Flavia did not know that the last time my mother had stayed at a nursing home, after her fourth heart attack—when Flavia received no reply from my mother nor from Oscar about her friend's condition—was also the time that my mother refused to have a telephone in her room. This effectively prevented me, Flavia, and others unable to travel to Bremerton from communicating with her. It seemed pretty clear then that Oscar was closest to my mother's heart, as he was the only person she allowed to visit and speak with her. Only after he'd walked out did she call for me to come and take care of her. Perhaps I'd become the person closest to her heart by default. None of this could I express to our last remaining old family friend.

When Flavia seemed ready to end our conversation I handed Mom the phone so they could say goodbye. At first she looked reluctant, but her face brightened when I put the receiver to her ear. Making an effort to produce a resonant tone, she said slowly, *Goodbye, long-time friend. I'll be seeing you again.*

Tears fell as I marveled at the simple confidence of my mother's farewell. When she passed the receiver back to me her voice had lost its timbre. *Well,* she whispered, *that's done.*

We were silent awhile, letting the moment settle. Then I stood up, arranged the necessary items on her nightstand, emptied and cleaned her commode. She looked pleased that I was doing the business at hand, after we'd soldiered through something momentous together.

Having learned that my mother had not answered Flavia's letters during her most recent sojourn in the nursing home, it seemed reasonable to ask why she'd refused to have a telephone installed in her room. It had hurt terribly to be unable to reach her, and forced to call Oscar for information. When pressed, he'd told me that no one at the facility was optimistic about her recovery. I was afraid to lose her with no chance to say good-bye, and as the days passed I became ever more miserable and desperate to speak with her. After I'd made several calls to the nurses' station, they spotted Oscar pushing my mother in a wheelchair down the hall, and transferred my call to a cordless phone that could be handed to her. I heard a nurse say firmly, "Your daughter wishes to speak to you."

When I heard her say *Hello dear*, I managed to say "Mummy," but was overcome by sobs of relief that I was at last hearing her voice—and unable to conceal the pain that she'd made it so difficult to speak with her until then.

Oh, grow up! she barked, handing the phone back to the nurse, who tried to console me by saying that my mother was not feeling well. In a few days, though, she was well enough to be released, and Oscar drove her home.

When Flavia asked if I knew whether my mother had ever received her letters at the nursing home, I told her I didn't know. Afterward, I began to wonder whether Mom had told Oscar not to respond to her. My concern for Flavia rekindled my distress that my mother might have stonewalled both of us. Surely, I thought, the Hospice staff would support my asking why she'd cut herself off from her own daughter and possibly her oldest friend. So I did.

Mom hesitated. Then, begrudgingly, she admitted it had been wrong to do so. *I was angry that I had to learn to walk all over again, repeating the same exercises I'd been given years before.* A long pause. *I was mad at God for not letting me get it over with and die right there.*

– And if she'd had her way, she'd have died without seeing or speaking with me. So, was Flavia right to say I was the person closest to her heart?

In a rather flat tone my mother acknowledged that when my call was put through to her from the nurses station, it had been *inappropriate* to tell me to grow up. – Not unkind, or even cruel, just inappropriate. Nothing resembling *Sorry I hurt you. Sorry I shut you out, when I wanted to die, and might have died having shut you out.*

That night we watched a documentary about World War One on public television. We learned about Kaiser Wilhelm's shriveled arm, for which he may have compensated with military displays of power and pageantry. How the introverted, spiritual Czar Nicholas I longed to be a devoted family man rather than ruler of Russia. The insanity of 27,000 French troops clumped together in bright blue uniforms, slaughtered in one day by the Germans as they entered Alsace. Archival photos appeared on the screen, exposing the squalor and futility of trench warfare. Mom and I took it all in, sharing an appreciation of the fabric of history that wove back to her father, who'd possessed books by some of the war correspondents mentioned in the documentary. Two of his brothers were in that war, she said. One was killed, and one survived, only to die in the flu epidemic of 1918.

Mom explained that Queen Victoria had carried the gene for hemophilia, which she'd passed along to Czar Nicholas' son and heir. That wasn't mentioned in the film, I said. She replied as if it were common knowledge, *Oh yes, and the whole royal family was syphilitic as well!*

The program ended at eleven, past her bedtime, but she didn't feel nearly as tired as previous nights. Her feet and legs were less swollen and, she noted cheerily, she'd been *voiding plentifully* during the day. *Have you been spiking my food with parsley?* she teased. Parsley was a natural astringent that I'd naively thought might replace the diuretics she'd rejected, in order to prolong her life. It did not prove powerful enough.

CHAPTER FORTY-ONE

Blessings and Betrayals

In our second month together my mother was still getting up and dressing herself, which seemed normal to me but extraordinary to Lucy, her Hospice aide. Mom still read the daily paper and a pile of murder mysteries from the library, and played Scrabble with friends. In the evenings we watched TV. Every Friday she had me drive her across town to her hairdresser's, her only outing. Lucy took me aside and murmured, "She's doing this for you, you know."

When I shrugged it off as her usual routine, Lucy said, "Take it from me, most people in her condition would stay in bed all day, not bother to get dressed, and forget about reading anything." She was amazed that my mother still had her hair done every week. "Rachel is well past the point where most people don't keep up appearances."

Another week passed. Mom noted that her body was retaining ever more fluid, and whatever could not be excreted was filling all available space. When her feet were elevated in bed, excess fluid seeped from her legs toward her abdomen. She even felt it squooshing around her bottom.

November 9th I recorded in my journal the first time she accepted my offer to help her get undressed and prepare for bed. I accompanied her to her bathroom and followed her directions how to soak her dentures. Handing her a hot wrung-out wash-cloth to slowly wash her face, I opened and set out her jar of face cream so she didn't have to reach for it. As we stood together at the sink, she rested her head on my shoulder. I put my arm around her, kissed her cheek, and saw tears in her eyes.

It occurred to me that she would not be able to stand and move about much longer, even with help. So I put my arms around her and took perhaps my last opportunity for a really big hug—sensing how thin she'd become, apart from the fluid reten-tion. When I released her she stood there as if unsure what to do next, so I held out my arms again and offered, "One more for the road!"—squeezing her frail frame so heartily that she whispered, *Careful, dear!*

You can go ahead and prepare my bed now, Mom suggested, as she stayed behind in her bathroom. From her bedroom I heard some barely audible sniffles, but she was dry-eyed when she entered. I blinked back tears as I helped her into bed. Silently, as on previous nights, I applied lotion delicately to the taut skin of her swollen legs. As ever, she sighed a grateful *Ah!* when I rubbed her toes.

In a brief moment of composure I said, "I'm so glad I can be with you, Mummy." She made a little sound and gave me a tender look.

A few hours later, while I was recording this precious mem-ory in my journal, I thought I heard her coughing, so I went back to check on her.

"Are you okay, Mummy?" I asked at the doorway to her bed-room, not so loud as to wake her, but audible if she was already awake.

How very nice of you to look in on me, she answered clearly. She seemed alert, not groggy, but said she'd been sleeping and had not coughed. With motherly concern she noticed it was 1:45 a.m., and asked if I was going to bed soon.

I stroked her forehead and said, "I'm very proud of you, Mummy." *That's nice, dear,* she replied. Such tenderness filled the air that angels might have hovered among us. I withdrew and returned to my journal, to give thanks for this moment.

That weekend I decided, for the first time in my life, to go to a movie alone. "The Associate," a comedy about women making it on Wall Street, was playing at the Silverdale Mall. It starred Whoopi Goldberg, who guaranteed a few laughs. I'd wanted to see it with Mary-Jo, but she had a fulltime job and needed to look after her father. When Mom's friend Ada Mae arrived to play Scrabble, I excused myself and drove to the Silverdale multiplex.

In my 20s, 30s and 40s I'd spent many solitary weekends, too embarrassed by my lack of dates or close friends to dare going alone to the movies. But as my half-century mark approached I felt justified to enjoy doing so. I pulled confidently into the mall, bought my ticket and a large bag of popcorn, took a seat, and surveyed the Saturday night audience. There were quite a few other loners amidst the couples and clusters of friends. The movie dropped us into a vat of alternate reality, where our shared laughter helped me celebrate this small private milestone.

Before Mom dressed in the morning, she would sometimes ask me to choose an outfit from the variety of slacks and colorful blouses in her well-organized closet. I did my best to mix and match, but she preferred her own taste. Each week I laundered her clothes and returned them to her room. One morning I was hanging up her clean blouses and pants, when I noticed her face contorting anxiously as she watched from her bed. She pointed to the sections of her closet meant for blouses and pants, insisting I not get them confused. This seemed unreasonable.

"Since I have not yet mixed up your clothing," I replied coolly, "why don't you wait until you see me misplace something before you get upset about the possibility that I might do so?"

Oh Becky, she groaned, *you don't know how it feels to have an active mind and so much desire to do things, but not the physical means. I would like nothing better than to put my own clothes away and do things for myself. But I just can't.*

Sad for her and ashamed of my snippy retort, I decided from that moment forward to oblige any and all fussing from her— praying that if I ever became helpless, there would be someone who'd take unbegrudging care of me. In subsequent days, Mom said she found it reassuring to hear my brisk footsteps whenever she called.

On a mid-November morning the Hospice team convened in my mother's bedroom to go over the steps I should take when she died. Nurse Shawn started by asking what was the first thing I should do at the moment of death. The question pierced my heart and caught me off-guard. Tears fell down my face, and I could not answer. My mother was not pleased.

No! she shouted. *I don't want any tears! I want this to be a positive experience!*

Shawn, Lucy, and Dee the social worker looked at each other, concerned. "Rachel," Dee said, "we are doing our best to help make this a positive experience, but your daughter's feelings are only natural." The first thing I should do, Lucy explained gently, was to call either Shawn during the day, or whoever was on duty as the night nurse, who'd make all the necessary calls after that. Later, Lucy told me, after our meeting they'd discussed how tough my mother had been on me, and what a high standard she kept for herself.

Weeks passed before Mary-Jo had a free afternoon to spend with me. She took me to a vintage clothing shop in Port Orchard, where I spotted a large floral shirt in pinks, blues and purple that Mom could wear over her slacks, hiding the bulge of fluid in her abdomen. Mom seemed to like the shirt, but looked sullen watching TV after supper while I worked at the computer. Earlier than usual, she asked me to prepare her bed, and headed for her bathroom. I turned on her electric blanket and the heating pad for her feet, folded back the sheets, and fetched the lotion for her swollen legs. When she appeared in the doorway, she declared bitterly that she was all alone with nobody who cared for her.

This dying thing is not easy. It would be a lot easier if you'd be nice to me...

What? I asked myself. How was I not nice, bringing her a lovely shirt from my first outing with Mary-Jo? Was it not nice to do some paid consulting work occasionally instead of watching TV with her? Did she resent Mary-Jo's going somewhere with me rather than spending the time with her?

"Stop it, Mom," I blurted. Though she was far too weak to subject me to another lecture about being a selfish, uncaring daughter, I had an irrational fear that once she got going, she'd be unable to stop, and I'd be unable to bear it. But stop she did, staring back at me, slowly choosing her words.

Okay, if that's what you want...and I ask you to ask yourself if you think you are being loving and kind by what you've just said.

I held my ground, answering firmly, "I have no doubt about that." She could search for any negativity in my attitude, but there was none. I knew I'd taken the best care of her as I could, and had a right to spend a few hours with my closest friend in the area. After some silence, during which I smoothed lotion onto my mother's distended legs, I said softly, "I am always here for you, Mummy, but I understand that you feel lonely at times." I reminded her that my afternoon outing with Mary-Jo was the first chance we'd had to see each other since my arrival, and I needed to get out for more than short walks and trips to buy groceries. Reluctantly, she agreed that I needed some personal space.

The next evening, as I returned from a walk, Mom announced brightly that she'd examined some papers from the wastebasket near my computer. *Why Beck,* she said in a tone of incredulous, faintly sheepish, surprise, *I've just realized that what you're doing is important work. And I see that you're very good at it!* My consulting project was a fundraising strategy for a group of historically black colleges and universities. The discarded memos she'd read were about scheduling a meeting of their presidents, rather than the ideas I had in mind for them, but it was amusing that she'd gone through the trash rather than ask me what I was working on. Had she picked up this sleuthing technique from whodunits?

At the time I was unaware of the extent to which she'd complained to others over the years, that my nonacademic work in New York was inconsequential—perhaps why she'd sounded so surprised.

I'd put off calling the Hospice volunteer who'd been assigned to take caregiver breaks with me. Hospice provided another volunteer to visit my mother while I was out with her. Why hadn't I seen the brilliance of this plan before? After Mom's reaction to my afternoon with Mary-Jo, it was time to make contact.

A few days before Thanksgiving, Nanette, a freelance journalist, took me to explore an impressive new organic market in Poulsbo. As we examined a display of artisanal cheeses, she mentioned that her mother, who'd died three years before, had also pushed herself to get up and dress every day as she neared death. Her mom had also been a powerful presence, who'd convinced everyone she was a marvelous person, while being extremely critical of Nanette. Nanette, however, lived with her husband the four months she'd stayed near her dying mother, who'd been moved to an assisted-living facility.

"Not living under the same roof made a big difference," Nanette said. "I wasn't trapped, like you are." Hospice, I thought, could not have found me a volunteer more simpatico.

Having heard that my mother read crime novels, in her next visit Nanette brought Mom two recently published ones from her collection, plus *The Nine Tailors*, a classic Dorothy Sayers mystery, for me. As she left, she told me to call her anytime during the week. I mentioned that she'd already given me the four hours a week she'd signed up for with Hospice. "Forget about the time limit," she said. "Let's just be friends."

I liked her instantly. We were close in age and spiritually compatible, but there was an implicit social divide in my being single, while she'd been happily married for 22 years to a successful newspaper executive, whom she'd met when she was a reporter. I had no status as a part-time humanities professor and consultant in the unglamorous field of fundraising. Despite the Bard's warning that comparisons are odious, I could not avoid thinking that Nanette would have to like me for myself, if our friendship was to endure.

Thanksgiving Day appears in my journal as one of our happiest. After a morning thunderstorm, sunshine burnt away the clouds. I stepped outside to sweep away the leaves that had blown across the carport. John, the man who checked my mother's oxygen absorption and delivered a full tank each week, drove up with his little son in tow. This came as no surprise, since the one we called "oxygen man" had grown very fond of my mother, and was making an off-duty visit. His boy was delighted to run out onto the deck and examine the crab shells dropped there by gulls. His wife had baked us a pumpkin pie, John said. He gave Mom a bottle of port wine he hoped she would enjoy. I was glad she'd have their special company while I took a walk.

How strange, I thought, that another John had brought her these loving farewell gifts on Thanksgiving Day. It was almost like my brother had sent him.

Trudging up to the crest of a hill overlooking Puget Sound, I wondered if I was ready for the end of my time on planet earth with my mother. In the distance the Seattle ferry glided into its terminal. Beyond that were outlines of warships docked for repairs in the Naval Shipyard. Across the Sound and behind a scrim of clouds and smog, Mt. Rainier loomed in ethereal majesty. I recalled a trip to Tacoma with Mom, when a sudden glimpse of Rainier around a bend caused her to veer, awestruck, off the road, barely avoiding a crash.

On the downhill trek to her home, I contemplated the indefinitely small number of days that my mother would be there awaiting my return. Then I noticed a black dog following me. It circled around at a polite distance, as though offering to escort me back to face the immediate present, perhaps the future. Was this another sign, from a canine instead of a hummingbird? The dog kept within a twenty-foot radius as I absorbed the panoramic views from the high streets of Manette. It trotted ahead of me down the winding driveway to my mother's place, where I thanked it and gently told it to go home. It turned obediently to withdraw. But as I neared the carport I noticed that the dog had stopped to watch me, almost like the final hovering of the hummingbird. It gave me a soulful look as I opened the back door and waved it good-bye.

When I came inside, I made an offhand comment to Mom, that the folks who lived on the hills above her in Manette had a clear view of Mt. Rainier. In raw envy, she growled, *I know!* Though her beachfront home on the Washington Narrows was enviable itself, she had clearly pined for more than a roadside glance at the great mountain worshipped by natives as Tahoma. What else, I wondered sadly, had she yearned for, that she could only glimpse in passing? To cheer things up, I mentioned how well put-together she'd looked for the unexpected visit of John and his young son. She'd put on lipstick, earrings, and purple slacks that set off the floral shirt I'd got for her in Port Orchard with Mary-Jo.

For Thanksgiving dinner, I heated up the turkey and stuffing I'd purchased at Boston Market—known as "the yuppie Macdonald's"—and steamed the greens and squash from Mary-Jo's garden. Mom requested tiny portions, just to keep me company and to be able to tell Mary-Jo she'd tasted her homegrown vegetables. I tried a slice of John's wife's pumpkin pie, but forgot to open John's gift of port wine, to my regret. Searching for something to talk about, I said it was very thoughtful of Nanette to bring us those murder mysteries.

Mom nodded somberly, and in an oddly appreciative tone, reminisced that she had read one whodunit after another to get herself through the loss of her first baby.

It was the hardest thing I'd ever gone through, losing that child. The thing about murder mysteries is you get to see them solved. Many are quite well written, underrated in fact as fine literature. I kept reading them until I was well enough to work on the farm again.

Long ago she'd told me about the wonderful nurse she'd had in Everett General Hospital, where incredibly, after 36 hours of labor, no doctor offered to end her agonies and save the baby by performing a Caesarean section. He'd been perfect in every way, she said, but could not emerge from the birth canal, no matter how long and hard she pushed. He died of suffocation. My mother was inconsolable. A kindly nurse suggested that she take her mind off her terrible loss by reading the paperback thriller she'd just finished and still had in her purse.

It could have been the same nurse who, in one of Mom's favorite stories, had urged her to think of something she could be thankful for. Evidently, my mother—an ocean away from her home country and the family who'd have comforted and done everything possible for her, and perhaps disillusioned with her choice of an American husband—could think of nothing that warranted thanks, least of all her own survival after a tragic labor. In Mom's account, while giving her a bed bath, this nurse noticed a mass of dark moles spattered like globs of paint across her back. "Well, dearie," she suggested, "you can be thankful these moles are on your back and not on your face!"

As a child I'd heard almost nothing about my mother's heartbreaking, needless loss of her first child, my unnamed elder brother. Eventually she was told that she lacked the hormone that allows the birth canal to open. Thus Johnny and I were delivered by crudely performed C-sections that left wide, jagged scars on either side of her belly. In the same clinical manner that she now described her retention of fluids, she'd informed me that after two of these procedures she was unable to bear more children. But thanks to that kindly nurse, my mother could distract herself from these and other disappointments, anesthetized by the suspense and resolution of murders most foul. I used to wonder why she no longer read poetry or serious literature. She now provided the answer.

Mom was impressed by Mary-Jo's studious apprenticeship to her father, a master gardener who used to light up and enter a zone of joy whenever he discussed the avocation he shared with my mother. When he became too frail to tend his garden, Mary-Jo took over, and won several blue ribbons at the Kitsap County

Fair. By Thanksgiving, Mom's sense of taste was fading, yet she claimed to have never eaten such wonderful string beans and zucchini. My tastebuds were fine, and I agreed. Unspoken was our awareness that this would be our last Thanksgiving together. We'd been unable to share one since I'd left for college.

During the dinner it occurred to me that I'd heard all my life about my grandfather's side of the family, but knew almost nothing about my grandmother's, the Evanses. When asked, Mom rattled off the names of her mother's seven brothers and sisters, the first time I'd heard them. Aunt Lucy was the eldest, Mom's mother's godmother, who had raised her younger siblings after their mother died—my maternal grandmother being the youngest. Lucy's lengthy sacrifice robbed her of opportunities for marriage, or soured her outlook on it. She never married, and lived alone in the many-roomed house she'd inherited. She wore a red wig, Mom said, *just to please herself.* When she'd visited Aunt Lucy as a girl, she'd been forbidden to move about the house before nine in the morning or after ten at night. *At first I thought Lucy was rather tyrannical. Then I figured she mustn't have wanted me to see her without that red wig.*

"Why didn't you tell Johnny and me about these relatives?"
You never asked.

"But Mummy, how would we know enough to ask about them?"

Rather than answer, she launched into an anecdote about her Uncle Ebenezer, one of her mother's brothers, renowned for his disputatious streak. It was family legend that Uncle Eb had argued with someone about another man's last name, when his interlocutor knew the man in question and insisted that he, not Ebenezer, was correct about the man's name. Uncle Eb famously shouted, "Even if he told me himself I wouldn't believe it!" Mom found this especially amusing, and gave me a knowing glance. She'd occasionally remarked that I'd inherited an argumentative streak from her mother's side of the family, the Evanses. Her mother's Welsh lineage, she claimed, had been tainted by interbreeding with the English—in particular, the Mannings, who were known for mulishness. Whereas the Williamses were pure Welsh, ergo implicitly of better stock. In my mother's view, her mom, Alice Evans Williams, was *the best of a sorry lot*. It was the only favorable remark I heard about my maternal grandmother.

The name Manning, like Painter, Mom explained, dated back to the Norman Conquest. However, she stated with greater pride, the Welsh people were *autochthonous*—a fifty-center for sure. She paused for me to ask what that meant, but I'd come across the term once and looked it up. Then I regretted not giving my mother this last chance to increase my vocabulary.

Washing the dinner dishes, I noticed that the indestructible General Electric toaster I'd grown up with had been replaced by a toaster oven. "What happened to our old toaster?" I yelled from the kitchen.

Gave it to the deserving poor.

"I hope you cleaned it out first!"

'Hope so, too. Can't remember.

She shared my concern, given its history. It had such a gleaming chrome exterior that, for no slovenly reason, we simply wiped off the outside, mindless of anything accumulating within. The first time it was fully cleaned was on Camano Island, after its sojourn on the berry farm, when Verne placed a tiny shriveled carrot on the kitchen table for all to observe. Mom laughed in amazement that a whole carrot had found its way to the bottom of our toaster. What size had it been before countless roastings? A few years hence, Mom gathered us round the toaster and held up a tiny mummified mouse by its petrified wire of a tail. Poor thing! We stared in sympathy and horror, then resumed forgetting to clean the toaster's innards. Toaster ovens do not produce comparable surprises. I hoped the deserving poor would enjoy them.

The day after Thanksgiving, Bob Madden, Edwin's once outcast son, called to wish Mom a Happy Thanksgiving. After he'd learned to design and build yachts in Port Townsend, he'd moved to Vancouver, Washington, closer to Oregon, where he was making a good living designing yacht interiors for the superrich. He'd settled there with his children and their mother, Katie. When I answered the phone, Bob asked how Rachel was. I suggested he might want to visit her soon, as I did not know how much longer she'd be with us.

In a while he called again, asking if it was okay to come over. "Sure," I said, unaware that he'd driven four hours straight and was calling from a payphone. He arrived in ten minutes, not having eaten but refusing my offer of lunch. He tried not to show his panic and fear, but Mom was so calm and normal with him that he began to relax. She sent me off on several time-consuming errands. When I returned, Bob was in good spirits and they'd shared a meal of Thanksgiving leftovers. By then she'd offered him some frank talk, which she summarized after he left.

We were both delighted that Bob and Katie, the mother of their two sons, had got married after fifteen years together. But Bob was restless and longed to take off for Paris to study art, leaving his two boys in their mother and grandmother's care. Katie had finished college and had a good job, and her mother was an active veteran of the Peace Corps.

Mom advised Bob to look around and see the world and universe as having some design to it, even possibly a Creator. Though he'd rebelled against religion, she suggested he ask the Creator for guidance as to what he should do next—as she was doing in her present situation. *Bob accepted this*, she said proudly, *because it wasn't religious sounding.* She recommended that he think less about himself and his artistic ambitions and more about Katie and their sons. I hoped he'd follow her advice, but eventually discovered that he hadn't.

I'd been impressed by Bob's response when I mentioned what had happened with Oscar Cooper. "Oscar isn't very mature," he'd said. Mom nodded, saying she'd told Bob she was *too old to be jilted,* and did not want Oscar back.

Since Nanette arrived for my sorely needed breaks precisely when another Hospice volunteer appeared to entertain my mother, she and Mom had never gotten acquainted. So before our next outing I brought Nanette into the living room where

Mom sat ensconced in her recliner, awaiting the arrival of her own Hospice volunteer. I introduced Nanette as the wonderful new friend she'd heard so much about. Nanette responded graciously that it had been a pleasure getting to know me, and said, "You must feel fortunate, Mrs. Madden, to have Rebecca as your daughter."

My heart nearly stopped when my mother replied in a steely tone, *It's all well and good for you to speak nicely about Becky, but you do not know the half of it. Why, in this very room, if you'd heard her screeching at one of her boyfriends, as I have, it would have curdled your blood!*

Nanette's face froze in the rictus of a half smile, formed in anticipation of a much warmer response from my mother. I have no memory of how she responded before our hasty departure, I was so mortified—struck with an unwanted foreknowledge that our friendship had received a mortal blow. When we arrived at the Boatshed restaurant, I had no appetite, but tried to comfort myself with my favorite dessert: blackberry cobbler à la mode, which suddenly had no taste. Despite Nanette's words of sympathy and moral support, I sensed that she was pulling back to protect herself from a friendship that might become toxic—as my mother had venomously implied. How could she not wonder why a dying mother, even one as difficult as her own, would feel compelled to warn away a potential good friend of her own daughter?

To this day I regret that Nanette did not stay in touch with me after Mom died. Within a year she'd changed her phone number and email address without notifying me. Though one cannot be sure, it is plausible that my mother successfully destroyed a friendship of mine that could have flourished indefinitely.

Shortly before this incident, Lucy commented to me, outside Mom's earshot, that dying was scary no matter how much a person might believe in an afterlife. "Besides, people are angry to be dying. I don't care how long they've lived. Nobody wants to leave this world they know and love. I sure don't want to go. I've still got places to go and people to see and a husband I love. I'd be angry as hell to have to die!"

I was grateful for this Lucy, who lived up to her name, shedding light on why my mother might have lashed out at me. But anger at having to die did not seem to account for the malice in my mother's response to Nanette. Wouldn't she want me to have such a fine friend after she'd gone? Why bring up an ancient argument—in which my defense against false accusations had been heated, hoarse, but hardly blood curdling—with a sadistic boyfriend I'd parted with fifteen years ago? In fact, she'd already met and warmly approved of the man I was currently dating.

Dee had advised me to be forthright with Mom about my feelings. So a few hours after Nanette dropped me off at the carport, I cleared our dinner dishes and said: "It really hurt when you brought up that crazy argument I had with Anton, after I introduced you to Nanette. It was so long ago, and so unrelated to the present. You seemed determined to destroy her good impression of me, when you knew how much I hoped we would stay friends. Why would you do that to me?"

After a long pause, my mother answered as if she'd been beleaguered by endless criticism: *Oh well, it seems I've made another mistake.* She sighed, took a deep breath, and exhaled with no hint of remorse, *I'm sorry.*

After this there was no way I could probe for why or wherefore. It was amazing enough that she'd said, this once, that she was sorry about anything where I was concerned, even if her tone had a cold, defiant edge. I withdrew to the kitchen to wash the dishes. After what happened with Nanette, it became harder for me to believe that my mother cared enough to want me to have friends after she was gone.

Two days later I noticed a change in the arrangement of seashells on the windowsill near the dining table. One of them was a sand dollar that Captain Madden had brought back from the beach at Midway, where he'd strolled shortly after heavy combat during the war in the Pacific. The keepsake had been turned upside down. Its wobbly new position hid the graceful looping design on its top half and exposed its darker, veined underside with its normally concealed vent hole. For a sand dollar, it was belly-up—perhaps an expression of how my mother felt about herself. I set it upright.

In early December, the Hospice people moved my mother from her bedroom in the back of the house to the middle of the living room, and into a more adjustable, rented hospital bed. They expected she would have two weeks at most to live, so why not place her where she could sit up and enjoy her magnificent view, receive guests, and be central to all the action? Shawn, Lucy, Dee and I quickly repositioned the living room lamps and furniture, and connected the medical equipment.

My room was on the other side of the wall from the living room, so I redirected my listening for sounds during the night that signaled my mother's need for attention. One night a man's reedy voice interrupted my sleep: "Becky, go to your mother!"

I sprang out of bed to check on her, but she appeared to be sleeping. To make sure she hadn't called out to me, I asked softly if she needed anything.

Thank you, dear. Nothing you could give me. But nice of you to ask.

I told her I'd been woken up by a man's voice.

Oh? Her face brightened. *Was it Edwin's?*

"No, it was Verne's."

Really? That's interesting. She looked quizzical rather than doubtful whether I'd actually heard this voice. She seemed flattered to have Verne looking in on her after so many years. It struck me as odd. Why would Verne make his presence felt, waking me up when there was no need? Then again, why not? Verne had been married to her much longer than Edwin. In his own way, maybe his feelings for her had run deeper.

In time my disapproval of Verne—as Mom's cold fish suitor, husband, closeted addict to tranquilizers, and temporarily maniacal park ranger at Illahee who'd cost us the best home we'd ever occupied—faded. I hesitated to judge. Marriage to my mother had given his life focus and respectability. For ten years he'd helped our family survive. Mom had never disparaged him or displayed resentment of their secretly Platonic marriage. Considering her loyalty and discretion for the thirteen years they were married, it was credible that Verne's spirit would make known his concern for her suffering.

By early December, Lucy came every other morning to bathe my mother, but no longer helped her out of bed to dress her. On Friday, December 6, Lucy drew me aside and said she hoped my mom would make it through the weekend. "I told your mother, 'Now Rachel, you're not allowed to die on your birthday.' [December 8th] 'And you can't die on Becky's birthday, either.'" [December 9th] The Hospice staff believed she could not survive much longer.

Lucy put her arm around my shoulder. My eyes filled with tears when she recalled how concerned they'd been when Dee, Shawn and she gathered in Mom's bedroom over a month before to review what I should do at the moment of death. "Rachel's reaction to your tears was really hard." Lucy had grown very fond of my mother, so I did not mention Mom's devastating response to Nanette when I introduced them.

Before she left, Lucy signaled for me to wait in the hallway while she returned to the living room. "You know, Rachel," I heard her say, "you made the best decision having Becky come out here." Mom said nothing audible, though she might have given Lucy a polite smile. No matter, I was grateful for Lucy's endorsement, and walked with her out to the carport.

"It's a mystery to me," she reflected, getting into her car, "why some patients hang on so long." Leaning against the steering wheel, she looked up and asked, "Do you know any reason why your mom would want to?"

Not wishing to burden her with troubled thoughts, I shrugged. "Maybe she's trying to live until Christmas?" Lucy lifted an eyebrow, slowly shook her head, and drove off.

In fact, I'd already brought up the subject of Christmas with my mother. *Ha!* she'd snorted. *What makes you think I'll be around by then?*

The next day, for no apparent reason, she was able to move her legs and feet, even to raise her edematous left arm, whose fingers and wrist had gone down to normal size for the first time in weeks. *This is a miracle,* she stated calmly. *I hope it isn't another Phoenix episode. There seems to be no cause for this improvement. Except that there is a God, whose will we must obey.*

She insisted on turning herself from one side to the other without my assistance, so I could apply lotion to her back. Having done this, her newfound energy was spent. She lay still awhile. Ever factual and precise, she stated that her heart would have failed just then, were it not for the pacemaker. She considered it a warning not to abuse what was left of her body.

The greatest poverty in my life has been in energy. To use a terrible expression, I was nigger-rich with the little energy I had, and it's taken a terrible toll on my health. For my benefit, she recalled something she'd read years ago about the Hawaiian Kahunas, who warned against mistreating *"little sister in the body."* She knew I tended to push myself when my body needed rest.

That weekend Doreen, my old friend from high school, came to visit, bringing her teenage daughter Catlin. I was touched that Doreen had remembered my 50th birthday was approaching. She brought me a handmade ceramic sugar bowl—in purple, my favorite color—from her collection of vintage American pottery. In the hallway, out of Mom's view, I gave Doreen a grateful hug. She confided this would be Catlin's first experience of someone dying.

They sat close to the hospital bed in the living room, and Mom asked Catlin and Doreen about their activities. Her face lit up when she heard they were both learning to ride horseback. *When I was a girl in New Zealand, there were no paved roads. What few cars there were could only be driven in the summer, mostly on dry riverbeds.* Almost everyone traveled on horseback and horses, she noted, could be moody, cunning creatures. In her experience, if a horse did not like its rider, it would inhale plenty of air when it was cinched up and saddled. Then, at an opportune moment, such as going down a steep incline, the animal would exhale, causing the saddle to slide forward and the rider to fall off. This was new to our guests, and me. Mom's charm and good humor kept the atmosphere free of gloom.

Doreen noticed a watercolor hanging in the hallway, and fondly recalled a time she'd traveled to Seattle with us, when my mother bought two watercolors, the one she was looking at and another that she asked if she could see. I had no recollection of the trip, let alone the other watercolor. It felt as though my fickle brain had discarded a memory well worth keeping. To conceal my dismay, I pretended to recall the trip and conjectured that my mother might have given away the other painting.

As they were leaving Doreen said softly, "You're doing a good job taking care of your mom, Becky. I know it must be difficult."

"Especially when the visitors leave," I murmured. She nodded—being the only friend who'd known since our high school days that the mother I would soon be alone with could be radically different from the one who, on her deathbed, had entertained them with vivid accounts from her youth. Maybe that was why I'd lost some of the memories that Doreen retained.

The Hospice team were amazed that Mom survived the weekend. Sunday had been her birthday, and on Monday, my birthday, Mary-Jo brought over an entire dinner, ready to serve. She wanted to carry on her family's tradition of celebrating my mother's birthday with a festive meal at their house. Earlier that day Mom told me she had neither taste nor appetite. I said I hoped she would not mention this to Mary-Jo, because the dinner meant so much to her.

I'll do my best to fake it. She followed through by sampling and praising every dish. During the meal she remarked that, as a nurse, she'd been repelled by hospital scenes of weepy family members standing around the beds of terminal patients. As Mom saw it, a person's death was often *a blessed release from suffering, and their family should be thankful for it.* Apparently for Mary-Jo's benefit as an evangelical Christian, my mother opined that such displays of sorrow seemed to contradict the Christian faith.

In defense of grieving people, Mary-Jo replied, "One reason people cry when someone is dying, Rachel, is they know how much they are going to miss that person." She said it meant a lot to her to have someone besides her parents who really cared for her. She also wanted my mother to know how much she'd enjoyed the year when she came every week to clean her house. "You know, Becky," she explained years later, "I offered to take that job when Rachel lost her housekeeper, not for the income but because it would keep me in regular contact with her."

Over John's port wine after dinner, my mother stated—a fact she had not shared with me—that in her will she'd stipulated that Mary-Jo would be her heir if anything happened to me.

"Oh Rachel," our friend responded happily, "for me that is a perfect example of the thought being what counts." As her father leaned back in Mom's recliner, Mary-Jo pulled a chair close to my mother's bed, held her hand, and asked if they could exchange one of their favorite memories of times they'd shared. She started first, recalling how thrilled she and her father had been to ride the monorail with my mother across the vast fairgrounds in Puyallup, Washington's largest state fair. Why had Mom never mentioned this special trip to me?

My mother reached further back in time, to offer what she described as her favorite memory—though it was not something she'd experienced with Mary-Jo. Before Mary-Jo returned to Washington to take care of her parents, she'd become so involved with Reggie Cantwell and his associates in Canada that she'd moved to Victoria to serve on his staff. Since Mom and I had attended several seminars in British Columbia when Mary-Jo was present, Mom asked if she remembered my then boyfriend, Anton Lee, another seminar participant from New York.

Mary-Jo's warm expression faded. "Of course, Rachel. I knew him well."

Speaking as if I were not present, but clearly relishing the grip she had on our attention, my mother spoke of the same argument I'd had with Anton that she'd brought up in her recent, horrendous response to Nanette. This was a week or so after I'd told her how much it hurt me that her words seemed calculated to ruin Nanette's good opinion of me, for which she'd claimed to be *sorry*. Was she now trying to poison my longstanding friendship with Mary-Jo?

The two of them gave as good as they got, Mom recounted, perhaps sensing my horror that she would dig up this ancient altercation yet again. *I thought to myself, Becky has finally met her match.* My mother uttered the last four words as if she'd felt gratified that I'd apparently failed to overcome his twisted accusations. Anton and I had stayed overnight at her place after attending the seminar, and planned to drive with another meditator back to New York. With a smirk of pleasure, Mom described seeing Anton and me off at her door as we began our return trip. It had been her own private joke, she recalled—which she especially enjoyed—to wave at us and say, *I can see you spreading sweetness and light all across the country on your way home!*

I was appalled that, so close to death, my mother chose to share this disparaging anecdote with Mary-Jo, her father nearby. It meant that her recent apology had been far from sincere. Why had she not chosen any of the much happier times she'd shared with me and my companion of several years—a much wiser, kinder, and more admirable man? Mercifully, Emil Kaiser had dozed off in the recliner. I stared at Mary-Jo in distress, but she kept a neutral expression. Within minutes she and her father bade my mother a tender good-bye, and I thanked Mary-Jo for the lovely birthday dinner she'd brought to us.

Three hours later, after putting her father to bed, Mary-Jo called. "Becky," she said anxiously, "I didn't see any way to change the subject after Rachel got started. I hope you won't let that last experience ruin your memory of the evening." She wanted me to know that twice in the past few years she'd tried to broach the topic of what she considered to be a destructive, hostile element in the way my mother spoke about me. "But each time I got close to the subject, Rachel cut me off, saying, 'Oh, Becky has never understood me.'"

I asked her if she thought it bore any relation to why God was not allowing my mother to die just yet.

She thought awhile. "Well, my dear, that's entirely possible."

Mary-Jo and me at her home, bedecked with ribbons she'd won at the Kitsap County Fair. Photo by Emil Kaiser.

CHAPTER FORTY-TWO

The Life Force

My mother showed extraordinary improvement several days before her death. She was amazed to be able to lift her own legs up into bed, though she had to catch her breath afterward. A full day was blessed by her increased energy and the special warmth of her company. My journal records how grateful I was for this happy time.

Still lacking appetite, she declined the lunch I offered. Instead, she was determined to tell me something she'd long withheld. Though she glossed over a few details, the gist became clear: on the berry farm, my father had ordered her to have sex with at least one of his followers. Aghast, I asked why.

Roger had painted himself into a corner. To his followers, she explained, he'd been pontificating that in order to grow spiritually a man needed to be intimate with—in his terms—*a woman of advanced spiritual attainment.* One of the men closest to him insisted that he identify such a woman. Alas, my father could think of no one but his bride, whom he'd been praising as the only woman he knew who possessed "mental integrity."

The Theosophists who hung around your father felt they were too enlightened for old-fashioned mores. Given his conduct before marrying her, and his reputation as the "Brother for Love," he'd have lost all credibility if he claimed to be in an exclusive relationship. Mom seemed to brace herself for my inevitable question.

"So who was it?"

Wayne Trubshaw.

I was speechless. Though he'd been somewhat of an ally to me, Uncle Wayne had always been—at least in my memory—an oddly unattractive man: heavyset, clumsy, peevish, and prone to bloviating about crackpot esoterica.

My mother continued. *This arrangement continued until Roger's death. By that time Wayne and Frank were insisting that I marry one of them. I refused to discuss it, and told them I was not going to even think of marriage for at least a year. The only way I could resolve their rivalry was to marry someone else.*

Till then I'd either assumed, or been led to believe, that when Frank's leg had healed and he stopped drinking, he'd returned to his wife in Florida. I was too young to remember how long he'd stayed with us, much less to notice that he was about my mother's age and especially fond of her. I finally understood why Mom had made her gobsmacking assertion, when I was at Columbia University and about to fly at Frank's expense to Florida for a Painter family reunion. *If anyone tells you otherwise, you are your father's daughter, not Frank's.*

Now I learned that my half-brother had lingered on the farm after our father died, hoping to take his place! Even so, Mom did not clarify whether Papa had also ordered her to consort with Frank, perhaps to help him "grow spiritually" enough to stop drinking. I was so shocked about Uncle Wayne that I didn't think to ask.

Regardless, it cast new light on why for many years Frank persevered in his efforts to locate Johnny and me after he returned to Florida. Johnny was a toddler when Frank appeared at the berry farm, but Frank was living with us when I was conceived.

I married Ray Draine to avoid marrying Wayne or Frank.

Ray at least was better looking, divorced, claimed he'd been on the wagon for years, and took us to meet his sister in Seattle, whose family seemed happy and thriving. He hadn't let on that he expected marriage to make him full or half owner of the berry farm. When his assumption proved false, he might have gone on those binges just to spite her.

We'd been married only six months, when Ray left on a hunting trip in my car, with the farm's money. She left out the fact that it was one of several so-called hunting trips.

I did not tell her about the sounds I'd heard through the wall that separated the master bedroom from the one I shared with Johnny. Her cries of *Oh Ray, don't!*—the sound of muffled thuds—and the agony of a four-year-old powerless to defend her. Nor did I mention Ray's pulling into the farm's driveway after his final disappearance, finding me alone and offering to take me with him. It would have been too sensitive, and perhaps raised the question why I'd been left alone so much.

Another question I didn't ask was why she had to marry Verne, another "recovering" alcoholic. Were types like Ray and Verne the only people looking for work as farm managers in those days? As I grew older, such queries gradually dissolved into an acceptance of my mother's need to survive. With two young children and a barely sustainable farm to run, how was she supposed to meet what she called *congenial men?*

CHAPTER FORTY-THREE

Is This the Moment?

A few nights before my mother died, I lay exhausted, unable to sleep, staring at the mosaic globe of translucent Capiz shells Mom had installed three decades before as the ceiling light fixture in her new home's guest room. Its iridescent thin shells concealed the simple light bulb within, transforming its wattage into a glow of mysterious elegance, as my mind replayed an extraordinary tête-à-tête with Mary-Jo.

With a look of grave humility, my friend admitted to having been cruel to her mother. I had no idea of this, but knew that Lucille, her mom, had suffered from bipolar episodes most of her life. As a girl, Mary-Jo had been sent to live with her grandmother or an aunt for months at a stretch. When she and her parents lived under one roof, Lucille's mood swings had been a constant strain.

"I just hated the way I lashed out so harshly at my mother," Mary-Jo said. "I finally asked God why I did so, when I loved her so much." Then came a time, after she'd finished verbally lacerating her mother, when she became aware of a dark feeling of satisfaction and enjoyment within herself. "That was when I realized that a demonic entity was working through me, because that ugly feeling of satisfaction would only come from the devil."

I lay there sifting through whatever I could remember of the worst times I'd spent with my mother—though my mind had suppressed or obliterated much of her soft-spoken, relentless monologues, and my utterly ineffective responses to them. Had I felt anything resembling satisfaction or pleasure in whatever I'd said to her? No. As sports fans used to say, you can't win for losing. Maybe some fans of horror movies find pleasure in being terrorized, but probably no one who's experienced real-life trauma.

Not to give myself a pass, though, considering my tendency toward bluntness. No doubt I'd overstepped the bounds of tact when trying to resist what felt like strangely dishonest, twisted— but frighteningly intense—attacks on my character and goodness. It was impossible to feel satisfied, let alone enjoy, the futility of explaining how and why I hadn't intended to be selfish or inconsiderate of my beloved mother. It was true that I'd focused on my studies and music, because I loved music and learning things, and being a good student seemed the only way I could make something of myself.

To be honest, studying and music practice were refuges from the stress of being criticized and accused of not loving her. Lacking my brother's effortless charm and humor, I could not prevent classmates from mocking me for being pudgy and brainy. Turning inward meant I'd failed—as Mom put it—to bring sunshine into their lives. There was nothing in this for me to feel pleased about, because what she'd really wanted from me, or thought she wanted, was for me to be *consistently* cheerful at home.

Unlike Mary-Jo, I never had a clear insight that a dark force too powerful for me to handle alone was driving my mother, trying to destroy our bond of love and trust. But I knew instinctively that the mother who really loved me was the one who'd answered my cry every night when I'd wet the bed, never chastising or accusing me of failing to control my bladder. That was not the person who spent hour upon hour berating me for not appreciating her, who expected me to remain cheerful at home without realizing that she was undermining my capacity to be cheerful.

All I could do was cling to my own sense of truth and fairness to myself. This meant trusting my gut-level perception that her persistent accusations and platitudes—despite being couched in righteous-sounding terms—were unloving and demoralizing. If anything, I wondered if the kind of dark gratification that Mary-Jo had perceived in herself had been experienced by my mother, without perceiving that it was malevolent. Had she felt some vicarious gratification years ago, when Anton had reduced me to hoarse, helpless protestations? Or after she'd dropped that poison pill into Nanette's good opinion of me? Or when she, closer to death, told Mary-Jo that her favorite memory was a snide private joke she'd made about me and a sadistic former boyfriend, as we set off on a cross-country drive back to New York.

"I knew I had no power within myself to defeat this force," Mary-Jo told me. "I could only be set free by commanding it to leave me in the name of Jesus. When I did this, it left."

Wow, I thought, if only I'd known enough to try that with my mother! But I hadn't thought of our fraught relationship in this way, until that conversation.

Over the years since—in Mary-Jo's words—she'd asked Jesus to be her Savior, I'd been awed by her personal relationship with God. She'd resolved a swath of problems, major to minor, by asking for and receiving understandable instructions—often accompanied by Biblical citations—from the Almighty. What most helped her understand what had been going on with her mom, she'd mentioned in our talk, was an insight gained from a passage in Scripture. The gist of its first part was that God's love remains in us as long as we love each other.

Mary-Jo waited before telling me the second part, as though it might be hard to accept—that God's love reaches its perfection in us. She was thinking about this passage, she said, when it occurred to her that one of the deepest forms of love is the bond between mother and child, especially mother and daughter. "I looked at it this way, Becky. Satan would do his utmost to destroy love's potential for perfection. So he would target the deepest and potentially most loving of bonds with the most relentless afflictions."

My friend added: "I believe Rachel's relationship with you has been attacked by a spirit of destruction, like what happened with me and my mom." She also believed that God had prepared her to address this matter with me from a position of strength, because she'd been given this revelation, and had been freed from the evil spirit that had tormented her relationship with her mother.

To me she seemed like an avenging angel. The more so because, after the birthday dinner she'd prepared so lovingly, Mary-Jo had witnessed the spiteful pleasure my mother took in recounting what she'd chosen as her most favorite memory, her sarcastic *private joke* about me and the long-gone, sadistic Anton. I'd also described to her my mother's withering response when I'd introduced her to the Hospice volunteer Nanette. Mary-Jo prayed for God to take away my hurt, and asked that nothing would divert her from speaking directly to my mother about this. As our prayer ended, I sensed something akin to a balm of Gilead, in the strong and tender friendship that had developed between us.

That night, before sleep came, it occurred to me that I'd reached my 50th birthday with no one noticing except Doreen when she'd visited earlier. Apparently, in all the years Mary-Jo and her parents had celebrated my mother's birthday, Mom had never mentioned that my birthday was the day after hers. If she had, I felt sure, our friends would have included me in the birthday celebration at our recent dinner, which took place on my birthday. As she read this passage in an early draft of this memoir, Mary-Jo assured me that she had not known about my birthday.

I stared up at the glistening Capiz shells, envisioning parties thrown for people I knew in New York who'd reached the half-century mark. But the part of me that felt it had lost out was rebuked by another that considered it petty and self-indulgent. Far better to give than receive, it scolded; I should renew my thanks for this chance to be reconciled with my mother.

My conscience won out, but it hurt that my 50th birthday never came up at any point during our final days together. Yes, Mom's impending departure from this world was a far more compelling focus of attention, but was I not the closest person she'd be leaving behind? Was reconciliation still possible? My hopeful side floated the possibility that this disappointment was a mere dust mote compared to having an ally in a winnable struggle against a long entrenched spirit of destruction.

Twenty-four hours later, just before Mary-Jo's promised phone call, I found myself doubting whether she should confront my mother, given the sense of finality in their exchange of reminiscences after Mom's birthday dinner. Though my mother's anecdote had seemed calculated to turn Mary-Jo against me, I was afraid to pass judgment. During our days alone together after this occasion, my mother had taken pains to impart bits of wisdom she thought would most help me. Every morning she complimented me on the oatmeal I cooked for her, and thanked me for fixing all our meals. Every night she told me how good it felt when I applied lotion to her swollen legs and ankles, and rubbed her toes. *Thank you, dear,* she'd say, *for your ministrations.*

When Mary-Jo called, she said she'd prayed for guidance in her determination to challenge the spirit of destruction in my mother, but she had not expected God's response, which came to her clearly: **At this time fellowship is the better way**. She waited for me to absorb this, but I'd been in instant accord while she was voicing those enormously kind, wise words.

The next morning a flu bug took advantage of my fatigue and depleted immune system. Dragging my leaden body through the necessary tasks, I passed my mother's bed. Lifting an edematous hand and forearm, she said, *Bless you, dear.*

I came to a woozy halt, and leaned on the metal frame of her hospital bed. Having never received a blessing from her before, I replied, "Oh Mummy, bless you, too. You are so brave." The exchange of blessings seemed to wash something out of the air, leaving behind a memory to be cherished.

My flu peaked that afternoon, and I had to lie down to muster the strength to prepare supper and clean up afterward. Mom was propped up in bed as the midday sun lit up her vista of snowcapped mountains beyond a sparkling shoreline. She wasn't sleepy, and was not yet being given drugs capable of altering her consciousness. She assured me she'd be fine while I rested, and if she got bored she'd skim the newspaper I'd left with her. I nodded gratefully and trudged into my room, leaving the door ajar in case she called.

Two hours later I awoke from a dreamless void. I must have moved slightly, because I heard my mother chirp, *Oh, good!* She'd been listening for the first sound that I was awake, so eager was she to tell me what had happened. She looked radiant as I entered the living room, and patted a place for me to sit on her bed. During my nap, she said, she was awake and resting peacefully when a young man she recognized as the singer Michael Jackson let himself in through the sliding glass door from the deck and invited her to come with him. She told him she was surprised and flattered by his visit, but that she wasn't able to get around anymore. To this he replied, "No problem. I'll help you," and extended his hand.

Michael Jackson, my mother continued, transported her to a palatial estate and ushered her into a stately hall lined with magnificent paintings and sculpture. *He offered me anything I wanted,* she recalled in an amazed voice. *I realized they were among the finest works of art the world had to offer, so I thanked him sincerely, but declined.* Then he led her to an elegant banquet table arrayed with crystal bowls full of wonderful delicacies. *And Becky—you'd appreciate this from our berry farm days—there in a pyramid arrangement were the most perfect ripe raspberries!* Her hand carved the air to outline the fruit's formation. We knew too well how difficult it was to keep raspberries fresh in those days, how quickly they could wilt and become moldy. Putting them into a pyramid display would have taken extreme skill and incredibly robust raspberries.

I could imagine how marvelous they would taste, and told him that, with my background, I appreciated them as much as anyone could. But I did not have the appetite, nor did I wish to disturb such a beautiful arrangement. She wanted me to understand that she'd made it clear to her gracious host that her lack of appetite was in no way regrettable.

After this legendary artist had shown her around and been turned down for every splendid thing he offered, my mother said she asked how she was going to get home. *He said, "Don't worry, I'll take care of that."* Before she could wonder how, he'd taken her hand and was effortlessly helping her back into her bed in Bremerton. Then he bowed, let himself out through the sliding glass door onto the deck, and disappeared.

This was not a dream, Mom insisted. *I was wide awake the whole time. What do you think it means, Beck?*

Her gaze was luminous as she waited for my answer, though she seemed quite content with her own opinion. Whether or not she'd been awake, or in an alternative reality, the tribute she'd just received created a moment of unique openness for us. I gave her edematous hand a gentle squeeze.

"Well, Mummy, I think it means you've reached the point in your life when the world and all its treasures are no longer desirable. It's a special blessing to be given such a vision."

Glowing, she nodded. *That's what I think, too.*

This experience of heightened reality gave no access to spirits of destruction. Discord was impossible. When Mary-Jo heard God telling her that fellowship was the better way, He/She might have already planned for Mom to share this experience with me.

The next morning she described her vision to Lucy, who passed it on to the entire Hospice staff. Lucy told us they were jubilant.

Another day or two passed, and my mother, who prized lively conversation, began to doze off when friends came to see her. As Christmas approached, she recalled something vaguely biblical that amused her, concerning Shadrach, Meshack and Abednego.

In her vague recollection, they might have been the three wise men who'd journeyed to see the infant Jesus. Somehow their names had been reduced to *"Rack, shack, and to bed we go."* We chuckled, and she dozed off again.

On Tuesday, December 17, she asked me to turn up her oxygen to the highest setting. Even with that, she struggled for breath.

Becky, she rasped, *I fear I haven't been a very good mother.* She seemed to be in earnest, perhaps beyond fishing for praise.

I was silent. Would she say something more, to put our troubled past into perspective, to help me face the future without her? I waited for anything she might add to render this uncharacteristic statement more intelligible. When I did not respond right away, she said, *I've tried my best.*

Transfixed, immersed in awareness of her suffering, and the starkness of her words, I knew she was too weak to be asked why, in years past, she'd told my close friends that I did not love her, or why, in a very recent outburst, she'd virtually warned a valued potential friend away from me. The most essential question I did not think to ask was if she was able to acknowledge that I loved her—since she'd once seen fit to cancel the F she'd given me as a daughter.

Several thoughts flashed across my mind, in a few seconds.

One was the ancient Eastern belief that we have all been reincarnated so many times that virtually everyone has been our mother in a previous lifetime. Perhaps I'd been her mother and had chosen to return as her daughter to complete some unfinished business. My life to this point might have been a test of whether I could maintain my integrity beyond this moment. Another was the possibility that my mother's nearly endless dissatisfaction with me had stemmed from other wounds, deep in her heart, that had never healed. As far as I knew, she'd lost the man she called the love of her life and married my father instead, only to lose her firstborn son in childbirth, then my father, and the farm she'd inherited from him. Her second husband had abandoned her, triggering a nervous breakdown that put her in jail, then in a psychiatric institution, while her children were placed in foster care. Her third husband had made only a pretense of affection, and the fourth condescended to marry her only after his health failed. A brain tumor had taken her second son's life in his prime. Finally, the desertion by her elderly boyfriend forced her to rely on me, whose love she'd been discrediting since my adolescence.

There were other possible components of my mother's remorse that I did not know about at this moment. A decade would pass before Mary-Jo informed me that, in the years she and Lucille Kaiser had known my mother, they did not hear her say "one good word" about me. Lacking such essential information at the time of my mother's vague but genuine confession, I had yet to understand why, after Mom's first trip back to New Zealand, Aunt Gwenda had sent me a letter insisting she knew in her bones that I was a good person. Maybe my mother's obsessive complaints against me lay behind her damning phrase, *same old Becky*, that I'd accidentally overheard in a phone call—almost certainly to my brother—during our trip to Canada, which she refused to explain. Perhaps it accounted for why my mother's other close friends in Bremerton never seemed pleased to greet me when I visited her every summer.

Returning to the moment at hand, I realized that my mother must have labored greatly to express this nebulous regret. Seconds had passed, her gaze clung to me for a response. "It's difficult being a mother," I heard myself say, "and it's very difficult being a child. It's impossible to be perfect at either one. We just have to forgive each other, and accept our limitations." This did not seem enough, so I added, "Considering all the difficulties, you've done very, very well."

She looked away. Was she disappointed that my response hadn't been more effusive? Did she share my regret that she could not be forthcoming as to why or how she hadn't been such a good mother?

Earlier that evening we'd watched a slapstick stunt on the TV show "Home Improvement," and she'd let out a short *Ha!* Not much breath, but real amusement. It was the last time I heard her laugh. An hour or so later she smiled, hearing me chuckle during another comedy, whose dialogue she couldn't hear above the hiss of the oxygen tubes. During the evening I kissed her forehead and stroked her brow. Before she went to sleep, when I leaned in to coax her to swallow a bit more milk with her sleeping pill, she whispered, *Good-bye, dear.*

"Goodnight, Mummy," I murmured. "Pretty soon you'll be able to hang out with Johnny instead of me." Her eyes widened a little, then relaxed. I readjusted her oxygen cannula, and she kissed the air to thank me.

The next day Mom's friend Helen Scales, a retired public health nurse, came to help take care of her. Helen brought a flannel sheet that she warmed up in our dryer and put over my mother. Mom made an effort to smile, whispering, *That feels nice.* Helen explained to me that nurses used to put warm flannel sheets over post-surgical patients to comfort them. A kindly touch, rarely if ever done in today's hospitals.

I left Helen with her while I tidied up the dining area. From the corner of my eye, I noticed Mom raise her arm and point to a spot near the ceiling. Helen told me later that, as my mother pointed, she'd said, *Look! There's an angel!* – a beatific smile on her face. Helen said she looked at the spot and saw nothing. No matter. I was happy for Mom. She'd told me she'd always wanted to see an angel, and envied those who'd been granted this special grace.

That night I lay on the sofa next to my mother's bed while she slept fitfully, once calling out, *Somebody help me!* Twice she cried, *Becky, do something!* All I could do was tell her I was right there and ask what I should do, for which she had no answer.

Still later, she pleaded, *When are they going to come? It's so hard to be waiting.*

Not knowing who *they* were, and guessing she might be hoping for angels, I replied, "They'll come at the perfect time, Mummy." Stroking her forehead, I suggested that God might be using her to give others a chance to serve, such as Helen and the

Hospice people assigned to us. She listened as though open to any reason for her prolonged agony.

Hours passed. Into the dark, after much labored breathing, she asked, *Is anybody there?*

I grabbed her hand. "I'm here. I haven't left you."

I'm glad somebody cares, she whispered, returning the firm grip.

"It must be very hard for you, Mummy."

Slowly, she gasped, *My dying is very hard...and so has been my living.*

More time passed. I was bewildered when Mom seemed to snap awake, pleading, *Does Karen have the baby? Are all the sheets ready for the baby?*

Was Karen the nurse who'd comforted her after her 36-hour labor, when her first son had died trying to be born? Was it Karen who'd given her a paperback murder mystery, hoping it would distract her from devastating grief? Maybe Karen was the one who'd told her to be thankful the multitude of large moles on her back had not chosen to appear on her face.

I felt privileged to be near my mother in the throes of this flashback—as though I'd been folded back in time with her—so she would not be alone as she relived the most agonizing experience of her life.

Nurse Shawn stopped by the next day to ask if my mother felt the same about artificial interventions. Mom made it clear, charmingly, that she still had no desire to be resuscitated. *No big schlamozzle.* Her exact words. I teased her for trying to sound like a New Yorker, and asked if she knew what schlamozzle meant. She gave me a smug smile, as if her own usage had been perfectly fine.

After Shawn left, I looked across Mom's hospital bed at Helen and wisecracked, "If there is a big schlamozzle, Mom, Helen and I will flip you up and down a few times on the draw sheet. You might not enjoy it very much, but we will."

Mom gave me a twinkly look. Helen chuckled and rolled her eyes.

Later that afternoon the Hospice chaplain appeared to say good-bye. After meeting privately with my mother, he stepped into the kitchen to bid me an eloquent farewell, praising my mother's grace, charm, and the breadth of her life that she'd made so vivid in what she'd shared with him. He'd been fascinated by her accounts of nursing in the days before Dr. Foley had invented the inflatable bubble to keep catheters from slipping out. He'd learned from her that enemas had been invented after observing the behavior of migrating birds. He'd been transported to another time, edified, and blessed by the chance to break bread with her.

John the oxygen man arrived shortly afterward. He connected two tanks with a Y-tube so Mom could greatly increase her intake, and showed me how to put a facemask on her so she could breathe through her nose and mouth. On the way out he paused to say, "I really feel for you. I've been coming here a couple years now, and she's *really* nice." I choked up, waved him a silent good-bye, and he assured me he'd be on call if needed.

Late at night, December 18, I was keeping vigil on the sofa near my mother, who'd been sleeping more deeply with the new oxygen mask. According to Shawn, she wasn't expected to live another 24 hours. Helen was asleep in Mom's bedroom. I'd called her that morning, afraid that Mom might die if or when I left the room. Helen came immediately, stayed with me throughout the day, and was taking a well-earned rest.

A sudden commotion jolted me upright. Mom had yanked off the oxygen mask and was thrashing about trying to rid herself of her catheter, bedclothes and nightgown. "Now Mummy, you mustn't take off your nightie," I said groggily, with a hint of whimsy. "You have to be decent."

Even in her far-gone state, the look she gave me registered the trace of humor. I replaced her covers, checked that the catheter was still in, and reminded her that the mask was now her sole source of oxygen. She kept her nightgown on but squirmed away from the mask.

The sound of my voice roused Helen, who thought it best to increase the amount of morphine recently prescribed to reduce my mother's discomfort. Mom accepted the morphine sulfate tablet, but struggled to keep the mask off. *I don't want it,* she gasped, *even if it kills me!"*

"Rachel dear," Helen answered kindly, "we're trying to help you."

Mom replied clearly, *I know you are,* and paused, perhaps hesitating to tell us to remove the mask anyway, then drifted off into what we hoped was euphoria. Helen urged me to get some sleep while she kept vigil. She stayed with Mom the rest of the night, administering morphine at half-hour intervals.

Thursday morning, December 19th, Dee informed me that, uncharacteristically, Lucy had asked to be reassigned. In Rachel's case, she explained understandingly, Lucy had not wanted to see her patient die. I recalled Lucy's breezy "All in a day's work!" when she'd told me how used to death she'd become. Not so easy, it seemed, when my mother was her patient.

Nanette appeared in the late afternoon, and insisted on staying with me until Mary-Jo could come in the evening. Thursday was Mary-Jo's day off, the only time she could be with us, but she had to take care of her father first. Just before she arrived, Nanette and I heard thick gurgling sounds in my mother's throat. Frantic, I called the Hospice night nurse and asked her to bring an aspirator of some kind. She said she'd try. When Mary-Jo came, Nanette left, saying, "You're the only one they'd come to do this for."

At once Mary-Jo sized things up. "What exactly were Rachel's last wishes about this oxygen?" she asked. "Did she say anything to you about it? Because frankly, it's the only thing keeping her alive."

As I began to tell her that the night before Mom had told us to remove the mask even if it killed her, I realized, in horror, that Helen and I had been prolonging my mother's life against the intent of her living will. Mary-Jo looked at me, saying calmly, "I would support you one hundred percent if you decided to remove this mask." Thinking it best to do so when the night nurse came, I lifted it briefly to wash my mother's face.

A knock on the door, and the remarkable Hospice night nurse, Jean Strum, appeared. Tall, sturdy, middle-aged and unassuming, her presence combined humility with serene confidence. "For Hospice patients," she assured us, "oxygen is not meant to prolong life, only to provide comfort." What mattered was to follow my mother's wishes.

The thought arose that I'd been responsible for 24 hours of unnecessary suffering because I could not bear to remove that mask. On the other hand, the past 24 hours had extended my mother's life and made possible her last contact with Mary-Jo.

Sensing my trepidation, our friend bent down close and asked, "Rachel, would you like us to remove the oxygen mask?" Up rose my mother's less swollen arm. Her hand made an emphatic pushing-away gesture. It reminded me of the times she'd tossed out straggly plants that no longer beautified her home. A similarly brisk stroke ordered the terminus to her own life.

I detached the mask and turned off the oxygen. Nurse Jean called the hospital for an aspirator to clear my mother's throat. Mom was breathing more slowly, looking relieved to be free of the mask. Would I be willing, Jean asked, to drive to the hospital and pick up the aspirator? I answered quietly, "I'm not leaving my mother." She then asked Mary-Jo, who said she was willing to go. There was no tension in this exchange, only gratitude on my part that I had a friend who loved me enough to do this.

The nurse stood watch nearby as I stroked my mother's silky white hair, freed of the brown coloring that had coarsened it until recently. "Okay, my darling beautiful Mummy," I murmured, "it won't be long now." Only a few minutes of her life remained, but I knew she received these words straight from my heart.

Jean knelt beside me and held my mother's wrist for a pulse. We heard her take in a sharp, full breath, after which she did not exhale. I looked at Jean and asked, "Is this the moment?" She applied her stethoscope and heard a faint heartbeat. When Mom exhaled deeply, the nurse listened again, and heard nothing.

I watched to see if my mother's body would show a wave of life leaving it, as I'd seen happen when my pet bird died. No such wave passed through her body. It simply acquired a stillness, and remained warm, especially her head. With wordless tact, Jean stepped out of the room. I cradled my mother's face in my hands and wept, silently giving thanks for the gift of her life, that she had been my mother, and that my prayers had been answered in the weeks I'd been given with her. To her spirit, who I sensed had not left the room, I said, "Please forgive me, Mummy, for all the times I've hurt and disappointed you. Remember that I do love you and have done my best to be here for you."

Minutes later, Mary-Jo returned to find her old friend gone. Rather than sorrow, she expressed warm acceptance, and confidence that we'd done right to act on my mother's wishes. She said she was glad to be with me so soon afterward.

My mother's face had taken on a wondrous expression—emanating serenity, dignity, and a childlike sweetness. She seemed to radiate a benediction upon everyone around her. Nurse Jean gently bathed my mother's body, and said she'd heard about her from others on the Hospice staff. It was an honor to meet her, she told us, if only at the moment of death.

When Jean was finished I walked her out to her car, and noticed that someone was in it waiting for her. He was sitting in the dark, not even passing the time with something to read. "Oh, that's my husband," Jean said. I said I hoped he didn't mind the wait. "That's all right," she explained. "He's used to it. He's retired and likes to feel part of my work, which he believes is important." I assured her it was, thanked them both, and returned to the house, where Mary-Jo hugged me and said she had to leave to help her father go to bed.

I stayed up alone with my mother, tidying up the living room, doing the few dishes. Occasionally I touched her still warm head. Mostly I just existed, sharing our last private time together. About two a.m., I turned off all the lights except her favorite lamp, stroked her forehead, and said, "Goodnight, my precious Mother"—the only time I'd ever addressed her by that formal term.

Before getting into bed, I opened a prayer book I'd brought with me that contained a long series of traditional prayers for the dead. I read them all in earnest, praying that her soul was blessed and forgiven of any offense that might detain her from a happy and smooth transit to her next phase of existence, preferably heaven.

There was no longer the hiss of an oxygen tank, nor the labored breathing of this most loved person I'd tended for such an evanescent span. As I waiting for sleep, there were no indoor sounds to listen for, so I became more aware of the embrace of nature: soft waves on the shore and wind stirring the leaves of nearby trees. There would be no other night like this, just the two of us. Her spirit seemed to linger before embarking into the unknown.

I sent my personal radar out into the ether, for any signal that something was left unsettled between us. What came back was a feeling that my mother's spirit was trying to strengthen me for the time ahead. To fend off sorrow for losing her incalculable presence, I reflected on the Bard's words she'd taught me in childhood: *"Judge not the play until the play is o'er. Its scenes have many changes. The last act crowns the play."* She'd first given me these lines to slough off the taunts of grade-school bullies, then the mortification of being a wallflower at high-school dances. As I got older, what seemed like betrayals of her love for me became part of our shared drama, including some penultimate episodes before her death. But they paled in importance compared to the tender moments we'd shared as I took care of her—her spoken blessing, her eagerness to share a most wonderful vision, the fear she'd expressed that she hadn't been a very good mother, and her tender farewell.

Helen returned at eight the next morning. She pulled a chair up next to my mother's bed, held her cool hand, and sat alone with her while I prepared to face the world.

On an impulse, I called Oscar Cooper to ask if he'd like to come and see her. He thanked me and arrived within minutes. Letting himself in, he approached her body and delicately placed the fingertips of one hand on her forehead. It seemed to signal his love and hope for her forgiveness. Oscar took a last look at her serene face, thanked me again, and let himself out. It felt more probable than ever that a mysterious Providence had impelled this man to walk out on my mother, perhaps for my sake. Why else would he make that insane demand that she not renew her fire insurance policy or else he'd leave her? Was there not something in Scripture about God sending a *lying spirit* into King Ahab so he'd be defeated in battle?

Moments later, Mary-Jo appeared with her father for a last good-bye. He, too, did not linger. Better for him to remember the happy times, some captured in his daughter's photos, when Rachel the equally expert gardener conferred with him amid rows of his prize vegetables, their faces hidden under straw sunhats, as though trading insider stock tips.

About eleven that morning I wondered when I'd be capable of calling the mortuary to have them come for my mother's body. You can do this, I told myself, and dialed the number. Twenty minutes passed while I dreaded their arrival. Then two sons from the family who owned the funeral home drove up to the carport in a black van. Their gurney could not make the turn from the carport into our entry hall, so they had to carry out my mother's body wrapped in a white sheet. There was no time for me to embrace her, so I placed my hands tenderly around her head after they'd wrapped it. As they carried the body out like a beam under their arms, I reached out and squeezed her toes one last time, knowing that, underneath the sheet, her toenails were neatly polished from the last pedicure I'd given her. I grieved not to be able to perform any more of what she'd called my *ministrations*.

Following the two men out, I watched them place her body on the gurney to be lifted mechanically into their van. To my surprise I heard myself demanding in a concerned tone, "What are you going to do with my mother's body?"

The older brother answered stiffly, "We'll place it in a controlled temperature room, then in a casket for burial." I then blurted out what sounded like a warning: "You must treat her body with care. She is a great soul." Taken aback, he assured me they would. Locking onto his gaze to hold him to this, I thanked them.

Hands clasped under my chin, I stood bereft, as the large black lozenge slowly ascended the driveway in first gear. It was similar in shape to the white ambulance I'd followed from the nursing home in my mother's car, the night she'd saved her own life, refusing to take the sleeping pill provided by the night nurse who'd accused her of hyperventilating. No need for me now to drive behind, tapping the horn to reassure her of my presence.

Whether her spirit was hovering above the scene, next to me, or far away, I could no longer sense. What I felt clearly was that my role had become much more solitary. The appreciation she'd voiced in her final days, validating my presence in her life, was becoming a memory. By coincidence, the black van inched up past a car on its way down, driven by my mother's reclusive neighbor, Mrs. Hudson. As soon as she pulled into her adjacent carport, she stepped out and walked toward me. Avoiding eye contact, she stood next to me, gazing out in the same direction, where the van had just disappeared.

"I know how hard it is," she said. "I've lost my husband and a son, and it seems like yesterday. I feel for you." I mumbled thanks and went inside.

On the stripped hospital bed in the center of the living room lay the exposed egg-crate foam mattress that retained the indentation of my mother's body. I leaned across it, resting my head on the area that had supported her heart, and sobbed, understanding what an older colleague at work had told me, decades after she'd lost her own mother. Despite her appearance of maturity—having raised a family and become a grandmother—she still felt like an orphan without her mother.

I'd forgotten that Helen Scales had remained inside while Mom's body was taken. She emerged from the kitchen, placed a hand gently on my back, and said, "Becky dear, would you like to spend the night at my place, just for a change? You're welcome to stay as long as you like."

Years before, Mom had told me that Helen had called her when she'd come home alone from the hospital, suffering from unbearable post-surgical pain. She and my mother were both nurses, but a long career in public health administration had left Helen with little hands-on experience. My mother rushed over and put Helen into a soothing sitz bath, staying with her for several days until she could manage on her own. Helen had never mentioned it to me, but she may have tried to return such a favor to her good friend's daughter.

It would be a lovely respite, before I faced what Mom had called *the repercussions.*

CHAPTER FORTY-FOUR

Hindsights

Helen Scales' unassuming, elegant home was tucked among tall evergreens overlooking Bremerton's Oyster Bay. A narrow patch of forest had been cleared on her property for a glimpse of the bay without lessening the sense of nestling among the trees. Helen gave me her own small bedroom, whose windows faced east to welcome the morning sun, needing no blinds for privacy. Unused to having forest sounds so close, I was awakened at dawn by the rumble of what has been aptly named a conference of crows. I'd never before heard their rasping, pumping chant, infused with a spirit of tribal intelligence. No crows appeared in the small clearing where Helen had placed two lawn chairs and a side table, yet the sound was so intense there had to be quite a gathering in the surrounding woods. What were they proclaiming in their sage, powerful unison? Had they recognized me from my walks in the hills of Manette? Had some of them observed the black van leaving my mother's house and knew of her demise? I wouldn't put much past a crow. Once one of their New York brethren joined me on a bench in Central Park and flew off with half the sandwich I'd brought for lunch. With reason, a Native American tribe bears their name.

That morning I phoned Rosemary, one of my mother's closest friends, who'd been expecting my call. When I mentioned my concern that Mom had been kept alive a day or two longer than she would have wanted, Rosemary said, "A few weeks ago Rachel told me, *If only I could stop the oxygen and get it over with, but I don't want to frighten Becky.*" Helen confirmed this, saying, "Rachel was worried because you'd never seen anyone die, especially a loved one."

Rather than feeling remorse, it occurred to me that even if Mom had martyred herself tolerating the oxygen a few days longer, during that time she'd seen an angel above the foot of her bed. She'd been transported to a princely estate by someone she recognized as Michael Jackson, and turned down without regret some of the finest artifacts and delicacies the world had to offer. And she'd lived until a Thursday evening, Mary-Jo's day off, so she could die in the presence of the friend she'd loved as a second daughter.

By far the most haunting memory was two days before she died, when she was too far gone to elaborate on her stunning near-confession, *I fear I haven't been a very good mother*. Sitting comfortably in Helen's high-ceilinged living room, absorbing the sunset over Oyster Bay, I pondered why Mom could not have raised this crucial matter a few days earlier. What sprang to mind was Tolstoy's "The Death of Ivan Ilyich," the story of a Russian judge dying of liver disease, who gradually realizes that he'd spent his life pursuing the dubious rewards of a career in the Russian courts, passed up his chance at true love in his youth, and denied his wife and children the care they deserved. As death approaches, Ilyich's unloved wife makes a dutiful appearance at his bedside. Ivan tries to say "Forgive me," but all he can get out before expiring is something like "Forego." Tolstoy softens his readers' disappointment by having his omniscient narrator say what really mattered was that the Merciful One heard what the dying Ilyich meant to say.

The fear my mother had expressed as she neared the end was as unfathomable to me as Ilyich's last word to his wife. Only the Merciful One knew what she meant. Considering how she'd been blessed by multiple acts of grace—and would be even in the matter of her burial—I had to believe that, overall, God was well pleased with her life.

Over breakfast the next day, Helen reminisced about her friend Rachel's unlikely membership in an exclusive club for professional women. They'd disregarded her modest professional background as a practical nurse, though perhaps not her status as the widow of a Navy captain. Her friend Rosemary had nominated my mother, basing it on her outstanding work as a volunteer at the Welfare Department. At club meetings, Helen recalled, "Rachel had all those dignified ladies in stitches. She told us about a woman in New Zealand who'd changed the pronunciation of her name so it would be more suitable in high society."

"Oh, you must mean Mrs. Sidebottom," I replied, attempting a posh British accent: "That would be Mrs. Sid-ee-bo-TAHM to you." Helen laughed as though she'd heard it for the first time.

Her favorite was a tale Mom must have got from Captain Madden, about an admiral's wife who'd accompanied her husband to China, where she bought a fancy medallion at a bazaar. Determined to impress the Asian dignitaries they were meeting in their travels, she hung the medallion on a thick gold chain, accessorizing a Mandarin- collared sheath dress she'd had made for her from Chinese red silk shantung, slit high up one thigh. She wore the ensemble to a State Department reception, where one Chinese diplomat after another scurried away, pretending not to understand when she asked them to translate the characters on the medallion. Finally she got her husband to corner the Chinese ambassador, who answered the admiral with inscrutable patience: "It says, Licensed Prostitute, City of Shanghai."

"I would have worn that thing with pride!" Helen whooped. Slowly shaking her head, she recalled, "No one could get those gals to let their hair down like Rachel. We really missed her when she stopped coming to meetings. After awhile I couldn't be bothered."

Helen accompanied me to the funeral home to choose a headstone and provide them with an epitaph to engrave on it.

We were greeted by one of the owners' sons who'd come for my mother's body. Before showing us photos of sample headstones, he brought us to meet his mother at the main desk. She gave me a quick, cordial greeting and nodded to her son, who escorted us into a meeting room.

Everything had been settled with the funeral parlor, I thought, when the next day an older man—perhaps the family patriarch—called to offer me a "choice of caskets." I'd already selected, on my mother's precise orders, their least expensive model, similar to the pine box she and I had once chosen for Verne. Providence, however, seemed to have arranged otherwise. So I returned to the funeral home.

From the older man's circuitous explanation, I gathered that a law greatly favoring the mortuary business required families who arrange for a viewing of their loved one's body before it is cremated, to purchase outright, rather than rent, the casket used for the viewing. After the cremation they could either—some choice!—keep the casket for future use, or donate it to the funeral home to offer to another family, at their discretion. In this case, anonymous donors had purchased a plush, satin-lined, polished metal casket with a beautiful rosy lavender finish, artfully trimmed in chrome. They did not wish to keep it after the viewing of their departed loved one, so the funeral home decided to offer it to me, "to expand your choices," as the man diplomatically stated. Lavender was one of Mom's favorite colors. Had we been richer and less leery of the mortuary business, we could not have chosen a more suitable model. He opened their catalogue to verify its much-higher price, and asked me to choose between it and the model I'd selected.

"It's perfect," I said without looking. "Thank you very much, and please thank the donors for me." Thus—no disrespect to Mom's disapproval of price gouging by the funeral industry—her body was put to rest in the manner Providence felt she deserved.

Assuring Helen I was ready to return to my mother's place, I drove back to the empty-feeling house and began placing overseas calls to our family Down Under. First was Aunt Gwenda, who'd become hard of hearing and forgetful. Her voice sounded chirpy, almost cheerful, at news of her sister's death. She asked me to wait while she found a pencil to write down Rachel's age and date of passing in case she forgot.

It was the second time I'd ever spoken with her. The first was sixteen years earlier, during my mother's second trip to New Zealand. At that time I'd been dating a charming Australian man who'd met my mother when she was visiting me in New York. He was a Harvard Ph.D. and scientist who played a fine game of tennis, liked poetry, and spoke confidently that we'd be married someday. Ironically, before Mom left for New Zealand, she predicted I would no longer have much need of her because she was convinced that this fellow—who, unbeknownst to us, was bipolar as well as a recovering alcoholic—was a perfect match. I'd thought so, until he dumped me for a former Harvard student he happened to visit in Mexico City on a research trip. The agony of suddenly being dropped for another made my long-distance call to my mother rather desperate. Gwenda was delighted to speak with me, but realized I was too distraught for chitchat. Mercifully, she did not ask what was troubling me, but explained that my mother was out on one of her daily walks and would return in an hour or so. I was too upset to call again.

I could still hear Gwenda's younger voice, how pleased she sounded to hear from her American niece, and regretted that I couldn't make more of that earlier opportunity to talk with her. Now she was 86 and losing her faculties, while I gushed about growing up listening to her wonderful letters, and my hopes of meeting her and my other New Zealand relatives some day.

"Well, Becky," she replied, "I can assure you of a very warm welcome, but I may not be around to greet you myself."

Not long after Mom's death, Gwenda was diagnosed with an inoperable aortic hernia and sent home to die. She had not been expected to survive a week, but after forty years of yoga she was unusually fit, and lived another two years. In Gwenda's last letter to Mom she joked about reading the same copy of the

Reader's Digest over and over, because she instantly forgot what-ever she read. Gwenda died in her sleep at 87—nearly equaling my mother's age. As Providence would have it, she'd just enjoyed a long visit with her daughter Heather, who was due to return to Australia in the morning. Thus Gwenda, too, got to spend some quality time with her daughter, but how different was her peaceful passing from that of her sister Rachel. By all accounts, Gwenda and Heather's relationship had been consistently supportive and harmonious. It must have disturbed my aunt to hear her sister speak about me so disapprovingly.

In case Gwenda forgot, I called her son Grahame an hour later. He said he'd got the message, but his mum didn't remember who'd called her. Though we hadn't spoken since he and his fam-ily stayed with Mom in Bremerton on his sabbatical from Waicato University in 1975, I felt close to Grahame. He and my brother had bonded instantly when Johnny came to be interviewed for the position of New Zealand's director of flight safety. The two cousins shared the same deadpan, hooligan sense of humor, and felt like brothers. Johnny's main reason for wanting to move to New Zealand, I suspected, was to be near Grahame.

Johnny, I'd heard from Mom, had been weeks at Walter Reed Hospital, unable to speak due to a botched biopsy, when Grahame unexpectedly walked into his hospital room. As soon as Johnny saw him he sat up and said "Grahame!" Then his muteness returned—making that his last spoken word. Grahame said the three most important men in his life were his father, his brother Stuart, and my brother. Each passed away before his time, and each had a fantastic sense of humor.

Not wanting our conversation to end, I said wistfully, "Too bad my mum never spoke with Douglas Elliott when she returned to New Zealand…"

"Hold on," Grahame interjected. "Rachel did speak with him. By phone, on her first trip back here. I know because I placed the call."

My stomach received this as a sucker punch. "Are you seri-ous? She never told me!" Frankly, I was more at peace with my mother's death than with this posthumous news flash. "Do you have any idea what they talked about?"

"Not a clue. After I put through the call we all left the room so Auntie Rachel could have her privacy."

I was heartsick. I pressed Grahame for even his faintest impression of Mom's facial expression or demeanor after the call. He remembered nothing.

"Amazing," I concluded, trying to mask my disappointment. Of all the things Mom chose not to share with me, this felt the worst. I'd grown up hearing about her one true love, torn away from her by the war and the tiny error of a telegraph clerk. How could she not tell me about this historic phone call?

Mom was newly widowed on her first trip back to New Zealand. During her sister's years in the States, Gwenda had kept tabs on Douglas, learning that late in life he'd married a woman with similar expertise in gardening. Douglas was still working at a regional newspaper when Grahame reconnected him with his former fiancée.

Up till then, the last time they'd talked in person was when the previously humiliated Rachel Williams had brought her handsome, wealthy new fiancé, Geoff Whisker, to meet her friends and former coworkers in Palmerston North. She'd made a point of stopping by Duncan & Davies, the plant nursery where she and Douglas had spent perhaps the happiest four years of their lives. After her triumphant return visit with Geoff, who would soon be lost to her in a shotgun marriage, she and Douglas had communicated only in writing. As far as I knew, their correspondence had ended with the fateful cable she'd meant to sign **LOVE RACHEL**.

I tried to imagine what kind of words my mother had exchanged with the man she'd called the love of her life. Maybe there'd been no outpouring of emotion, just awkward British reserve. Douglas might have answered during a hectic moment in the newsroom, and could not give her his full attention. If so, I could understand why she'd preferred not to discuss it, but that did not dim my disappointment. Eventually I was able to research Douglas's career in New Zealand, and found that after many years of bachelorhood Douglas had married the gardening columnist at the newspaper where he worked as a photographer and writer of obituaries. He'd published a popular book on native New Zealand flowers, and hosted a weekly radio program on gardening. Mom was 59, Douglas 56, when she first returned to New Zealand. Before she left, I asked if she would try to see him. *No*, she'd replied firmly. *I don't want him to remember me as an old woman. Nor do I wish to ruin his marriage.*

When I returned to New York after Mom's death, I told a fellow literature professor about this painfully unknowable conversation. She believed that my mother would have dropped everything and stayed in New Zealand, if Douglas—married or not—had shown any interest in her. The reason my mother said nothing about it, my colleague wagered, was that Douglas had shown no interest.

I did not buy that scenario, preferring to conjure up a dialogue similar to the last lines of Marguerite Duras's memoir of her Chinese lover. This young man's father had arranged for him to marry a girl from an equally rich Chinese family, and he could not face the certainty of being disinherited if he disobeyed. Many years later, after they'd both been married and raised families— the Chinese man telephoned Marguerite in France. She recognized his voice instantly, and after a brief, halting exchange of essentials about their years apart, they reached a deep silence. Duras ends her book when her former lover breaks the silence, telling Marguerite that he has always loved her, and will love her "beyond death."

Though deeply moved, I was also vexed by the way Duras concluded this intimate memoir. Was I the only reader who wondered how she could have deprived her once great love of a response, after he'd bared his soul to her? Surely she'd said something equally heartfelt to him. Or had she? Had Duras decided, in artistic terms, that his confession would make a more effective final line of a book, so she omitted her reply because it might sound anticlimactic, even banal—especially if it had amounted to 'I feel the same for you'? But what if she'd written down exactly what had transpired—and done something that seemed unthinkably heartless? Had she actually remained silent, and simply hung up after he'd spoken? Didn't her former lover—and her readers—deserve better?

So, in the scenario I imagined for my mother and Douglas, they exchanged words similar to those of Marguerite's Chinese lover, one to the other, with equal tenderness.

Much later, it occurred to me that I'd never told my mother about Steve Devere's soulful farewell kiss in the subway car, the impassioned end of our future together. I had to admit that parting from Steve had been too private, too sad, and too precious to share with her. If she'd felt the same about her last spoken words with Douglas, I had to forgive her.

After a day spent making phone calls, Mary-Jo suggested we go see the movie "Jerry Maguire." In the title role, Tom Cruise plays a fast-talking sports agent who unexpectedly discovers evidence of his own integrity. Afterward, with Maguire's slogan "Show me the money!" ringing in our ears, we sat in my mother's car to chat. I joked about what Mom might have said about Jerry Maguire, saying I wished we could still communicate somehow. Her scowl took me by surprise.

"Becky, Scripture forbids us to talk with the dead," she warned, citing chapter and verse.

Taken aback, I asked what was the harm. The only consolation for my loss, I suggested, would be to establish a bond of love and support that extended beyond physical reality.

"We should express our thoughts directly to God," she insisted. Otherwise, our attempts to communicate with the dead could be poisoned by evil spirits who prey upon our vulnerability after losing a loved one.

"But Mary-Jo, can't we ask God to protect us from evil spirits?"

Though unwilling to deny that anything is possible with God, she stuck to her position.

"I've asked Johnny to help my friend in New York find a parking space when he comes to see me, and he's had incredibly fast results, in one of the world's toughest places to park. How can that be evil?"

No answer.

Our disagreement was resolved, in my view, late on Christmas Day after my mother died, when a severe blizzard hit western Washington. My friend from high school, Doreen, and her husband Jim had invited me to Christmas dinner in Everett with Jim's parents, where, though orphaned, I was treated like family. After the meal, the late-afternoon sky darkened as we drove back to Doreen and Jim's place near Tacoma. During a comforting round of herbal tea and conversation, I glanced out the window at what looked like a cosmic pillow fight. The dark sky had been displaced by a mass of roiling white rags, blocking all perception beyond some faint outlines across the street.

Concerned for my safety, Doreen and Jim urged me to spend the night. I was grateful, but a commanding voice inside my head told me to drive back to Bremerton. It felt authoritative, and maternal. Against my friends' judgment I headed out to my mother's car, which I was beginning to realize was now mine. Jim reminded me of the turns I needed to take before I could enter the southbound highway. Once on it, visibility was blurred at best, and sharp winds buffeted the sturdy '84 Camry. Already the hulks of heavier, supposedly safer vehicles could be seen at the odd angles where they'd slid off the shoulder. A palpable aura of danger stopped me from turning on the radio for company. I was alone in the car with the elements, and a sense of my mother's protection.

Get behind that maroon car, I felt her say. *And keep the same steady pace.*

I did. Its deep color remained visible through the swirl of flakes. Together, the maroon car and I negotiated gale-force winds that howled across the Tacoma Narrows Bridge. Safely on the other side, the car uncannily chose the exit to Bremerton. Abandoned vehicles were littering the roadside, but the maroon car and trusty Camry forged safely into West Bremerton, where we stopped at the traffic light on Callow Avenue. There we separated, it going straight while I turned right toward the old Manette Bridge and East Bremerton. I crossed the bridge with no cars in sight, and signaled left onto an empty Wheaton Way. As I wound down the narrow access road to my mother's house, the tires were cushioned by a five-inch white carpet. Pulling into the carport, I could almost hear my mother sigh in relief as the wheels rolled securely onto firm dry concrete.

Well done, dear! her spirit seemed to intone. We'd made it through a perilous storm—she in her new position of permanent safety, helping me keep safe in my sphere of impermanence.

Over a foot of snow fell during the muffled night, the first arm of the storm. During a brief lull, the Hospice volunteer who'd kept my mother company while I took breaks with Nanette called to ask if I was okay. Though I barely knew her, she offered to take me shopping for provisions in her four-wheel-drive SUV. Had my mother triggered her concern for me from the Other Side? I'd just returned from the supermarket when the blizzard resumed, dropping another two-three feet and snowing everyone in. But, unlike at Doreen and Jim's place, my electricity and heat stayed on. Toasty warm and well-stocked in the home Mom had left to me, I felt blessed.

After Mary-Jo heard about this, she said it was probably an angel who'd helped me rather than my mother's spirit. I reserved judgment.

Snowed-in and alone, I had little choice but to tackle the tasks at hand. Seated at my mother's place at the dining table—with the best view of the waterfront—I gazed fondly at the antique oak china cabinet she'd bought for $25 at a garage sale on Camano Island. I remembered how she'd applied paint remover and taught Johnny and me to gently scrape away the dark layers of old paint that masked its golden-grained beauty. We watched it start to glow as we varnished it on the gravel outside the boatman's cottage at Monaco Beach. Now it was a family heirloom that only I remained to cherish. I had to steel myself to pack its contents. Was my mother's spirit consoling me as I wrapped her precious china teacups in bubblewrap, grateful for how well they must have been packed to have stayed intact on their journeys from England to New Zealand, then to North America and our series of homes in Washington. Wherever her spirit was, I told myself, Mummy might be viewing her beautiful hand-painted pieces of Royal Albert and Royal Worcester rather like ornaments that were no longer her style.

Mary-Jo offered to store the china cabinet at her father's house. With no idea how to transport it there, she utilized her direct channel to God. Presto! It turned out her father's neighbor had a son with a husky friend and a beat-up old van. The two young men arrived with Mary-Jo one day, joking and chuckling with her while they wrapped the cabinet in old quilts, laid it lengthwise on a dolly, rolled it out the door, up some boards into the van, and drove away. Done in two shakes of a lamb's tail, as Mom would say. All I had to do was watch, thank them, and wave goodbye.

Eventually I had the cabinet expertly packed and shipped to New York, where I would serve tea in her lovely old china cups after dinner parties, hoping she would enjoy seeing them in use, as she had not been able to do in her lifetime.

Next I was drawn toward the shallow single drawer in the side table next to my mother's recliner. There, it seemed, she'd stored only the dearest and most telling documents of her life. On top was a much-handled envelope that held two letters from my brother. One was computer-printed in early 1982, and described his new Coast Guard assignment in New Orleans—the post he would never hold because of a fatal brain tumor. His words pulsed with optimism. It was probably the last letter Johnny sent her while still in good health. The Coast Guard had awarded him a position that might have compensated for his loss of the flight safety directorship he'd so desired in New Zealand. He was to become District Planning Officer for the 8th District, Pensacola to New Mexico, the high-powered right hand to the District Chief of Staff. "Supposedly it's a 'stepping-stone-to-Admiral' type job," Johnny wrote. "I'll settle for Captain!" He died at the latter rank.

The same envelope held a much earlier, handwritten report—on Coast Guard Academy letterhead—from the sailing ship Eagle in 1963. In it, Johnny reported having nearly finished his summer training cruise on the Eagle, about to be transferred to a modern cutter so other cadets could have their turn. He hadn't written to me about this, so I was reading about it for the first time.

> I'll tell you what we do on board as much as I can. We're divided into duty sections, 3 of them. A section stands a watch & then waits 2 & stands another. The watches are 12-4 a.m. midwatch, 4-8 a.m. morning watch, 8-12 forenoon, 12-4 p.m. afternoon, 4-6 p.m. 1st dogwatch, 6-8 p.m. second dog, 8-12 evening. While your section has watch, you may do anything from engine room watches to signalman or radarman. If you don't have anything specific assigned, you are in what's called the ready boat crew. That's designed for man overboard when a boat has to be lowered. Actually all you do on ready boat crew is stay on deck at all times & do various ship's work like chipping paint, scrubbing decks & polishing brass. In general, we get stuck with all the stuff no one else wants to do. That's why it's commonly called "ready boat screw."

The letter had tea stains on it, Mom having read it so many times, probably to her friends. My brother could not resist a jab at Verne, who'd never approved of his table manners:

> I've stood all the engine room watches now & I was a mess cook all day today. Boy do mess cooks ever clean up on food. Tell Verne I had 3½ steaks

for dinner & about half of a cherry pie. Not
counting all the vegetables, milk (a quart) too.

His natural humility emerged when he admitted how much
he'd learned from the enlisted chief petty officers, and how
strange he felt to outrank them.

As I sorted through our mother's effects alone, I sensed the
compassion my brother would have felt for me. My heart was sore
as I read how Johnny closed his letter from the Eagle. He told
Mom that the mail on the Eagle was "pretty unreliable," depend-
ing on whether they were near land. "I got a letter from you on
board, though. Boy, it's even better to get letters here than at the
Academy." I would have gladly written to him. But alas, we didn't
have a close relationship.

Mom had not shown me this delightful photo he'd sent her
as a cadet:

How easily he could charm her, though he panicked at the possibility of incurring her wrath. On one of his summer leaves from the Academy, we got into a lengthy tennis match and forgot that we'd promised Mom to be home for dinner. We were slugging it out in a fading sunset, the ball ever more difficult to see, when I asked Johnny what time it was. At once his carefree ferocity froze into dread. "Oh shit, we're way the hell late. What'll we tell her? Think up a really good lie." It almost felt like we were kids again, except for the swearing

I thought maybe we should stick with the truth. How bad could it be to admit we'd got into a long match and lost track of the time? He looked at me as if I'd never entered the real world. "Go ahead. It's your funeral."

Mom was glad to hear we had a good game. She'd even kept dinner warm for us. Relief flashed across Johnny's face, his jaunty confidence and appetite restored. One of my fondest memories was the quick nod he gave me, as if to say, Nice shot.

The only letter from me that Mom kept in this drawer was crisp and clean, no evidence of repeated readings. On the envelope, postmarked April 1983, she'd written: *Letter from Becky outlining our problem as she sees it.* The marked-up contents made me cringe. I'd taken great care to express my near despair that I would ever be understood and accepted by her. If I chose the option of silence, I wrote, it would only "indulge my demonic feelings of hopelessness when it comes to you and me."

My use of the term "demonic" evoked the Cantwell seminars, especially the one my mother and I had attended together that year. Mary-Jo had been there with her then-husband. So had my then-boyfriend, the aforementioned Anton. One night they and a few others gathered in the dorm room Mom and I were sharing, to offer their concerned opinion that my mother was ignoring ample evidence to the contrary when she'd gone around telling them and others at the seminar that I did not love her.

My letter had been excruciatingly blunt. I reasoned that, in telling my closest friends that I did not love her, she had been "game-playing," with "an element of deceit, perhaps even hypocrisy." In thick pencil, my mother had circled *game-playing*, *deceit*, and *hypocrisy*. When I summed up my feelings in a sentence that described her words and actions against me as a "betrayal of my sincerity," she'd circled *betrayal* and excluded from the circle "of my sincerity," the phrase necessary to its meaning. By highlighting those extreme-sounding terms apart from my context, she'd rendered suspect my anguish and turned herself into the injured party. Unacknowledged was the pain she'd caused by refusing to accept—or to appear to accept—the reality of my love for her, and my honesty in expressing it. It was the only letter from me in this special drawer—chosen from the multitudes I'd sent through the years, in which I'd poured out my gratitude and affection for her.

Therefore, I was oddly comforted to discover a short passage my mother had clipped from a letter from her sister. In it Gwenda stated, "I can never understand, Rachel, the way you speak about Becky."

As I've mentioned earlier, I'd been struggling with various drafts of this memoir and had shared some early chapters with Mary-Jo, when she reluctantly confided that in all the years she'd known my mother, she had not heard her say one good thing about me. After spending nine years in New York, Mary-Jo returned to Bremerton to take care of her parents, and told her mother Lucille that the Becky she'd come to know was very different from the daughter their friend Rachel consistently complained about. "I knew better than to argue with Rachel about you," Mary-Jo eventually told me. "Except for the one occasion when I could draw from first-hand experience. Rachel had been going on about how you were thoughtless and ungrateful to her, when I reminded her of the Christmas we'd spent together in New York." She recalled that she'd witnessed my giving her a beautiful pendant of a fossilized ancestor of the chambered nautilus, the shell whose name was the title of the poem I'd memorized and recited in her honor. Mary-Jo asked my mother how she could not appreciate the love I'd put into that gift and the effort I'd made to memorize one of her favorite poems. "Rachel," she recalled, "just gave me a frosty look and was silent."

Mary-Jo had no desire to revisit my mother's complaints, but I pressed her for some examples. Staring at the floor, she said, "Oh, Rachel would run on that you were socially inept, had very few friends, made unfortunate choices in men, had nothing resembling a career despite all your education, and…that you were a drain on her financially."

"Gosh." I tried to take it all in. The items on that list were mostly true, except the last, but Mom had never framed them in such a way to me. In fact, she'd insisted that career ambitions were elusive, and being happy *is an inside job,* outside the trappings of worldly success. I was stunned to learn that she'd considered her modest gifts of money over the years a hardship, since I'd kept myself afloat on my own earnings after leaving Columbia's doctoral program, after which she'd cheerfully offered to pay off one of my two college loans when I was earning enough to repay both. As for having few friends, and some disappointing relationships with men, well, so had countless daughters whose mothers did not hold that against them.

Mary-Jo added, "I used to think you'd be better off not knowing about this. But since you are trying to understand your mother, I've decided it's best to tell you. As much as I loved and admired Rachel, I never understood how she could speak the way she did about you." —Almost the same words Gwenda had written in the passage Mom had clipped from one of her letters and left in that drawer.

Reading through the items Mom had carefully culled and kept next to her recliner, a thread seemed to connect Mary-Jo's revelation about my mother to the first letter I'd received from Gwenda, shortly after Mom returned from her first trip back to New Zealand, 25 years after she'd left. My initial response had been to shrug it off, wondering why Auntie Gwenda had felt compelled to assure me, though we'd never met, that she knew in her bones that I was "a good person." Only after I'd connected it with my friend's long-withheld experience of having heard nothing good about me from my mother, could I appreciate my aunt's concern for her faraway niece, and her brave attempt to counteract the perpetual disparagement she'd heard about me from her older sister, whose wisdom she had never previously doubted.

A few years before Mom's death I might have been overwhelmed by this realization, but now it emerged as two fitted pieces of a larger puzzle. Now I could refract their significance through a stronger prism, having demonstrated my love in ways my mother could not easily deny. Though she could not bring herself to acknowledge that I loved her, she had blessed me before she died, thanked me for my ministrations, and shared with me a wondrous vision of freedom from desire for even the finest things of this world. Equally important, in her death throes she'd struggled to voice her regret that she had not always been a good mother.

By then I'd earned enough of a sense of my own integrity that I began to search for something beneath the hurtful history of my mother's complaints about me to others—evidently, at least in Mary-Jo and Lucille's experience, untempered by any positive statements. I began to ponder whether a deep unhappiness lay buried beneath her bitter dissatisfaction with me, which could have taken root before I was born. Throughout her life with me she'd emphasized positive attitudes and building happiness from within. Paradoxically, she might have ignored her own standards of positive thinking in her litanies of my shortcomings—expressed to others, but consciously concealed from me. Why?

Midway through my last days with her, there was ample time for us to sort through the box of photographs with the roll of neatly-captioned labels given to my mother by Roberta and Maureen, the two women she'd traveled with to England and Wales. I thought it would be a perfect last project we could share, a chance for her to reminisce about this historic trip, as she helped me match up the photos and labels to place in a quality album I'd bought for that purpose. I'd hoped to learn more about our Welsh ancestors and homeland, so I could pass on some family history to her grandchildren. Proudly showing her the new album, I asked if she would look at the photos and tell me more about the trip.

No. Certainly not.

This hit hard. I fought back tears.

Observing this, Mom added: *It was a very unhappy time, one I do not wish to revisit.*

This was news to me. I'd saved her enthusiastic postcards from the trip, and longed for a fuller account. After some hesitation, she described being made to sit with Maureen's short husband in the back seat as they passed through the Lake District, stopping at Tintern Abbey and other legendary sites. She was so moved by the experience that she began to recite by heart some classic poetry about those places. Roberta, a teacher of English literature who might have appreciated these verses, was instead irritated, and shouted, "Rachel, why don't you just shut up!" Mom's imitation of this putdown made painfully clear why she had no interest in elaborating on this trip. She said the only way she'd kept her spirits up was to take long walks alone after dinner, communing with the surroundings and reciting the dear rejected stanzas to herself.

I packed up the box of photos and labels and was about to toss out some apparently unrelated pocket datebooks from a few years before the trip, when I glanced inside one and saw that Mom had used its blank pages to record her private reflections during the trip. Her words were scrawled diagonally across each page, addressing someone:

> *My darling, here I am at last on the Kew Bridge, looking down at the swirling waters. My heart reaches back across the years, to when you wrote me how you loved to walk here and stand in this very spot. You promised we'd take this walk together one day, you'd show me all the trees and flowers you loved, and we'd look down into the waters with our future ahead of us. Now I am here alone, having spent most of my life away from you, and wonder where your heart is. Mine has never left you.*

Her postcards to me had overflowed with fascinating details about historic battlefields, ruins and cathedrals, and how it felt to stand upon the very stones where Thomas à Becket had been slain. But in these recycled datebooks she'd recorded her sad, solitary pilgrimage to the haunts of her lost love. Since she'd taken this trip to England and Wales shortly after her first return trip to New Zealand, I wondered anew what she and Douglas had said to each other in their final conversation. There was more to unpack.

"But first, there was a memorial service to attend. The Christmas blizzard had made a funeral impossible, so I arranged for a service to honor my mother's life in the church she'd attended with Captain Madden. Mary-Jo gave an inspiring eulogy, describing my mother as an extraordinary human being who'd lived one of the most interesting lives she'd ever heard or read about. Meeting her when she was 31 and Rachel 65 made a great difference in Mary-Jo's life. Their friendship, she said, took away her fear of growing older, as she watched Rachel live her life "with joy, intelligence, energy, wisdom, and a wonderful appreciation." Her example convinced Mary-Jo that dying is a natural part of life—"an extraordinary thing to be able to say about someone."

My friend's memory of trading her favorite Scripture verses with my mother—she reading aloud from her Bible while Rachel recited her choices entirely from memory—was remarkable in several ways. Besides being proof of my mother's amazing capacity to memorize poetry as well as biblical passages, it also revealed the depth of their friendship. (As Rachel's daughter, I'd never experienced anything like the above exchange.) One of Mom's favorite verses was Proverbs 3:27: *"Refuse no kindness to those who have a right to it, if it is in your power to perform it."* Mary-Jo said it "so aptly describes the way Rachel lived her life. She never preached God's Word. Instead she heard it, accepted it, and did it. I know all of us here have been touched by her kindness."

I fully supported Mary-Jo's sentiments, but I had a couple problems with that verse from Proverbs. First, are we capable of judging who does or does not have a right to our kindness? Second, if we have *not* been shown kindness (and their equivalents, justice and respect for our character) by persons who justifiably might have deemed us worthy of such treatment, are we not challenged to consider whether they had the capacity to refrain from doing us harm?

CHAPTER FORTY-FIVE

Old Love Letters

Had my mother left any other important papers somewhere else? After I'd sorted through the drawer next to her recliner, I checked her bedroom. No papers in her closets or chest of drawers. I was about to call quits when I opened the single shallow drawer in her dressing table, with its miscellany of items she hadn't got around to editing. Inside were two lace-edged embroidered handkerchiefs, a pair of white silk gloves, and the hand-carved butterfly pin I'd given her when I was a girl—still in its dainty little box of patterned cardpaper. At the back was a packet of letters bound by a desiccated rubber band that broke when touched.

All but two letters were addressed to Miss Rachel Williams from Douglas Elliott. One looked as though it had been wadded up and thrown, then retrieved and returned to its uncrumpled envelope. There were also three cables—two from Douglas and one from my mother shortly before she married my father. Had Mom left these here for me to find, or forgot she had them? Discovering them felt as supernatural to me as the hummingbird who'd tapped on the sliding glass door to my mother's kitchen. Within moments, I was communing across half a century with the spirit of a man I'd grown up hearing about. As I entered his lost world it felt as though he was consoling me for having lost her—as he had, long before.

Like a scene from a classic movie, I replayed the episode in the Western Union office that my mother had etched into my psyche since childhood, and had shared with our friend Mary-Jo and perhaps others. In it, Rachel Williams arrives at the telegraph office in Everett, accompanied by her host, Roger Painter, who was not yet her husband. A clerk takes down the words she wants cabled to her fiancé in New Zealand, and gets flustered when he's never heard of that country. Miss Williams pays for the cable and is heading out the door when the clerk remembers the wartime requirement that all cables must include the sender's first and last name. Assuming his customer and her escort are married, he calls out, "Sir, what's your last name?" The man, who is almost out the door after his companion, shrugs and answers "Painter." The clerk then makes a simple, unwittingly disastrous fix: he removes **LOVE** from the woman's signoff and adds **PAINTER** after her first name. This causes the poor fellow who receives the cable to believe that his betrothed has married another man—and she never hears from him again. I could almost hear an ominous film score in the background—deep dissonant chords over rolling tympani, ending with a cymbal crash.

Almost as graphic in my mind was Mom's account of how shocked she'd been, on her first trip back to New Zealand 25 years later, when her sister Gwenda blurted out, "Rachel, I've never understood how you could have been so cruel to poor Douglas." What did she mean by "poor Douglas," Mom reported asking Auntie Gwenda, when—according to what she'd told me—it was Douglas who'd broken *her* heart by not responding to that cable, which left her vulnerable to the avid courtship of Roger Painter to marry him instead! It so happened that Gwenda, on behalf of her sister, had welcomed Douglas when he returned to NZ from London to marry Rachel, who was on a paid luxury excursion to Canada as a reward from her wealthy employer. Gwenda became fond of the brother-in-law she'd expected he would be. When she learned that Rachel had suddenly met and married an American, she wrote to Douglas to console him, expressing hope that he would not be bitter. Several months later Rachel's ex-fiancé responded, enclosing the apparently cruel cable he'd received from Rachel, which Gwenda had saved all those years and presented to my mother, who saw that it was signed **RACHEL PAINTER**, not **LOVE RACHEL**, as she had dictated to the Western Union clerk.

Only then, my mother claimed, did she realize that Douglas, seeing she'd signed the cable with a new surname, must have assumed she'd married someone else and had chosen to inform him in a particularly heartless manner. She figured the telegraph clerk assumed she was married to her escort, and asked for his last name to avoid further embarrassment, then removed the word **LOVE** and added **PAINTER** after **RACHEL**. This kept the word count and price the same, and wartime rules obeyed. *Too clever by half*, my mother would have concluded, in any other context.

That part of her story was probably true. But the rest of it was not, though its tragic tinge had long since bled into my own outlook on life. In the scenario Mom had described to me and Mary-Jo, she'd claimed that she'd waited in vain for Douglas to reply. And, desolated that he did not confirm his willingness to wait for her until she was allowed to return to New Zealand after the war, she succumbed to my father's pressure to marry him. I fully believed that this forlorn decision had set my mother on a nearly lifelong course of unfulfilled relationships, difficult marriages, financial struggles, and untold loneliness. My incomplete picture of what actually happened fed into my fear of the heartlessness of fate—that one could lose what was most precious through some unknown mindless error.

But now I had Douglas's side of the story in my hands.

The first letter, on brownish onionskin paper, was postmarked London, 23 August 1939, in a bluish airmail envelope addressed to Miss Rachel Williams, "Mangaotawhito," Private Bag, Ruatoria, New Zealand. Another hand, perhaps that of my maternal grandmother, had redirected it, "care of Gardiner, Duart Road, Havelock North, N.Z." Douglas had cunningly sent it to his former sweetheart's parents' address, because he'd expected her to already be married to Geoff Whisker. It began as though she'd started the conversation.

London, England.

August 23, 1939.

Dear Rachel,

No, I have not forgotten you. It just doesn't seem possible, my dear. I wonder if you feel the same. Every day I keep on thinking of you and sometimes I almost feel I must see you coming in at the door — that you have arrived here unannounced. Ridiculous, isn't it after all this time? Quite ridiculous but splendid all the same for I seem in some way to have part of you with me.

I was in the Cotswolds recently — a land of rolling hills and sweeping walls of stone running across the fields — from every cottage you smiled at me for the Madonna lilies were in bloom. And I think of you in so many small and odd little ways. Whenever I brush my hair I remember you saying long ago that my hair needed it to make it shiny or some such thing. If that's not ridiculous what is? Very occasionally I see a woman do some womanly thing that brings back an echo of the way you used to do and suddenly I seem to think of you complete. I say occasionally for no one I have seen does or says things quite as you used to do.

"The poor old world...almost looks as though it may topple at any moment, so in case—just in case—I am writing this short letter." He'd written to her before, he said, but hadn't posted the letters. Britain would not declare war on Germany until September 3, 1939, but by that August war seemed inevitable.

"If you feel you can write," he concluded, "I'd be terribly happy to get your letter. If not, well I must confess I shall be terribly disappointed. I can't help it so it's no use scolding me or screwing up your nose or clicking your heel on the floor like you used to." He closes, "Not good-bye but with all my love, Douglas." The Nazi bombing of London would not begin for another year, but Douglas suggested in a postcript: "If there is a bust up, it would be safer to write to New Zealand House, 415, Strand, London, W.C."

The day she received this, his former sweetheart evidently cabled that she was no longer engaged to Geoff, which elicited the following reply:

She telegraphed her acceptance the same day, for his next letter, also dated September 27, asked:

My Dearest One,

Is it true—really true? I've had to read and reread your cable just to make sure I haven't linked up the wrong words. And you wondered at my still caring! Good Lord, Rachel, it's not a matter of <u>still</u> caring... Even though it seemed hopeless I found myself caring more each year. I love you and you alone, and it seemed that that was all I should do. But now you are free and it's all splendid again.

In her private travel notes decades later, my mother had referred to the spot he described in this closing:

If only you were here – there's a dear little place nearby called Strand-on-the-Green – it's a kind of village along the bank of the Thames, like a fishing village, all on its own in the middle of suburban London – the moonlight will be all silvery there tonight and you can walk along the path beside the water, quite alone beside it, and hear it lapping against the dim boats. And we could walk there...and I could tell you again I love you.

Goodnight my darling,
Douglas

Two days later he insisted they say important things straight away, because letters took so long "even by air-mail." He acknowledged a subsequent cable he'd received from her, offering to join him in England if his work was there, and said he'd love more than anything to have her with him, but it would be too dangerous for her to make the crossing, with Britain about to enter the war in Europe. With war approaching, he'd lost his work in landscape gardening, and was surviving on odd jobs. Though he was eager to show her the lovely parts of England—to see them through her eyes as well as his—he felt there was "a lot of wrong all through the life of this poor country, and N.Z. is a long way nearer the right thing." Since he was "a colonial" in English, with poor eyesight, it was unlikely he'd be drafted soon, and his job prospects would be much better if he returned to New Zealand. Unfortunately, he was having trouble earning enough to pay for his trip home. He was even embarrassed that he couldn't afford to buy her an engagement ring.

This did not stop him from resuming the kind of candid repartee the two of them must have shared when they'd worked together at Duncan & Davies. "It all seems so futile," he wrote. "Already the atmosphere is becoming filled with hate and false patriotism." He promised to take her views of the war seriously if they differed from his. He begged her to forgive him for rejoicing at news of her broken engagement to Geoff—"When I came to earth I couldn't help wondering if you had suffered"—and asked how recently they'd called it off. "And why didn't I write to you before? Why must we be so careful of the proprieties? And yet you couldn't write until I'd written – you must have thought I had quite forgotten you."

I was touched to read that after her engagement to Geoff, Douglas expected to be a bachelor the rest of his life.

My eyes popped at his query: "Do you still write poetry? And do you still send it to papers?" Mom never mentioned that she'd written and published poems in New Zealand, though her love of poetry was obvious in the vast amount she'd committed to memory. Had life on the berry farm extinguished her creative energies, or had she needed a husband like Douglas to encourage her? His optimism was poignant, though perhaps a tad passive.

> I hope you are not worrying about how we shall work things out… But apart from it being rather useless to worry with all this war on, I think that we should feel quite confident considering what <u>has</u> happened – the fact that we've found one another again. The rest should fall into place of its own accord, shouldn't it?

I smiled when his letter expressed hope that she no longer burned her cheek with a curling iron, as she'd done when he was working with her. In England she would not have to curl her hair, but he urged her not to get an "Eton Crop," which makes some women look "just like men," wearing "tweedy, mannish costumes." On further reflection: "I don't mind how you have your hair so long as it's still you."

His fountain pen left a trail of ink ranging from black blobs to faintly legible scratches. He asked if his "little one" wanted "some chirruping youngsters?" *He* did, he wrote, "with all my heart." He believed New Zealand would be a better place to raise children, because of England's problem with "class distinction."

When they first met, she was a nurse trainee at Palmerston North Hospital. But a tubercular spot was found in an x-ray of her lungs, and she was told to quit hospital work. Since she could not afford a sanitarium, the next best option was to find work outdoors. I'd assumed, incorrectly, that Douglas had got her the job at Duncan & Davies.

Having never seen my mother walk like that, I was surprised to read that Douglas used to be thrilled by the "swinging way" she used to stride "down the drive at D&D's." He longed to walk with her back in N.Z.: "Here in London I never feel free – the wind itself is different, a kind of tortured thing that throws itself hopelessly against the house walls – it doesn't sweep freely and it has no sweet cleanness in its touch." In his letter of October 4, 1939, I was surprised to discover that Douglas had visited Mangaotawhito: "There you dwelt among a thousand hills and there was something grand to look at," while in England much of the countryside was closed off by hedges.

A small photo of Mangaotawhito my mother
brought with her from N.Z.

"Dearest Miracle," he addressed her, in a letter confessing he couldn't let her go in his heart even when she was engaged to Geoff. Did she remember telling him he'd have to wait for her until the unlikely event of her divorce? Halfway round the world from her, he had to pinch himself at the twist of destiny that brought them back together. His optimism pierced me with melancholy. How much he'd loved her, how blessed he'd felt—and how they were to remain apart, at least physically, for the rest of their lives.

His early letters were written before he'd received his first letter from her, which had evidently expressed her difficulty writing, and said they had "no real need of words." Douglas replied, "No real need, but I was mighty glad to get yours." He was glad she'd cabled him to accept his proposal, to give him, he quoted her, "some tangible sign of the 'me' who has always been yours." Hmm, I thought. Had she always been his?

In truth, she'd been quite taken with the dashing, artistic Geoff Whisker. Among her private things I found a box of old photos from New Zealand, including one of Geoff at work as an artist, probably in his hotel room near the Sydney School of Art, taken shortly before he was accused of impregnating a judge's daughter on the ship over. The man's magnetism seems to radiate from the antique décor, as if he were acting in a period drama. It must have been Geoff who'd told my mother that she needed four

more inches of leg to be properly proportioned—a criticism she repeated to others the rest of her life—lastly to Lucy, her Hospice aide.

Douglas gently invited her to tell him what happened to end her engagement with Geoff, and worried that it had been painful. "I want so very much to heal you of <u>all</u> the past—for I too hurt you, I know." Righto, I thought. No need to mention his mother's screaming "Get that woman out of my house!"—which he'd shamefully obeyed. I was impressed by his concern that she'd been badly hurt again. None of his subsequent letters indicated that she'd told him about Geoff's shotgun wedding.

Was her job "nursing this mental case" difficult? For it didn't sound like "happy work" to Douglas. "It's just you through & through to try to forget your own troubles in helping someone worse off." Had it not occurred to him that she'd taken a position of nurse companion not only to avoid further exposure to TB, but to put distance between herself and him, and his mother?

As the weeks passed, I gathered, his fiancée's fears mounted that they would never see one another again. So he offered her "a lecturette on being optimistic." Even if peace did not come soon, "as God has brought us so far he will surely complete the work." In November 1939, shortly after Great Britain declared war on Germany, Douglas reported being safe and sound, but wished the world "would come to its senses and see the hopelessness and utter futility of all this force, force, force."

During his lengthy wait for another letter, Douglas combed through his diaries and found an entry for the day they first met: October 1, 1932. That afternoon he and two friends had tea, then "went over to see a nurse in hospital—and she had a boil on her chin, poor thing!" A later comment may have explained what caused the boil: "Rachel is leaving the hospital as she cannot bear to see the patients suffering from lack of mental comfort!!" Douglas of 1939 added: "The exclamation marks are mine—Editor." At first I thought my mother might have given this as her reason to quit hospital work, rather than the spot on her lung. But since she'd always emphasized compassion and kindness to the suffering, the boil on her chin could have resulted from rage at the hospital's indifference to patients' "mental suffering." I could not forget her unceasing patience and tenderness during the years I'd wet the bed.

Douglas quoted from his diary that in December 1932 "Rachel Williams came in and we enthused over books – she, like me, is mad enough to like 'Alice in Wonderland.' Loud cheers!" "Don't blame me for these remarks," his older self wrote, "they are exactly as entered." As the 1939 London winter set in, he rhapsodized:

> Did you like your walk with me this morning?
> The snow crunched under our feet, becom-
> ing firm and a wee bit tacky. I took you round
> to all the places I thought you'd like the best

> in their wintry mantle – down Sutton Lane
> past the Queen's Head and along to Chiswick
> House ground where you saw the pale blue
> sky broken into pieces by the network of lime
> branches in the long avenue. ...Then we went
> along to Church Street, past the house where
> Thackeray's Becky Sharp went to school, till
> we came to the quaint cottages which used
> to be the Burlington Arms – the hostel where
> traveling folk used to wait to be ferried across
> the Thames.

At teatime he invited her to snuggle up against his knee after he'd poured boiling water into his little yellow teapot: "What could be grander than that?" What a devoted husband he would have made, I thought, this man who called my mother his "green-eyed goddess" and shared her passion for both nature and literature. Setting reason aside, I imagined how much better our family life would have been if he'd married Mom, rather than Papa and my weird succession of stepfathers!

Douglas's letter of 8 January 1940 confirmed our bond. In it he worried that his personality could never match her radiance and magnetism. We'd both loved her deeply, and each of us had feared not being able to fulfill her expectations. Douglas had found it frightening how much other people loved his fiancée, and worried that they'd be expecting the man she'd chosen to be equally wonderful. He mentioned that a cousin of his had recently met Rachel, and wrote to him so full of her praises that it seemed she (his cousin) had never expected his fiancée "to be so superior!" Still, in other letters it was clear that he had friends in England who cared for him, visited when they could, and invited him to join them for holidays.

What made his beloved so special, he opined, is that she made it a joy to do things together, "making all the lovely things doubly lovable, and all the sad things only half so sad." I had to concede that he and others had experienced more of my mother's buoyant qualities—at least since I became the object of her *night-mare monologues*. I shared Douglas's appreciation of the friend-ship they'd both found in books, and dwelt wistfully on a line he'd written about how marvelous it would be when they could read together again. I believed he'd have understood my sadness that she could not put aside some of her criticism of me to read my own writing, or a few of the great literary works I'd suggested as a break from all those murder mysteries.

Douglas recalled that they each owned copies of *In Tune with the Infinite*, a book she'd told him she could have written herself. "But Rachel," he pleaded, "if you feel that you could have written that, why not write something now? Hundreds of people are hungering for sympathy and understanding and good humour – why not give it to them on paper as well as in person?" Indeed, what had stopped her? The answer seemed buried under layers of circumstance.

Foremost, she'd come under the sway of a spiritual Svengali—my father—who'd subordinated her abilities to his. Plus, he'd purchased a farm that required most of their energies to function. After he died, and after Ray Draine left her, she mar-ried Verne, whose absence of physical affection for her she'd hid from everyone except me—and only mentioned once, after his death. After the winter of 1955 destroyed their crops, she had to sell the berry farm and take what British society would consider a degrading job for someone descended from Welsh landed gen-try—charwoman. That and raising two children left no time or energy to exercise her writing gifts, except perhaps in letters. If Douglas had provided her financial stability and encouragement, what books might she have written?

He reminisced about the time, early in their four-year friend-ship, when she'd asked him about "the opportunities for a girl in horticulture." I'd assumed that Douglas had found her a position at the renowned Duncan & Davies nursery, but his letter revealed the initiative had been hers. It's possible that my mother participated in an early wave of feminism, as the first woman employed by the largest supplier of plants and seeds in the Southern Hemisphere.

Mom had described Douglas as a shy young man, tied to his mother's apron strings, who took four long years to realize that he loved her. His letters proved otherwise. He wrote that after she'd inquired about employment with Duncan & Davies, he'd confided to his diary that his thoughts were "rather full of Rachel Williams," wondering what kind of salary a man needed "to make marriage possible"! Had his so-called shyness resulted from knowing that his mother disapproved of her strongly?

When the London mail brought no letters from her, Douglas reported that he'd distracted himself by attending a speech by a Member of Parliament and fellow Christian Scientist, who'd predicted that Hitler's power would come to an end without much fighting, because the Maginot and Siegfried Lines were pretty well invincible. "So, my darling," Douglas mused, "perhaps it won't be so very long before peace comes again—and it seems very likely to be a truly wonderful peace, the beginning of world federation." Well before Chamberlain's famous speech, Douglas was hoping in vain for "peace in our time."

Still waiting to hear from her, he reminisced about two brothers, friends of theirs who'd been called into the war. "Remember the fun we used to have going up to see them at Vogeltown?" he asked. "Isn't it queer how the things that are past are so absolutely past. It hurts sometimes to think that we can never see them the same way again." I was with him on this. Besides the pain of losing my mother, it hurt that I would never see her letters to this man she'd called the love of her life. Even more, I regretted never having met him. Yet something wondrous had not been lost. Here was I, miraculously reading letters that my mother's lost love had intended for her eyes only. His love for her arose ageless from the yellowed pages.

Douglas was a gentler, humbler soul, uncursed by charisma. He became a kindred spirit, closer to my heart than my own father. I knew—reverting to magical thinking—that if Douglas had been my father he would not have shoved me away when I was a toddler—as Uncle Wayne remembered Papa doing—causing me to fall on my back in front of the roomful of people who'd come to hear him speak.

On December 4, 1939, he responded to a pensive letter from his love, who'd evidently wondered whether they were gambling that the "magic" they'd once shared would be there when they finally got together. Oh dear, I thought, even before she met my father, she might have tried to prepare Douglas for the worst.

All at once Douglas received a batch of her letters that the New Zealand censors had held back, and Douglas admonished her not to worry so much:

> Remember what we agreed—that if God means this union to be complete we can rely absolutely on him. ...I really don't think that even that old bogey, death itself, can stop me loving you – so that you'd really have just as much of me as you do now – except for a few scrawly pages of writing every week or so.

I got goose bumps at the thought of his faith, his trust, and the fluke of my access to his scrawly pages, long after death had claimed him.

These pages informed me that my mother had promised Douglas she would stick with him even if he were imprisoned as a pacifist! It sounded ominous, however, when he mentioned that she'd urged him to read a book entitled _Act Now_. When I saw his casual reply that it was out of stock, I wanted to yell at him across the chasm of time: Did you try other bookshops? Or reserve a copy at the library?

He threw cold water on the good news that he'd found steady work in a "newsagent-sweets-tobacconist's shop," stating that his wages weren't enough for her to join him. That letdown was hardly tempered by his quoting a customer who'd said he resembled James Stewart in the movie _Mr. Smith Goes to Washington_. Had she seen it? Despite my fondness for Douglas, if he'd been a character in an epistolary novel I'd have feared for his chances.

My sense of impending doom grew when Douglas reported that his father had finally responded to the news of his engagement: "Not altogether approving, in spite of assertions to the contrary!" His dad's claim to desire only the happiness of his younger son seemed dubious. If he'd wanted Douglas to be happy, why not offer to help him come home and marry the woman he loved?

Douglas started to say he regretted that his father hadn't helped untie him from his mother's apron strings, then rebuked himself for blaming his parents for his own "faults of character." Unacknowledged, I thought, was the likelihood that his father's lack of enthusiasm reeked of the same "class distinctions" Douglas found oppressive in England. I suspected his dad might have helped him return home, had his son not planned to wed a woman who was not "one of us, my dear."

Sadly, his case was not enhanced by turning down the offer of a loan from a Mrs. Collins, for either his return fare to New Zealand, or Rachel's passage to London, claiming he didn't want to return home with a debt hanging over him. When his fiancée assured him she was willing to risk joining him in England, he responded, "My darling, you have friends and love where you are now—things that matter so much in these times, and if you came over here and something went wrong with me you'd feel it worse…and if anything went wrong with you I should feel responsible for your coming here." Scrawling "Don't worry" three times, he asked her to send him a photograph of herself, saying he felt "a bit like a dog in the manger when you tell me SIX other men have proposed to you." Really? Perhaps she'd exaggerated a bit, but after such dithering, I could hardly blame her for what she did next, which made me shudder.

Douglas's letter of March 1940 waxed lighthearted about news that she'd consulted a fortuneteller, who told her she would move to America. "That would be a bit of a lark, wouldn't it?" he wrote. Evidently this psychic predicted that Rachel would have two children: a boy and a girl, born in the States. My pulse tripped as I realized I was reading about a prediction of my brother's and my existence! Then came a wave of nausea, as I saw

Douglas's comment about the prediction: "The girl seems to be of no account, poor dear, but I see the boy is singled out as an outstanding character because he takes after his mother."

I was dismayed at how accurate this medium had been. Johnny had indeed proven to be a hero, saving many lives; whereas my life till then seemed to fit the bill "of no account." I had to wonder, was Douglas simply responding to what the fortuneteller had said, or had he elaborated on it to tease his sweetheart?

A more haunting question took hold: Had this prediction influenced my mother's decision to marry my father rather than Douglas?

When I told Mary-Jo about this letter, she wondered whether, by seeking out a fortuneteller—which the Bible forbids—Rachel had opened the door to a destructive spirit that would plague her relationship with me. What else but a spirit of evil, she asked, would predict that Rachel's daughter would be of no account?

Douglas's next letter reflected on the years he'd squandered being "an idiot." Perhaps part of their separation had to be, "but the cruel part should not have been...no, my dearest thing, I should not have been cruel." Of course, he felt no need to go into detail. They alone knew what had been cruel about his behavior. Nonetheless, as he "translated" it, knowing that his beloved Rachel loved him "after all that" proved she'd forgiven him.

Had she, really? Some wounds do not heal.

In late March 1940, Douglas finally accepted a loan from "the Henrys" for his passage back to New Zealand, though he felt their generosity was a tribute to Rachel rather than himself. With some irony, he noted that he'd be on a freighter passing through the Panama Canal, while she was crossing the Pacific on a luxury liner destined for Canada. In the same letter he commented on her fierce reaction to an idea he must have expressed in a letter she had not saved, in which Douglas had naively expressed his regret that Geoff Whisker had not notified him when he and Rachel were no longer engaged. Apparently, just before she sailed for British Columbia, she'd replied sharply that she'd have never forgiven Geoff if he'd cabled Douglas about their broken engagement. Douglas responded in clueless amazement:

> Here am I thinking I can hardly forgive him for not cabling. Think how much time we wasted, and if I hadn't been a bounder and written to a Rachel I already thought to be a married woman, I should never have had all this glorious thrill of life. Just shows—don't ask what— it just shows…

Given Douglas's excruciating reluctance to accept a loan to return to New Zealand, I had to think that my mother had seriously pondered their different social background. Was it petty of me to wonder why he'd turned down an earlier loan from the Irish-named Mrs. Collins, and accepted one from the English-named Henrys? Douglas seemed oblivious to her growing doubts:

> I think your 'expoundation' on the rich man and his difficulty entering the Kingdom of Heaven is fine. I had not looked at it in the light of the rich not struggling and suffering and conquering and so feeling at one with all men. And yet that explains more clearly than ever why Jesus told the young man to go and sell his goods and <u>follow</u> (feel with) him.
>
> Gee, what a woman. The idea of asking a man if he feels pricklings of resentment when you write about such things! My Rachel-one, the exchange of ideas is to me one of the unique things that set love apart. A housekeeper can feed me and darn my clothes, there are women-in-the-street if a man wants that alone, but it's the voice of heart answering heart, of mind answering kindred mind that is the greatest thing of all.

Profound indeed, but quite possibly his idealism was based on limited experience, and insufficient empathy. Maybe she hadn't given Douglas all the details, but why would she feel compelled to offer the above "expoundation," had she not been horrified by Douglas's notion that Geoff should have tipped him off re her sudden availability, as if it were just a heads-up among upper-crust men?

Before embarking, he posted lines both joyful and heartrending:

> Well my Rachel, the great time we've prayed for is coming much closer, and soon I'll be able to hold you close and just make you feel my glad heart singing its love song to you. ...But whatever happens you know I love you, alone and always. What a dull man—never to have loved any other woman.

After she'd "lost" him, I wondered if my mother found consolation in this passage:

> And even if this did happen to finish the chapter I want you to remember that I was happiest with you in those long past years—even when sometimes I almost hated you! What a confession...but those happy times were deeply happy and you became so very much a part of me that ever since, including the 4 years I've been away from you, I've kept that part and treasured it... So remember that, won't you, Rachel...that you've already given me great joy.

He enclosed a photo of himself holding a camera, as if taking her picture. His face looked pale, lined beyond his years, and poorly set off by owlish glasses.

Safely back in New Zealand by June 24, 1940, Douglas acknowledged receipt of her cable that she would sail in early August to join him. Poignantly, in implicit contrast to members of his own family, he reported that Mrs. Williams "seemed very genuine in her pleasure about our engagement." Strangely, he did not mention Mr. Williams, whose opinion Rachel would have valued more.

The next lines truly belonged in an epistolary novel:

> ...Dad brought me your double letter and oh my darling I loved every word. But you mustn't love me too much yet, in case you find you have been loving your own idea of me, as you say. Though I hope you haven't for I need you so badly—it seemed cruel that you should be taken away from N.Z. just as I was returning and I looked down onto the wharf when we arrived half expecting to see you there, though

my wretched common sense told me that was
very very improbable.

He thanked her for knitting him a fine sweater, "so warm
and solid-feeling—and I like gray, so suitable for my gray hair."
With the sweater came a welcoming letter from his future sister-
in-law Gwenda. When he realized how much Rachel meant to
her, Douglas wrote, he appreciated her message all the more. She
had to change her name "as soon as it can be done—yes just that,
Mrs. Elliott. You'd better write it two or three times on the back
of this page just to see what it feels like. I think Rachel Elliott
sounds very good. And it was so." I wished it had been so. Rachel
Elliott sounded far better to me than Rachel Painter. So did John
and Rebecca Elliott.

His uncertainty as to how and where she'd like to be wed,
and what they could afford, begged the sad question why his family hadn't offered to help. Even if traditionally the bride's family was expected to foot the wedding bills, his father might have
assisted, say, in finding them housing. Stoically, Douglas wrote
that he hoped to supplement his income by the sale of photographs and articles on gardening.

It remained uncertain whether Douglas would be called up,
but he worried about Britain's posturing:

> The war would get one down if one thought
> about it too much. I wish the British wouldn't
> boast so much just now. Poor old France did
> the same and it seems to me that that boast-
> ing makes their downfall all the worse, all the
> more humiliating to their honour. Boasting is
> a poor policy at any time but it looks specially
> bad in the present circumstances when these
> nations are fighting desperately.

"Here's a kiss for you --------- X. Did you get it? Goodnight—
All my love, Rachel Elliott—Your Douglas." Alas, as he was put-

ting those words to paper, the never-to-be Rachel Elliott was arranging to meet my father on a farm in Washington State.

A week later, Douglas announced his good fortune to be asked to take over the comfortable home of a widow whose two sons were leaving, one for the war and the other to be married. Both were friends of theirs, but the older brother had made the offer, which Douglas attributed to the latter's "weak spot" for Rachel. If they had any trouble recognizing one another when she returned, he suggested that she click her heels on the ground, like she used to in moments of exasperation. "I should recognize that," he writes, "—the heel-clicking." He'd mentioned that mannerism—perhaps seen only by him—in his first letter to her. It touched my heart that he spoke of it again in his last letter.

After all that had gone before, I was appalled by his final cable, July 31, 1940: MAY NOT MEET YOU AUCKLAND COME DIRECT NEW PLYMOUTH MARRY IMMEDIATELY ALL LOVE ELLIOTT. Though I'd come to love this chap, I was furious. Why on earth not meet her ship?? Saving on train fare? He'd made a royal case of eagerness to be with her, so why expect her to travel alone to join him for a quick wedding? I wanted to hit REWIND on the recorder of time and shout: Bad move, old bean! Time to be Sir Galahad, not Caspar Milquetoast! Nor Scrooge—when the wolf is at the door!

Destiny seemed to pin hapless Douglas down in New Plymouth, wearing his beloved's hand-knitted sweater, while the man who would become my father was opening his door to her, exclaiming "Those are the eyes!" as if she were a prophecy fulfilled.

August 1940 must have been steamy with courtship on the berry farm, for all letter writing stopped. The silence was broken by Rachel Williams' September 7th cable to Douglas. I stared at it, incredulous, for I knew by heart what my mother had recited to me as a child—MUST STAY FOR DURATION WHAT ARE YOUR PLANS LOVE RACHEL. All too well, I understood that she'd meant to close with LOVE RACHEL, and the fateful impact of the mistaken change in her last name. The actual cable in my clammy hand read as follows:

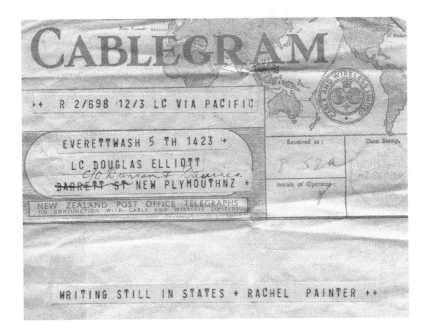

My stomach churned. Where was that question she'd told me she'd waited in vain for him to answer—the one jinxed by an unwitting error, that pulled the rug out from under the rest of her life? How could Douglas have broken *her* heart, when she'd told *him* to expect a letter? Reality was staring at me from the oxidized original cablegram: *The ball had been in my mother's court.* She, not fate or a nervous clerk, had called the shot. But that didn't mean "losing" him wouldn't eventually break her heart.

The next-to-last letter in the packet was dated January 27, 1941, from Douglas to "Dear Friend Gwenda." It had been wadded up and tossed somewhere, then retrieved. "Your letter," it said, "was here when I came in a moment ago and I have only just finished reading it and the one from Mrs. Barley." It seemed that Papa had asked Annie Barley, who used to do secretarial work for him, to inform Gwenda that her sister was unable to write due to "ill health." Most probably the health issue had been my mother's slow recovery from a near-fatal hemorrhage following the botched surgery to remove a genital "blemish" that my father had found unacceptable shortly after their marriage. Douglas commented on the "strange mistake" in Rachel's cable, being signed Rachel Painter when she was still Rachel Williams:

> Somehow [it] falls in line with the other rather supernatural experiences our dear old Rachel has bumped up against. ...Fancy her being so upset about missing the "love" – I believe I mentioned to you how ominous that omission was at the time. Well, anyway, Gwenda, the cable quite unintentionally prepared us for what followed, didn't it?

That was probably when Mom crumpled up the letter and tossed it in the round file.

In closing, Douglas thanks God that Rachel "seems to be improving...; nevertheless...I hope we soon hear from her in her own hand"—as though he still hoped she would correspond with him. He tells Gwenda he greatly appreciated her "sweet Christmas letter," and apologized for not responding sooner, though he'd managed to send her a card:

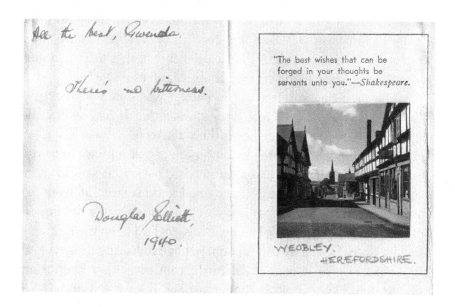

All the best, Gwenda.

There's no bitterness.

Douglas Elliott,
1940.

"The best wishes that can be forged in your thoughts be servants unto you."—*Shakespeare.*

WEOBLEY,
HEREFORDSHIRE.

In it he'd placed one of his photographs of England—an empty street scene to accompany his stark few words. This, too, Gwenda passed along to her sister.

After a month of mournful silence, Douglas wrote to Gwenda again:

> Well, now you know one of the things you were most worried about—I'm not the least bit bitter towards Rachel over what has happened. That would have been damned selfish and weak-kneed. I can't understand what she has done—we haven't sufficient information; but like you I <u>can</u> understand her doing it, if the "It" is something she felt to be right; and as that quality in her is something I always admired I feel it is only fair to respect it in her now.

Struck by his loyal regard for the fiancée who'd rejected him, my heart ached as I read his admission of a few lapses into self-pity, when thinking of "those two loveable and lovely things, 'home' and 'family.'" And, when he wondered whether he'd counted too much on his future with Rachel, feeling as though something he already possessed had been stolen from him. Though my own father had been the thief, I was in Douglas's corner.

The last letter in the packet was typed 28 years later, July 1968. It cleared up any lingering doubts about my mother's final correspondence with Douglas. Gwenda had written on the pretext of seeking gardening advice, but he went straight to the root:

> I was really delighted to get your letter. It's a terribly long time since we saw one another. I'm longing to know what's happened to Rachel. I've never heard of her or from her since *she wrote to say it was all off between us two.* [My emphasis.] So please give me the

full story up to date. I hope she is having a full
and happy life.

Here was unmistakable proof that the letter my mother
promised Douglas in her final cable had ended their engagement.
She hadn't wanted me, nor any others, such as Mary-Jo, whom
she'd told the same tragic story, to know how she'd "lost" the love
of her life. To my eyes, his love for her still glowed from the page,
even as he wrote that he and his wife Betty had been married for
eight years:

> We linked up too late to have a family but
> we have a lot in common and are very happy
> together. ...I left Duncan & Davies many years
> ago and have since worked for the local news-
> paper. ...Now I have so much writing to do
> that the only photography I do is for my own
> articles. ...Now, about your shrub...

> Very sincere good wishes – and please
> write again soon. Yours, Douglas Elliott

His familiar handwriting reappeared in the postscript: "Tune
in to 2ZP at 3 on Wednesdays" – his radio program on gardening.
That Douglas did not marry for twenty years after their
breakup seemed to validate what he'd professed in 1939, that
she was the only woman he'd ever loved—at least until he "linked
up" with Betty. Mom had told me once that what kept her going
in this country was her belief that *if worse came to worst, I knew
I could always go back to Douglas.* She'd sensed correctly that he
still loved her. Yet I could not imagine her returning to him as if
she'd failed to thrive in America. The grim facts of her marriage
to my father, had she been candid about them, might have dimin-
ished her in Douglas's eyes.

After her death, an Internet search disproved the reason
Mom had given me for having to stay in North America during

the war. The ship she was booked on to return to New Zealand in August 1940 was *not* the first passenger vessel sunk by the Japanese in the Pacific. I had not known it as a child, but should have remembered learning in school that the Japanese did not attack Pearl Harbor until December 7, 1941. A credible WW2 timeline did not mention any passenger ships sunk by the Japanese before then.

An archivist at New Zealand's Taranaki Research Centre was able to tell me that Douglas Elliott had written columns on landscape gardening until 1976, when he stopped due to ill health and died five years later at 69. My mother's first trip back to New Zealand had been in January of the same year he'd left his newspaper job due to illness. Was it possible that her telephone conversation with him—the closure it produced and the near certainty they would never meet or speak together again—had triggered the decline in his health?

When I came across this photo of my masterful-looking father with a group of visitors to the berry farm, I did not notice at first that he was basking in the gaze of his bride, in a scarf, almost unrecognizable among the guests. As my age passed that of my father when he died (63), it dawned on me that he'd hardly been a wizened old windbag when he and Mom were married. Instead, he'd been a virile mature man, whose counsel on matters of love and sex had attracted a variety of intelligent spiritual seekers. I began to consider that my mother might have been captivated by his wit and worldliness—even uplifted by hopes that her life would gain significance as his mate. After all, they were married ten years before his fatal accidental. On further thought, it seemed ironic and tragic that my father had been so preoccupied with theosophical ideas, so trusting that the farm hands had done what he'd asked them, that he'd stepped onto an unbolted plank and fallen to a prolonged, unnecessary death in his prime.

Reconsidering my mother's series of husbands, new sympathies arose for her as a widow blindsided by the handsome, secretly avaricious Ray Draine, who'd refrained from drinking until he learned that marriage would not make him full or half owner of the berry farm. His verbal and possibly physical abuse, then abandonment, had led to Mom's crazed search for him and the breakdown that got her institutionalized—and Johnny and me put into a foster home. I saw in new light why, after she'd hired Verne as her second farm manager, she'd ignored my warning at age eight against their marriage. Verne had been her only viable option. He'd been honest about his alcoholism, if not about his lack of genuine affection for her.

Decades passed before I faced the possibility that Verne might have been telling the truth in his creepy hand-on-my-knee statement that he'd always found me attractive. It may not have been a coincidence that a few days after our aborted chat on the sofa, he went on a rampage in the park truck that ended his employment at Illahee and lost us our best-ever home. Was there a causal link between the start of my mother's obsessive lectures as I entered puberty, and their ending with Verne's death?

I'd been exasperated by Mom's on-and-off romance with Capt. Madden, his arrogance and disregard for her, marrying her only when he needed a fulltime nurse. But there was no denying her love and selfless caring for him. I had no doubt that the Good Lord had answered my prayers, keeping Edwin alive long enough for her to receive his Naval officer's pension—the least the captain could do for her.

Without dwelling on the humiliating way Mom was dumped by her last male companion when he knew she was dying, the upside of Oscar Cooper's move was that it gave me the chance to care for her without having to cater to his whims. That in itself was a blessing, given how deeply we needed to be reconciled.

The above thoughts focused on my mother's sufferings with a succession of men in the States. I had to take into consideration that she also experienced humiliation and betrayal in New Zealand. I don't think she ever fully recovered from the indignity of being verbally expelled from Douglas Elliott's home by his dictatorial, bedridden mother—ending the happiest four years of her son's and perhaps my mother's life. Devastated but determined to land on her feet, she found work as a nurse companion to a society matron, and got engaged to a rich, gifted but sexually careless man, whose shotgun wedding she came across by chance in the society pages.

In other realms of heartache, my mother lost her first and second sons. The first in childbirth, and the second—the person she loved most in the world—when he was 39, the father of three daughters who did not communicate with her after their father's death.

I've mentioned these events earlier, of course. But it's different to reflect on what can emerge from accumulated pain. In time, I began to perceive that by lying about how she had actually lost Douglas, and planting the idea of victimhood by a stroke of fate, my mother could have distanced herself from the murk of her choices and compromising circumstances. After my father's death, the weight of her suffering was too great to reveal to her lonely little daughter on the berry farm. Why not step outside that moment in time, tap into her literary skills, and brew fact and fiction into an unforgettable tale?

But a tragic story about a child's parent, told to the child by that parent as true, has consequences. Especially if the child longs for that parent's happiness more than her or his own. My mother's half-true tale sounded a note of doom for my own chances at love, which resounded until after her death, when I pieced together the actual story. With all my being, I tried to understand why my mother, after my childhood, never openly acknowledged that I loved her, when my love for her had always been the clearest, deepest element of my identity—next to my trust in God. Why she would try to turn my closest friends against me, and probably my brother, as well as her sister Gwenda and at least some of her close friends, was something I could never align with her otherwise exceptional character, her wisdom and kindness.

This paradox led me to study the wisdom traditions of East and West, to search through a swath of scholarly works, books and articles in the popular press, and anything that seemed relevant in literature, for insights why a person as kind and gracious as my mother could sustain a nearly lifelong current of bitter disapproval regarding her daughter—beneath an outward display, often genuine, of maternal encouragement.

The year after my mother's death I completed my doctorate in comparative literature. My dissertation focused on women's perceptions of evil—the insights of women novelists and thinkers, taking into account traditional philosophy, theology, and moral aspects of psychology. I proposed that the lack of attention and harmful forms of attention lie at the root of destructive actions, whether hostile or uncaring, or both.

Throughout my research and teaching, I never forgot the significance of the article my mother once shared with me about healthy newborns abandoned in hospitals, who died despite being kept clean, warm, and well-nourished. That infants can die for lack of caring attention convinced me that positive personal attention is essential to life, and the lack of it has grave consequences.

In teaching and writing, I try to convey that giving more attention to *the play of attention* itself would help us discover more about the moral and physical problems of those who have not received the care they needed to avoid injuring others. Pain and anger at being deprived of attention, I believe, makes people susceptible to feelings and actions associated with malice, neglect of others, violence, and other forms of destructiveness, which strike many of us as being—for lack of a better term—evil. In writing about the metaphysics of attention, I try to examine the substructure of evil, and how people can overcome destructive forces by the power of alert, focused, caring attention.

I am always grateful that my mother shared with me her love of language, literature, and the study of human nature. She was a figure of wisdom wit and grace to many. But I must also live with the sadness that I no doubt share with countless others, of not being loved unconditionally by a parent or other very influential and revered person in our lives.

Whether or not my mother meant for me to discover them, Douglas's old love letters were a lasting gift. They did not solve the major enigma of my life, but they shed new light on key elements of hers, allowing me to enter a zone of shared love and compassion unbounded by time. I believe my mother spun a tale of tragic loss for her own sake more than anyone else's. She may have found consolation in eventually believing in the fabricated elements that she'd concealed from me and others close to her. Perhaps her litany of complaints about me was another way to divert the bitterness she felt about her own life—carefully hidden from those she wanted to inspire with her idealism and positivity.

As Douglas had intuited, she'd buried her pain and disappointment under a gardener's mulch of service to others. Although this won her deep gratitude and admiration, it did not seem to satisfy her desire for the kind of attention she craved. What kind of attention, maybe she herself did not know. Romantic love? A life partnership that encouraged and supported her talents? Lively companionship that conquered loneliness? A successful daughter whose struggles she would not have felt compelled to disparage for so many years? Your guess is as good as mine.

My dying is very hard, she told me near the end, *and so has been my living.* She had also shouted *No!* at my tears when the Hospice team asked if I knew what to do at the moment of her death. *I want this to be a good experience,* she insisted. Despite her brutal putdown of me to the Hospice volunteer I'd hoped would become a lasting friend, and the caustic reminiscence about me that she'd shared with Mary-Jo, in my presence, as her happiest memory, I believe my mother got her wish. We'd shared some unforgettable, precious moments. Overall, it had been a gratifying experience.

The night before she died, though struggling for air, she'd voiced the fear that she hadn't been a very good mother. Though I have no way of knowing what she meant, her remorse sounded real. The fact that she'd found it so difficult to say, and uttered it so near death that she hadn't strength or breath to elaborate, was significant in itself. But it did not solve the enigma.

Nevertheless, I found lasting significance in the bolt of fore-knowledge that struck when I was about ten, when Mom told me about her favorite patient in the mental hospital who, in a fit of degree of animosity, cursed and insulted her with shocking ferocity. When my mother asked later why she'd said those terrible things, the patient replied with amazing honesty: *Because I knew you wouldn't hurt me.* When I first heard this, an inner voice alerted me that this woman's answer would carry great meaning for my life. In Mom's situation, and eventually in mine, it begged the question: What kind of suffering led up to this kind of degree of animosity, unleashed on a kindly nurse whom the patient knew would not retaliate? In my mother's case—and I believe in my own—we played no role in causing that degree of animosity, though we received its blowback. The repercussions I had to absorb from my mother's pain were much longer-term. The bitterness she expressed to others about me was kept from me until it was too late to ask her about it—if she'd had the self-knowledge to answer honestly.

Friends have asked if I forgave my mother. Since my goal was to understand, and my heart was full of love for her, forgiveness was always there. But that does not mean there was no hurt and no regret. A very wise friend asked if there was something I would have wanted more than anything to hear my mother say before she died. Yes: words like *Becky, I know you love me.* Words to this effect she never said, even as her life was ending. Perhaps it was too difficult to acknowledge the extent to which she'd denied me this validation of my personal honesty and integrity.

Mysteries like this are unsolvable because one cannot know all the agonies of another's heart. It is hard to accept that, for some, accumulated pain can lead to open or veiled cruelty, and indifference to the pain of those on the receiving end—who are often chosen as the least likely to retaliate. They (we) may try to heal by pouring great care and attention into a quest for understanding. When this goal eludes us, our disappointment feels like failure. But that would not be fair to the depth and breadth of our unresolved efforts. There are consolations for wounds that never fully heal—a quicker eye for others' suffering; readiness to offer comfort when possible, and when not, awareness of ways to empower others through other channels of attention, such as moral support, indirect advocacy, and prayer.

Self-respect and integrity feel earned when we've devoted our best, most focused, persevering attention to finding the cause of a bewildering personal betrayal, even if it escapes our grasp. What remains, I believe, is a form of humility—a different feathered thing. When the hope for resolution is gone, we who have tried and fallen short are strengthened by the habit of paying close, caring attention. It opens us to insight—which at any moment can spread its mysterious wings, swoop down like a heron, or pierce the air like a kingfisher, transforming mind and heart.

***

ABOUT THE AUTHOR

Rebecca Painter has taught literature, writing, and interdisciplinary humanities courses for over twenty years. She has served as a development consultant to universities, scholarship funds and civil rights organizations. Her scholarly writings have appeared in peer-reviewed journals and volumes of essays on philosophy and literature. Her informal reflections on life, literature, and the power of attention are posted on the website *attendingmetaphysician.com.* She is currently working on a novel based on her long friendship with a spiritual mentor.

A devoted amateur pianist, Dr. Painter lives in New York with her husband, a structural engineer. They host a series of soirées for local professional and amateur musicians and friends.